INFORMATION
SECURITY
Design, Implementation,
Measurement, and Compliance

INFORMATION SECURITY

Design, Implementation, Measurement, and Compliance

Timothy P. Layton

CRC Press
Taylor & Francis Group
Boca Raton   London   New York

CRC Press is an imprint of the
Taylor & Francis Group, an **informa** business

AN AUERBACH BOOK

Information Security Risk Assessment Model (ISRAM™), Global Information Security Assessment Methodology (GISAM™), and Information Security Evaluation (ISE™) are copyrighted to Timothy P. Layton Sr. Any use of these phrases and associated text and illustrations must be granted in writing from Layton. He can be reached via e-mail at tim@timlayton.com.

Auerbach Publications
Taylor & Francis Group
6000 Broken Sound Parkway NW, Suite 300
Boca Raton, FL 33487-2742

© 2007 by Timothy P. Layton
Auerbach is an imprint of Taylor & Francis Group, an Informa business

No claim to original U.S. Government works

International Standard Book Number-10: 0-8493-7087-6 (Hardcover)
International Standard Book Number-13: 978-0-8493-7087-8 (Hardcover)

Visit the Taylor & Francis Web site at
http://www.taylorandfrancis.com

and the Auerbach Web site at
http://www.auerbach-publications.com

Dedication

---

*I dedicate this book and the effort that went into it
to the three most understanding and caring people I know:
Timothy Patrick Jr., Alec Michael, and Abigail Elizabeth
Layton. When times are good, they make me laugh
uncontrollably. When times are tough, the smile doesn't
leave my face because of the unconditional love and joy they
bring to my heart.*

Table of Contents

SECTION II   Analysis of ISO/IEC 17799:2005 (27002) Controls

Foreword

When Tim Layton asked me to write a foreword for his latest book on risk assessment, I was both flattered and humbled. I have had the pleasure of working with Tim on several large risk assessment projects and I have tremendous respect for his knowledge and experience as an information security practitioner. It is an honor to have a small part in this work. And the topic—risk assessment—is both timeless and timely. Risk assessment is the cornerstone of an effective information security program. Security at its very nature starts with a basic understanding of risk. Virtually every information security framework is centered on understanding the risks to the organization and managing them to an acceptable level. Yet today, it seems the concept of a risk-based security program is becoming lost.

The burden and fear of regulatory compliance are causing many organizations to lose control of their security strategy. Instead of being based on a sound understanding of risk, too many organizations are basing their security programs on externally defined criteria. I see this as a dangerous trend within the security industry. With security budgets and staff cut to the bone, it is essential that organizations focus their scarce security resources on the biggest threats to the organization. Unfortunately, the opposite is often the case. By focusing primarily on compliance with externally defined standards, an organization is abdicating its responsibility to understand and manage its business risk.

Without a doubt, compliance can pose a significant risk to an organization. However, striving to achieve compliance in the absence of a risk-based security strategy can only lead to failure. The myriad requirements of the various compliance statutes are vague and contradictory. It is virtually impossible to ensure compliance with every facet of every standard. A compliance-driven security program will likely be costly and ineffective in reducing real risk to the business. In truth, a risk-based security program is the best strategy to achieve compliance. A common theme through all compliance standards—GLB, HIPAA, SOX, PCI, etc.—is to implement security controls appropriate for the risk to your organization. I recently worked with a retail enterprise that was struggling to comply with the new Payment Card Industry Security Standards as defined by Visa and MasterCard. The auditing requirements of the PCI standard are particularly onerous. This organization had never taken the time to assess its own requirements for auditing and logging. In the absence of an internally driven requirement, its only option was to implement an auditing capability as defined by the standard. Not only was this prohibitively expensive, it probably was unnecessary based on the organization's actual risk. Had it conducted a proper risk assessment, it could have deployed a reasonable level of system auditing that would have met its business requirement and satisfied the auditors.

I view risk assessment as the best defense against compliance risk. Demonstrating that you understand and are managing the risks to your business will meet every audit standard. Don't let an external compliance body define your security requirements for you. Implement an effective risk assessment program and take control of the compliance monster.

This book will help you do just that. I know you will benefit from Tim's guidance on how to get the most from your risk assessment efforts. For today's information security leaders, there is not a topic more important.

Gary Geddes, CISSP
Strategic Security Advisor
Microsoft Corporation

Preface: The Business of Information Security and Risk Assessment

The heart of every information security program is always risk assessment. The information security risk assessment process is used to discover the extent of the potential threats and risks associated within the system or environment being evaluated. This may sound easy and straightforward, but consider a large organization leveraging thousands of vendors to help with its business operations and services. Heavily regulated organizations are subject to scrutiny that many other industries are not forced to integrate into their business models. The type of organization referenced in this example probably has tens of thousands of employees with operations spread across the country and possibly conducts business internationally. The executive management team must account for the complexities and challenges within its information security strategy. Management's strategy and program must make sure there is direct linkage to its business goals, vision, and objectives while meeting the myriad legal, regulatory, and contractual requirements.

Information security risk assessment is only one part of this strategy. Organizations typically have many other risk assessment strategies and programs such as legal and contracts, vendor viability, operations, compliance, and so on. Having a misaligned or inaccurate risk assessment process will lead to an ineffective information security program, which has the potential to be devastating to an organization and its customers. In decentralized business models, corporate guidance on information security risk assessment will ensure that business goals and requirements are being considered as part of the assessment process.

It is not enough to have a comprehensive information security risk assessment process and information security program. The information security program must be documented, measurable, and reportable. This requirement is obvious for publicly traded organizations as well as federal and government agencies. Being able to quantify risks to the business and linking a series of analytical controls and safeguards to the threats and vulnerabilities are good business practice and will satisfy even the most comprehensive audits and discriminating regulators. All organizations should be able to explain how they identify risk and what controls they have applied to help manage or mitigate the identified risks. This is a fundamental requirement for regulated organizations.

As described above, risk assessment is only one component of risk management. Risk management also typically includes strategic planning, decision making, impact analysis, threat and vulnerability pairing, asset identification, likelihood, risk analysis, risk identification, remediation, risk evaluation, and potentially a host of other elements depending on the environment and unique organizational variables.

The information security battle is won in the boardroom and not at the firewall. From a strategic perspective, management support such as funding, establishing a cultural norm for information security, and visible participation is needed for every successful information security program, independent of industry or organization. Executive and management support is one of the most important elements for successful information security programs next to users accepting and acting properly on the information security policies and guidelines. Identifying threats and pairing them with vulnerabilities and the design and application of applicable controls only materialize because management supported and ultimately funded the process. Information security is not about technology—it is about people and their actions. There is a raft of laws, regulations, and guidelines that organizations must follow and hence the current trend of information security governance. There is a direct relationship between information security governance and risk management.

Every organization must manage operational risk within the scope of its business model. The information security policy is the document that ties the business and information security together. A diligent information security risk assessment process makes effective risk management possible. Information security policies should be leveraged as a business enabler. The information security policy should allow the organization to comply with all applicable legal, regulatory, statutory, and contractual requirements and still operate with efficiency and effectiveness according to the organization's business plan.

After the policy battle has been won in the boardroom, information security management has an enormous challenge on its hands. This is where the rubber hits the road. All users, whether they are employees, contractors, consultants, external partners, or third-party vendors, must be made aware of the organization's information security policies so that they understand the risks of not complying with organizational policy. Establishing a suitable information security policy and an effective information security awareness program will do more to protect an organization than any firewall or piece of technology could ever offer. It will also keep the auditors and regulators at bay within the larger and regulated organizations such as banks, credit card companies, and insurance organizations.

In fact, a recent global survey performed by Deloitte & Touche USA LLP revealed that information technology-related controls have evolved to the point where hackers are starting to shift their focus back on human error again. For more information on this survey, go to the Deloitte & Touche USA LLP Web site at www.deloitte.com and search for "2005 Global Security Survey."

With globalization, a 24/7 working economy, increased complexities of IT infrastructures, growth of remote employees, proliferation of mobile computing devices, and an ever-increasing number of common vulnerabilities, it is no wonder organizations struggle to find a balance to protect their assets. For these reasons and probably a thousand more, it is important for organizations to have a clear strategy and plan for information security that are owned by competent professionals who possess the skills and experience to lead such a difficult and demanding charge. Having an effective risk assessment process at the core of the information security program will allow an organization to identify applicable threats, whether they are technology, operational, or compliance based, and start the process of risk analysis to design and implement suitable controls to address the identified risk.

The cost of having a competent, qualified, and aware staff does not seem so costly when an organization discloses a data security breach of 40 million credit card customers, like the one reported in June 2005 by a third-party processing company.

Organizations invest in information security for a host of reasons. From a business perspective, organizations are motivated to protect against competitive disadvantage. In other words, how damaging would it be for your organization if a competitor had access to private or confidential information or data? A direct loss such as business revenues is possible, and it is desirable for any business to avoid such losses. Loyalty from clients could be in jeopardy if a damaging incident is allowed to occur and reported to the public. For some organizations and, in particular, publicly traded organizations, disclosure of certain types of incidents is required by law. In 2005 several states formally proposed disclosure and notification legislation, and there is a growing trend for this kind of legislation across the United States.

Losses of the information security type have the potential to impact employee morale and motivation. Information security losses apply to every organization, regardless of whether the organization is profit seeking or government/civic in nature.

If management does not have a clear and documented process for decision making, information could be disclosed to unauthorized parties resulting in negative consequences. These penalties could range from loss of shareholder value to damages to the organization's reputation. In some industries, the organization's reputation is part of the brand and considered a critical part of the success formula. A documented security policy with supporting guidelines and standards effectively communicated to the right target audience can successfully address this risk.

Security incidents can lead to a disruption in operations and can cause direct and indirect losses as well. For some organizations, there may be legal liabilities for disclosure or unauthorized access to information and data, and civil or legal consequences may be applied.

Individuals can be placed at risk because of unauthorized disclosure of personal information. This type of information could range from personal name and address to social security number to credit and medical history. In 2005 there were several cases that disclosed security breaches of credit card data impacting over 40 million people worldwide. There were also cases involving the loss of patients' medical records via stolen laptop computers. These breaches and many others are available for review by searching on news.google.com. By typing the phrase "security breach" in Google News (news.google.com), thousands of matches will be returned.

According to the FBI, fraud is one of the fastest-growing crimes today. Congress is rapidly pursuing many new laws and regulations to help protect and deal with the unauthorized loss or disclosure of personal data including financial and medical data. It is not likely that any organization (public or private) wants that type of press. This may be the exception to the old saying "There is no bad press."

In some cases a breach in security controls could risk the health of customers and employees. These are just a few examples of why organizations are motivated to develop and implement a cohesive information security strategy that is in alignment with the business objectives and organizational mission. For some it may be a legal or regulatory requirement, and for others it may be a market differentiator to gain an advantage over their competitors. All the issues cited here should be included in a formal risk assessment process that an organization should undergo on a regular basis. Risk assessment is the process that helps identify the scope and scale of the information security strategy ensuring connectivity to the business and organizational objectives.

Risk assessment should be a part of the normal project operations of every new and existing project within an organization. There are many different types of risk assessments and the scope can vary greatly. The model presented in Chapter 1 discusses this issue and how organizations can adapt accordingly.

Information security could be compared to life insurance: most people think it is generally a good idea and the right thing to do for our families or organization, respectively. At the same time, if we did not have to make these investments, not many would be rushing to their insurance agents or technology vendors and consultants to donate their hard-earned capital. Information security within the landscape of today's business model is extremely complex and continues to become more complicated over time. With the ubiquitous use of information technology in almost every business model today, it is a harsh reality even without the new legal and regulatory requirements that an information security strategy must be connected to an organization's business plans to appropriately protect employees, assets, and future business plans. For industries such as finance, banking, insurance, and others, it is a painful reality that additional laws and regulations are inevitable to an already heavily regulated industry. If business stakeholders in these types of industries do not have a vision and plan to manage to the current and future legal and regulatory requirements, it will ultimately impact their shareholder value. The cost to perform due care and due diligence is much less from a proactive model as opposed to being reactive. This is one of the reasons why we are seeing new roles and titles such as chief risk officers, chief compliance officers, and enterprise risk management positions. The role of chief information security officer has finally caught on for many organizations and industries, and the second wave of awareness has just begun. Over time it will become more obvious that information security is connected to almost every part of the business, and the linkage and relationship to the business model are ways to enable and strengthen the business.

There is a growing acceptance within the industry as a whole of why organizations would want to use and implement the ISO/IEC 17799:2005 (27002) Code of Practice for Information Security Management. Many subject matter experts and consultants agree that if an organization adopts and implements the ISO/IEC 17799 as their information security standard, they will address many of the other legal requirements placed on them by the Sarbanes–Oxley Act (SOX), the Gramm–Leach–Bliley Act (GLB), and the Health Insurance Portability and Accountability Act (HIPAA). With little effort, it is easy to map the requirements from the SOX, GLB, and HIPAA laws to the current version of the ISO/IEC 17799 standard. For financial institutions the linkage and relationship to the FFIEC (Federal Financial Institutions Examination Council) and the OCC (Office of the Comptroller of the

Currency) are very obvious and apparent. Any organization would greatly benefit by adopting the ISO/IEC 17799 as its information security framework.

The latest official release of the ISO/IEC 17799 is the second edition, also known as ISO/IEC 17799:2005(E) (27002). The second edition was released in June 2005. In the foreword of the second edition, a brief disclosure was listed indicating that the current code of practice is proposed to be ported to a new ISO numbering scheme at some time in 2007. The new numbering scheme will be ISO/IEC 27000. The ISO/IEC 17799:2005 is proposed to be ISO/IEC 27002, and part 2 of the BS 7799:2002 is now officially the ISO/IEC 27001:2005.

Other standards addressing measurement and metrics (27004) and implementation guidance (27003) are also being discussed along with a few others. Anything referenced besides 27001 and 27002 is considered unofficial at this time. It is important to note the relationship between 27001 (BS 7799-2:2002) and 27002 (ISO/IEC 17799:2005). The 27001 provides a specification for ISMS (Information Security Management Systems) and the foundation for third-party audit and certification. The new 27000 series has been revised to work with other management systems such as the ISO 9001 and ISO 14001. ISO/IEC 27001 covers the ISMS as referenced above, management responsibility, management review of ISMS, and how to continually improve ISMS. This standard will help organizations define their information security policy, define the scope of their ISMS, perform an information security risk assessment, create a plan to manage the identified risks, select controls and safeguards to implement, and prepare a SOA (statement of applicability) for formal certification.

At a high level, the ISO/IEC 17799:2005 (27002) standard provides a series of systematic recommendations for information security management to apply to their business model and operations and determine which controls apply. As outlined in the opening section of the introduction of this book, the ISO/IEC 17799:2005 suggests that organizations should include a formalized risk assessment process sponsored by senior management.

The overall purpose of the standard is to provide a common basis and platform for developing organizational information security standards for all organizations independent of geography or industry. Moreover, the code of practice provides a comprehensive framework and series of controls for interorganizational partnerships and dealings. The standard is not a law or regulatory requirement, and it should be adapted and used in accordance with applicable laws and regulations to ensure maximum effectiveness.

I have visited several countries throughout Europe, and the organizations I have evaluated to date are very familiar with the 17799 standard. In the scope of my own personal experiences, their information security programs were fundamentally designed and based on the standard. With the roots of the 17799 standard being in the United Kingdom, this is not a surprising discovery. The widespread proliferation of the EU Data Protection Directive in Europe helps to further explain this phenomenon. European companies face the same challenges as American organizations as they relate to protecting their assets while balancing the most appropriate set of controls for their respective business models and complying with all applicable laws and regulations. In today's global economy, whether an organization is based in

Europe or the United States, does not release the organization from compliance requirements with respective legislation or governance.

Corporate governance is the rage with the Big 4 public accounting firms and their management consulting partners. Corporate governance is a fancy label for good business practices. This would include a comprehensive strategy to protect assets including information, data, and information systems. The ISO/IEC 17799:2005 (27002) standard provides a good framework from a business perspective to aid in this process. Organizational stakeholders in the United States are beginning to understand the value in the breadth and depth of the standard and how effective it can be within their organizations. With the release of ISO/IEC 27001:2005, this will help organizational leaders figure out how to design and implement a cohesive information security program that fits their business model. By using the standard as the framework for their information security controls, organizations remove a tremendous amount of risk from relying on their information security professionals, who might miss a critical element or might not possess the depth of knowledge or skill in all the required areas. The standard ensures that the industry best-practice controls are presented for review.

If an organization customizes and implements the ISO/IEC 17799:2005 (27002) standard, it is in effect minimizing efforts that would be required for applicable laws and regulations such as HIPAA, GLB, SOX, PCI, FFIEC, etc. If an organization has implemented any other ISO-based systems such as the ISO 9001 or ISO 14001, the integration into this type of system is very straightforward and should be very familiar to the management team. The basic building block of any ISO system is formal documentation and process. There are two core concepts to an effective information security governance strategy: document and demonstrate. Your strategy must be linked to a documented program, and the program must be measurable and reportable.

The formal documentation for the ISO/IEC 17799:2005 (27002) standard is the information security policy document; this document is the single point of focus on which all information security controls and practices are designed and built. The ISO/IEC 27001:2005 will help organizations get their arms around the policy document and provide guidance on where all the pieces fit. It is critical that every organization has an information security policy document and that these series of policies be in alignment with the organization's business objectives and account for all applicable legal, regulatory, and contractual requirements. A comprehensive information security awareness and education program is required to effectively communicate the information security policies. For more information on information security awareness and why this is a critical element to protecting your organization's information assets, refer to another book I have written, *Information Security Awareness: The Psychology Behind the Technology* (ISBN: 1-4208-5632-4).

Almost every information security manager and chief information security officer struggles with funding and budget issues. I argue that if chief information security officers leverage the ISO/IEC 17799:2005 (27002) and ISO/IEC 27001:2005, these concerns and hurdles would be lessened. By the very nature of the standard, an organizationwide approach is required. In effect, it requires managers and stakeholders throughout the various departments, groups, and lines of business to latch onto the information security strategy and integrate it into the operations of the organization. Assuming there is appropriate senior management support, this can help spread out the budget challenges to other groups and at the same time make a broader audience more aware of the importance and challenges for information security.

Information security for organizations today has shifted from a technology-oriented focus to a business practice issue, making it a critical part of almost every organization. With the pervasiveness of information security and the increasing legal and regulatory requirements placed on organizations, I was compelled to author a book on information security risk assessment and the ISO/IEC 17799:2005 (27002) Code of Practice for Information Security Management in an effort to help management and organizations lower their risks.

Introduction

The emergence of new laws and regulations in recent years has rapidly moved information security from a technology issue directly to the attention of executive management and the board of directors around the globe. Almost every industry—public, private, and government—is impacted by the recent formalization of new laws and regulations. Even private firms are feeling the downstream impact because their publicly traded clients are placing new information security-related requirements on their relationship because of these new laws and regulations. Until recently, organizations were never forced to provide evidence of compliance in the security of their information technology systems or security practices. Organizations are accepting the reality of this onslaught of activity driven out of the compliance legislation and regulations and starting to consider ways and methods to demonstrate compliance, reduce complexity, and control costs. With the evolution of the PCI (Payment Card Industry) standard, we are starting to see industries self-impose information security standards. Information security has finally matured to a position on executive management's radar that will likely not lessen any time in the near future—if ever.

According to the Privacy Rights Clearinghouse, a nonprofit watchdog group in California, 2005 was a record year for publicly reported information security breaches and incidents. From banks and hospitals to government agencies, nearly 100 major security incidents were reported, with over six in December alone. Major institutions such as Bank of America and the Federal Deposit Insurance Corp. reported major security breaches in 2005. Smaller and lesser-known firms such as ChoicePoint and CardSystems Solutions Inc. were victimized by hackers, setting off a major flurry of activity for millions of customers. Major colleges and universities across the country, from Stanford to Duke, reported unauthorized people stealing thousands of files with account numbers and other personal data belonging to students and school employees. In some of the most damaging breaches, an insider was involved in the compromise, confirming what many information security professionals continue to warn management about year after year.

The largest computer security breach ever reported in history happened in June 2005 when MasterCard reported that a hacker breached a virtually unknown credit card transaction-processing company, exposing an estimated 40 million credit card accounts. It is a little-known fact that large financial institutions and banks use small companies and vendors for trusted and critical operations such as credit card transaction processing. The security incident with CardSystems Solutions Inc. helped eliminate this little-known fact for the general public.

All of this might leave you wondering, why the rush of activity and breaches in 2005? No one probably has the answer to this riddle. I speculate there wasn't a large increase of security breaches and incidents in 2005—only an increase in their reporting to the general public. Only within the last year have new legal requirements been passed at the state level requiring organizations to report security breaches in certain industries under specific circumstances. As of January 2006 approximately 22 states have passed security breach notification legislation, with several other states in progress. Approximately 12 states have security freeze laws allowing notified or potential identity theft victims to prevent others from establishing credit in their names. It is a little-known fact that in many states people can establish credit in your name and you are held liable by the credit-granting institution and your personal credit file can be severely damaged in the process. You are left holding the bag for the unpaid debt. It appears that in too many cases, unsuspecting consumers are held liable until they prove themselves innocent, assuming their personal credit has not been damaged beyond repair in the process. Identity theft is a nasty and ugly scenario happening to a growing number of people. According to the FBI, identity theft is one of the fastest-growing crimes today. Finding the proper balance of laws and regulations to protect the innocent while still holding people accountable for their actions is a difficult concept that will not likely ever gain acceptance from everyone affected.

The ISO/IEC 17799:2005 (27002) Code of Practice for Information Security Management is fast becoming the best-practice standard and benchmark for measuring information security around the world. The ISO/IEC 17799:2005 offers a best-practice guideline and framework for implementing an information security program, but it stops short of providing guidance on how to apply or implement the standard based on an organization's unique requirements.

Each organization possesses unique attributes; therefore, each organization will face different threats and vulnerabilities. The controls of the ISO/IEC 17799:2005 standard should be applied only as a result of a comprehensive risk assessment that involves all appropriate stakeholders and parties in the organization.

The information security policy is a good place to start the review process because the security policy should be the focal point of every information security program. In the first two chapters of this book, a model for information security risk assessment and a comprehensive information security risk assessment methodology are presented and described in detail. These first two chapters provide information security professionals and management with direct guidance and an approach that organizations in any industry can use to evaluate and assess their information security risks at a holistic level including operational and management dimensions in addition to the traditional technology-oriented methods. The model can be thought of as basic building plans that every good architect includes in his or her review of a new project, and the assessment methodology in this example is considered to be the blueprint used by the workers to erect the structure and evaluate it once it is built.

It may seem obvious, but controls and safeguards must be designed and implemented as a result of a formal risk assessment. All too often, organizations go straight to "solving the problem" instead of assessing the environment before applying a balance of controls and safeguards meeting all of the organizational requirements including business, regulatory, contractual, and legal.

The information security strategy and program must be directly linked to the business strategy and mission to be effective and measurable. A senior-level executive should sponsor the information security program and ensure that the rest of the executive management team and the board of directors understand the information security strategy.

If the information security program is supportive of the organization's business goals and requirements, an effective and applicable information security policy is required. As discussed throughout this book, the information security policy must be driven by the organization's business goals and objectives; any applicable laws and regulations and all contractual requirements must also be determined and applied. To be effective in the information security journey, organizations must be able to quantify their risks, account for any applicable threat and vulnerability pairs, assess the likelihood of threats and their potential impact to the organization, and report the state of information security to executive management and the board of directors.

By continually assessing the organization's information security controls, the management team has a platform for higher-quality decision making. In some industries this can be critical from an operational perspective as well as for meeting compliance and statutory requirements. For public and regulated organizations, it is not an option any longer to be able to report on the effectiveness of information security and compliance.

The ISO/IEC 17799:2005 (27002) Code of Practice for Information Security Management is a logical framework on which to base an organization's information security program. As mentioned in the opening paragraph, a formal risk assessment process must be conducted to ensure that the correct risks are being addressed and the proper controls and safeguards are implemented and monitored. The information security program must be measurable and ultimately reportable to management and any applicable regulatory or legal party. The ISO/IEC 17799:2005 (27002) framework, if adopted and implemented properly, will prove to be one of the best investments an organization can make.

By using the ISO/IEC 17799:2005, organizations can leverage the code of practice as a competitive advantage within their marketing efforts. In addition, because of the nature of the standard, senior management will have confidence that its organization's information systems and operations are secured with international best practices. For global organizations this can be viewed as an asset and differentiator. By coupling the ISO/IEC 17799:2005 with a series of appropriate risk assessments and an enterprise risk management strategy, an organization can create an environment that will lead to a balanced and lower-risk atmosphere.

The concept of information security risk assessment will be presented and discussed throughout this book. The second edition of the ISO/IEC 17799:2005 (27002) Code of Practice for Information Security Management discusses the need and relevancy of risk assessment. I will present and describe an information risk assessment model and ultimately describe an evaluation process that organizations can adopt and apply within their unique environment and operations.

My ultimate goal for this book is to provide a flexible and adoptable information security risk assessment model and assessment methodology that organizations in any industry can adopt and apply to ultimately lower their information security risks. Nontechnical information security risks are often overlooked and do not get the attention they deserve. I will provide the concepts and information required to link these concepts to an information security assessment methodology that will ultimately quantify and qualify the various information security risks of an organization. The model, methodology, and assessment process, when implemented as a cohesive solution, is a means of providing decision makers with information needed to understand factors that can negatively influence business operations. The analysis and information provided as a result of the assessment process will enable business managers and leaders to make informed judgments concerning the extent of actions needed to reduce risk.

This book will be broken down into two sections. Section I will provide a model and methodology of how to effectively evaluate and measure an information security program using the ISO/IEC 17799:2005 (27002) standard as the control framework driven by a formal risk assessment model (ISRAM™) and assessment methodology (GISAM™).

A mixed-mode information security assessment methodology will be presented and detailed in the second chapter. Methodological concepts ranging from the development of an assessment scale, to linking threats and vulnerabilities, to likelihood and impact are all presented and accounted for. A business process known as ISE™ (Information Security Evaluation), pronounced like "ice," is presented in the third chapter; it leverages the components from GISAM ranging from the level of effectiveness of individual controls all the way through the development of reporting metrics and the structure of the management report. ISE is a concept that leverages the ISRAM and GISAM for the purpose of capturing and presenting critical data to management and organizational stakeholders. This chapter demonstrates how to leverage the information security risk assessment model presented in the first chapter and how to pragmatically conduct an effective review and evaluation of an organization's information security posture based on an international best-practice standard. All the elements (model, evaluation methodology, business process, and standard) work together to provide the necessary information an organization requires to make effective information security risk management decisions that directly relate to its business. The last three chapters of this section (Chapters 4, 5, and 6) present a proposed security baseline for all organizations, an executive overview of the ISO/IEC 17799:2005, and a gap analysis between the first two editions.

In Section II, a detailed analysis will be performed on each of the 133 controls within the 39 control objectives in the 11 different control areas spanning 11 chapters starting with Chapter 7. These 11 chapters can be used as a reference guide for information security professionals who are already knowledgeable about the new release of the standard. Professionals who are new to the standard or unfamiliar with the differences between the first and second editions should use this book in conjunction with a licensed copy of the standard to ensure a thorough comprehension of the intent and scope of the code of practice. Chapters 7 through 17 can be best leveraged when used in conjunction with the standard, independent of the reader's knowledge level. The second edition of the ISO/IEC 17799 standard can be purchased directly from ANSI in the United States via the Web at http://webstore.ansi.org/ansidocstore/find.asp? or via the telephone at 212-642-4900.

Information security managers and organizational stakeholders can use this book as a business tool to help them better understand the ISO/IEC 17799:2005 (27002) Code of Practice for Information Security Management and then apply their new knowledge within the context of their own environments to ultimately lower their risks and exposures. This is fundamentally accomplished by conducting a comprehensive risk assessment and implementing a series of appropriate controls. The risk assessment process is a living process that should continue to operate within the scope of business operations.

My wish and hope are that the information presented in this book will help information security professionals and their organizations lower their information security risks and exposures.

The Author

Tim Layton possesses over 20 years of experience in information technology, information security, and corporate compliance. Besides this book, he has written the ISO/IEC 17799:2005 Management Gap Analysis Report, *Information Security Awareness: The Psychology Behind the Technology* (ISBN: 1-4208-5632-4), and The SANS Institute's Security Awareness Train-the-Trainer curriculum and has coauthored a Cisco CCNA Boot Camp training course for an international training company.

Mr. Layton was the founder of two successful information technology and information security firms during the 1990s before starting Tim Layton & Associates, LLC, in 2002 and Risk Management Institute of America in 2005. Tim Layton & Associates, LLC (www.timlayton.com) focuses on providing risk management solutions and professional services for organizations. Risk Management Institute of America (www.rmiamerica.org) is dedicated to developing and providing organizations with risk assessment applications and tools for compliance (GLB, HIPAA, FFIEC) and industry standards (PCI, ISO/IEC 17799).

Currently, Mr. Layton travels internationally identifying and analyzing information security and compliance risks for organizations in a wide array of industries and delivers training on the same topics.

He focuses primarily on identifying critical information security risks and quantifying relevant threats and vulnerabilities in a format that will provide management with a platform to make quality risk-based decisions. Much of his work leverages well-known standards, frameworks, and security-related laws including ISO/IEC 17799:2005, ISO/IEC 13335, ITIL, CobiT, NIST, COSO, PCI, GLB, HIPAA, and SOX. He also provides training on these topics as well as information security awareness, secure network architecture and design, information security program design, disaster recovery, and business continuity planning.

Mr. Layton developed a series of information security and compliance models, assessment methodologies, and software tools leveraging the ISO/IEC 17799 Code of Practice for Information Security Management, CobiT, PCI Standard, SOX, and GLB. These assessment methodologies and assessment processes have been delivered and implemented internationally scaling across many lines of business. Mr. Layton is also the cocreator of a custom software program that performs penetration and vulnerability testing on network hosts and software applications.

Mr. Layton earned a bachelor's degree in business administration, graduating magna cum laude, before continuing to earn a master of business administration (MBA). He is pursuing doctoral studies in industrial/organizational psychology. He possesses a comprehensive knowledge of the laws, regulations, and standards regarding information security and corporate compliance on an international basis.

Besides his academic background and successes, Mr. Layton holds many information technology and security certifications such as the CISSP® (Certified Information Systems Security Professional), SANS GIAC (Global Information Assurance Certification), GCFW, GCIH, and GSEC, as well as several other vendor-related certifications.

Mr. Layton can be reached via e-mail at timlayton@gmail.com.

Section I

Evaluating and Measuring an
Information Security Program

1 Information Security Risk Assessment Model (ISRAM™)

This first chapter presents and describes a model for information security risk assessment. The purpose of this model is to provide a framework for organizations so they can easily modify and adapt it to meet their specific requirements. The chapter also provides some background information on information security risk assessment and why it is important in the overall information security journey. A model used within the context of this chapter is meant to provide the framework and fundamental structure for the definition of a formal information security risk assessment. This model presents the requirements and elements for information security risk assessment and provides background information for each component. An assessment methodology built on the ISRAM™ is presented and described in the second chapter.

BACKGROUND

Information security risk assessment is not a stand-alone process. It is the first step in a larger business process known as risk management. An information security risk assessment is specific to information security, and risk management is a larger business initiative involving many different types of risk assessments and other dimensions including analysis, mitigation, etc. Risk management typically includes many other elements within the organization. These elements and business processes can include but are not limited to strategic planning, decision making, impact analysis, threat and vulnerability pairing, asset identification, likelihood, risk analysis, risk identification, remediation, risk evaluation, and potentially a host of other elements depending on the environment and unique organizational requirements and variables.

LINKAGE

There is a direct relationship between the corporate information security policy and information security risk assessment. In fact, the risk assessment should fundamentally assess the controls and safeguards that were developed as a result of the policy. In many cases this is not true, because the policy is not accurate or completely up to date. A comprehensive risk assessment has the potential to uncover the need for new or revised policy statements. Policies can be thought of as rules governing the choices in behavior of a system or organization that effectively serve as a guide in the decision-making process. These rules can typically be grouped into three categories: technical, management, and operational. Within the context of the ISO/IEC 17799:2005 (27002) Code of Practice for Information Security Management, I have assigned each of the 133 controls into one or more of these three categories.

It is important to note that information security risk assessment is a business process and not a technology issue. Some dimensions within many information security risk assessments will be technical in nature, but the resulting analysis and output is written and developed for business leaders and managers to give them an accurate depiction of risks their organizations and businesses are exposed to. Ultimately, the purpose of any risk assessment, information security or otherwise, is to provide decision makers with information needed to understand factors that can negatively influence operations and outcomes and make informed judgments concerning the extent of actions needed to reduce risk.

RISK ASSESSMENT TYPES

There are many different types of risk assessments, and information security risk assessments for that matter. One focus of this book is to help organizations lower their information security risks within their business and operations. The information security risk assessment model presented in this chapter is aimed at the organizational level as opposed to a specific system or application. There is a distinct difference between an organizational-level risk assessment and other types such as application or system assessments. The issue of scope is critical to understand. Scoping is addressed within the framework of the ISRAM. This and other related information will be detailed later in this chapter.

For example, an organizational-level information security assessment typically reviews and evaluates the information security practices, operations, and controls of an organization to identify any weaknesses or holes that exist at the organizational level and within business operations. Therefore, the tools and scope of this assessment would be much different from an assessment of a specific application or system. A focused information security risk assessment on a particular system or application is much narrower and the scope of the review is different. The information security risk assessment model presented in this chapter will help illustrate this point and the differences. The associated Global Information Security Assessment Methodology (GISAM™) presented in the next chapter embraces the ISRAM and gives it life and purpose. The assessment methodology is focused at the organizational level and leverages the ISO/IEC 17799:2005 (27002) Code of Practice for Information Security Management as the control framework.

Technology and technical components can play a large role in helping organizations effectively lower their information security risks, but, in the end, information security is only one dimension of risk that organizational leaders and stakeholders must factor into their overall risk management strategy and program. For that reason, it is critical that the information security risk assessment process as well as the information security program be connected to the business goals and objectives of the organization.

This chapter presents a model for information security risk assessment that organizations can adopt and utilize within their own environment and operations—independent of industry. Models must be scalable and adoptable or they would be useless. The model must support the goals and objectives of information security as well as management to be considered effective and reliable.

RELATIONSHIP TO OTHER MODELS AND STANDARDS

The concept of risk assessment has been around for a long time and is not unique to information security. Many models and methods have been created and developed over the years. Probably the best known information security risk assessment and management model is the NIST (National Institute of Standards and Technology) Special Publication 800-30. The NIST SP 800-30 is published by the Technology Administration Department of Commerce and is considered public domain as well as industry best practice by many professionals and organizations. The International Organization for Standardization (ISO) has published a standard that addresses the topic of risk assessment and risk management as well. This standard is probably not as widely known as the NIST SP 800-30. It is currently implemented as five separate components in the ISO/IEC 13335 series, and it is under revision and will likely be reduced into two parts in the very near future. The ISO/IEC 17799:2005 (27002) makes a brief reference to the ISO/IEC 13335 in the new risk assessment section. Within this book I primarily leverage the information within the NIST SP 800-30 as well as a few other sources that will be cited as necessary and I will not include information from the ISO/IEC 13335 for practical reasons as well as copyright constraints. The risk assessment framework and model is critical to enable a successful information security risk assessment process. The model can be thought of as high-level guidance when developing action-oriented processes.

The NIST SP 800-30 was published in July 2002 and has been scrutinized and tested by many organizations and professionals since its release. The risk assessment model presented in the SP 800-30 is focused on federal and government-based organizations and, with some slight adjustments and modifications, it can be adjusted to suit private and public organizations as well.

In recent times the ubiquitous application and proliferation of information technology within most business models have created a heavy reliance on information systems, therefore creating a heightened sense of risk in this area. Risk is nothing new to the business world. The enhancements and advances in technology of the last two decades have forged new concerns and risks for organizations that did not previously exist. Almost every component of every business is somehow either tied to, or reliant on, an information system or component of technology. The attention to information technology risks has grown exponentially over the last 20 years as a direct result of the skyrocketing utilization of information technology systems and applications. With the continued use and reliance on information systems, the inherent risks and vulnerabilities associated with technology will continue to expand and over time will become more resistant to traditional risk management mechanisms.

For regulated industries, and in particular publicly traded companies, the issue of information security risk assessment is not an option. The ability for these organizations to identify and report on their information security risks is a critical component of their corporate governance and compliance requirements placed on them by the law and their regulators.

The ISO/IEC 17799:2005 (27002) Code of Practice for Information Security Management is the most widely used framework by organizations around the world for information security best practices at an organizational level. The 11 main security clauses, 133 controls, and 39 control objectives of the ISO/IEC 17799:2005 (27002) present a comprehensive approach and industry best practice for information security for organizations independent of industry. The 11 main security clauses include the following:

- Security Policy
- Organizing Information Security
- Asset Management
- Human Resources Security
- Physical and Environmental Security
- Communications and Operations Management
- Access Control
- Information Systems Acquisition, Development, and Maintenance
- Information Security Incident Management
- Business Continuity Management
- Compliance

Without diving into the details of the standard right now, it is fairly easy to observe that technology and firewalls are not the focus of this standard. This standard embraces and assumes that technology-based controls are part of the information security strategy and program—not simply the focus and driver. The standard presents a series of 133 controls that can be adopted and utilized by organizations. The standard helps organizations on many different levels. One of the most obvious benefits of the standard is that organizations can leverage the wisdom and knowledge of the global community on information security and be afforded the opportunity to evaluate if each control applies to their business model. I have personally witnessed many business leaders and information security professionals benefiting from the depth and breadth of this standard. The majority of business professionals, information security or otherwise, are under demanding and heavy workloads; therefore, they do not have the opportunity to fully explore each of the possible controls presented within the standard. It is extremely unlikely that a single individual or small group of professionals has the experience or depth of knowledge to think of all the information presented within the standard.

The ISRAM and forthcoming chapters were written with the ISO/IEC 17799:2005 (27002) squarely in mind. Ultimately, I create a theoretical framework for information security risk assessment, and within the second half of the book I illustrate and describe how organizations can adopt and apply the ISO/IEC 17799:2005 (27002) to assess their information security risks through the GISAM.

In essence, a theoretical framework for risk assessment and evaluation methodology is presented and discussed in the first section of the book and a series of chapters on the ISO/IEC 17799:2005 (27002) Code of Practice for Information Security Management is presented with the intent of demonstrating how the standard can be leveraged and utilized during the risk assessment process. The global intent is to help information security professionals and managers understand the relationship of an information security risk assessment model, the ISO/IEC 17799:2005 (27002), and an evaluation methodology that leverages both components for the purpose of identifying and communicating risks to organizational leaders.

TERMINOLOGY

It is easy to get bogged down in all these terms and technical jargon. I felt it was important to set a baseline of understanding by providing high-level definitions of the most relevant information security risk assessment and management terms before we move into the actual model. There are varying definitions for many of these concepts and phrases that I present in this chapter. To establish a baseline of understanding, I have included definitions for several of the information security risk assessment terms. The majority of these terms and phrases are understood to be industry standard, and their meaning and intent should basically be the same here or anywhere else they are used within the context of information security risk assessment.

- **Information Security Risk Assessment** — The business process of identifying potential threats, vulnerabilities, impact, and risks to the organization and the likelihood of their occurrence. Results can be expressed in qualitative or quantitative terms or a combination of both. Information security risk assessment is one component of risk management.
- **Risk** — The likelihood, impact, and consequence of negative events the organization must consider as part of its operations.
- **Risk Management** — A comprehensive business process an organization utilizes to identify, evaluate, and select controls and safeguards for the purpose of reducing, mitigating, or transferring known risks at a reasonable cost to the organization. The cost of a control or controls should not outweigh the value of the asset.
- **Risk Mitigation** — The prioritization and implementation of the identified controls to lower identified risks via the risk assessment process.
- **Vulnerability** — A flaw or weakness in an information system, associated procedure, or existing control that has the potential to be exercised (accidentally triggered or intentionally exploited) and result in a breach or violation of the information security policy. Vulnerabilities have no impact if a relevant threat is not present.
- **Threat** — The potential for a threat to be exercised, either accidentally or intentionally, for the purpose of exploiting a specific vulnerability.
- **Impact** — The extent to which an exercised vulnerability affects the organization.

- **Likelihood** — The probability an event will occur.
- **Control** — Management, technical, or operational mechanism addressing a specific threat and vulnerability pair.
- **Asset** — Anything, tangible or intangible, that has value to the organization.
- **Availability** — Ensuring that only authorized users have access to appropriate information and information systems when they require it.
- **Confidentiality** — Ensuring that information is accessible only to those authorized to have access.
- **Probability** — The extent to which an event is likely to occur.
- **Residual Risk** — The remaining risk after controls and safeguards have been applied.
- **Stakeholder** — Any individual or group that will be affected by, or can be affected by, identified risks.

RISK ASSESSMENT RELATIONSHIP

At a high level, most information security professionals would likely agree that the information security risk assessment process is utilized to determine the extent of potential threats and risks associated within the environment being evaluated. Furthermore, the information security risk assessment process could be described as a business enabler that supports management by providing them with qualified information that helps support their business decisions.

The risk assessment process is at the heart of the overall information security program. It helps business leaders and stakeholders identify and evaluate the applicable threats and vulnerabilities within the scope of their environment and operations. Additionally, the existing controls are evaluated and analyzed, and the impact to the organization is reviewed along with the likelihood of breakdown in security controls and safeguards. Finally, the risk level to the organization with the scope of the assessment is quantified and qualified, and a series of detailed recommendations and analysis is provided in a business-type report to the target audience.

As previously described, the most prevalent and common approaches and models would include the NIST Special Publications and ISO/IEC standards. In particular, the NIST Special Publication 800-30 Risk Management Guide for Information Technology Systems, along with a few other NIST Special Publications, details and provides information on the information security risk assessment process. The ISO/IEC 13335 parts 1 and 2 also provide a detailed information security risk assessment model and process. The U.S. General Accounting Office (GAO) has also published an information security risk assessment model and process. All three of the references described above can generally be interpreted at a high level in about the same way. Models for risk assessment, information security or otherwise, are fundamentally the same. The NIST and GAO models are considered public domain and can be utilized by organizations free of charge. Both are freely available via the Internet. The ISO/IEC 13335 is copyrighted by the International Organization for Standardization and must be purchased to be read and reviewed.

The ISRAM most closely resembles the NIST SP 800-30. I have modified and adjusted the scope and meaning of the various components of the 800-30 model based on my academic training and 20 years of professional experience. The ISRAM is clear and simple and could be easily adopted by organizations in just about any industry. The ISRAM provides the framework and basis for the assessment methodology (GISAM) that is presented and described in Chapter 2. I believe models and frameworks are relevant and necessary, but if professionals are unable to apply them within the context of their own organizations, it is unlikely the model will ever reach its intended target. This is fundamentally why I present and describe the GISAM as well as all 133 of the ISO/IEC 17799:2005 (27002) controls. The assessment methodology and the standard give life and a pragmatic purpose for the model.

By having performed a thorough information security risk assessment, you will always be one step ahead of your auditors. For larger organizations this can help save a tremendous amount of time and resources during audit time. Moreover, conducting a comprehensive information security risk assessment demonstrates the process of due diligence on the part of management and, in some cases, this is critical. Management and personnel should understand the level of risk that exists within their environment and operations. This knowledge could be the difference between a full-blown compromise and a "near miss." If the responsible people are aware of the risks and controls that have been implemented within their environment, it is reasonable to assume there will be an environment of heightened awareness with the promise of fewer information security incidents.

INFORMATION SECURITY RISK ASSESSMENT MODEL (ISRAM)

The information security risk management model should be easy to understand, applicable to an organization's business model and environment, and detailed enough to appropriately perform the function for which it was designed. If no one can understand the model, it will not be utilized or applied. If the model is too detailed or does not fit with the organization's boundaries or requirements, it will not be effectively utilized and unnecessary risk will remain within the organization's operations and environment.

The easiest and most efficient path to success is to adopt a best-practice model and modify it as necessary to meet your organization's requirements. This approach ensures that best practices are being utilized and, by integrating the model into the environment within the necessary boundaries and requirements, success is much more likely to occur, ultimately resulting in fewer risks. The ISRAM and the GISAM are examples of this approach.

My plan is to detail a comprehensive, yet simple, information security risk assessment model that can be adopted by organizations and applied within their own operations and environments to effectively lower their information security risks. The subsequent chapters provide details on how the model can be adopted into a

Information Security Risk Assessment Model (ISRAM™)

Scope & Type of Assessment

Threats

Vulnerabilities

Control Level of Effectiveness

Likelihood

Impact

Risk Level

Recommendations

Analysis & Final Report

FIGURE 1.1 Information Security Risk Assessment Model (ISRAM™)

risk assessment process and how both can leverage an international information security standard.

Risk assessments, whether they pertain to information security or other types of risk, are a means of providing decision makers with information they need to understand factors that can negatively influence operations and outcomes and to make informed judgments concerning the extent of actions needed to reduce risk.

The model presented in this chapter assumes that assets, tangible or otherwise, have already been identified as part of the information security program. Assets and their values are utilized during the risk analysis and risk management phase to help determine the cost-benefit relationship between the value of the asset and the cost of potential controls and safeguards.

The ISRAM will be broken down into nine separate elements and described. Refer to Figure 1.1 for the ISRAM.

An explanation for each component in the model will be described to help illustrate its purpose and intent. This model can be modified to adapt to your organization's unique needs and requirements.

Scope and Type of Assessment

The scope and type of information security risk assessment is a critical part of the model and sets the overall objectives for the risk assessment. Additionally, the model drives the methodology and processes associated with the delivery of the model. Each type of assessment should possess a unique scope and assessment methodology. The delivery of the model is the assessment methodology utilized to support the ISRAM. I have developed and created several types of assessments for evaluating and reporting on information security risks. The various assessment types include application, network, organizational, Internet, physical, third-party vendors, and merger and acquisitions.

Assessment Types

The assessment types listed in the previous paragraph are a result of my own professional experiences but likely apply to many other organizations. I will briefly describe the assessment in an effort to help provide additional depth to the notion that individual assessment types are required to appropriately measure and report risks to organizational stakeholders.

Organizational Information Security Assessment

An organizational information security risk assessment is the type of assessment that reviews the overall information security posture of an organization from a management, operations, and technology perspective. GISAM, the risk assessment method presented in Chapter 2, is an example of this type of assessment. The GISAM can scale from a divisional or business unit level all the way up to the complete organization for hundreds of thousands of employees. It is most effective if it is performed annually by unbiased subject matter experts with the findings communicated to senior management. The resulting analysis and information from this assessment empowers management by identifying high-risk items within their organization and providing a qualitative analysis on the state of their current controls and safeguards. Because the assessment focused on three main areas (management, technical, operational), management can be assured a comprehensive assessment has been conducted.

Application Information Security Assessment

An application information security risk assessment is focused on a specific application that is deployed within the organization but is not Internet facing. Each application should have its own information security risk assessment, and the resulting information should be utilized by management and application owners during the information security planning process. The application information security risk assessment is focused on the "software" elements and associated components including dataflow; transport and storage; system users; and security of the application code and configuration.

Network Information Security Assessment

A network information security risk assessment focuses on network architecture and associated elements. This type of assessment ensures there is defense-in-depth and containment of risk principles utilized during the architecture and design of the network being evaluated. The individual configurations of each network device are reviewed and evaluated, ensuring proper configuration and application of the most recent security patches. As with any type of assessment, a series of specific controls would be evaluated to identify threats, vulnerabilities, likelihood, and impact to the organization. An assessment methodology would provide the scope of details for the controls to be reviewed.

Internet Information Security Assessment

An Internet information security risk assessment is a special type of assessment. It is special because it appears on the surface to be a hybrid of the application and network information security assessments, and to a degree, this is true. The point of departure for this type of assessment is that the typical and associated threats and vulnerabilities are different from traditional networked environments. The appropriate controls and safeguards utilized in an Internet type of deployment are different from applications and architecture deployed within the internal organization. There are well-known unique risks with Internet-enabled applications and services that require an assessment that accounts for these unique factors.

Physical Information Security Assessment

A physical assessment is focused on the physical and environmental controls only. This type of assessment can be performed very quickly and has the possibility of yielding some very high-risk items. History is replete with examples of a breakdown in physical controls that ultimately resulted in serious and negative consequences.

Vendor Information Security Assessment

A third-party vendor assessment is driven directly by business requirements. Whether the motivation is legal, regulatory, or compliance related, the business drives the requirements. As part of management's responsibility, the assessment and reporting of third-party vendors' information security posture is becoming increasingly more common. The assessment methodology would follow the ISRAM, just as in any other type of information security assessment.

M&A Information Security Assessment

A merger and acquisition (M&A) assessment is most common in larger organizations or in organizations that perform this type of service. In either case, the information security aspects of a merger or acquisition can be accounted for in an assessment methodology. By their very nature, mergers and acquisitions are extremely sensitive and confidential. Information and data pertaining to the merger must be appropriately safeguarded and protected because a premature disclosure of information could have serious and negative consequences. Another perspective is that the acquiring organization must fully understand the information security risks within the applications, operations, and environment of the target company. An effective information security risk assessment methodology specifically targeted at this type of scope can produce information and data that are critical to the long-term success of the new organization.

It is up to each organization to define the scope and types of assessments that are appropriate for their organization. The methodologies and associated assessments are dynamic and should be reviewed at least twice per year to ensure they are appropriately meeting all the necessary business requirements they are designed to address. The knowledge gained from the ISRAM in this chapter and the associated method in Chapter 2 should provide a baseline understanding of how to develop additional information security risk assessments as needed.

The various assessment types that I have included are for reference purposes and can be utilized as a basis to create your own evaluation and assessment methodologies. In all cases, the ISRAM, or your own revised version, should be observed and utilized by the professional or group creating the assessment methodologies.

THREATS

During the information security risk assessment process, it is critical to identify threats that could potentially harm or adversely affect an organization's critical operations and assets. An organization should refer to reliable sources such as NIST SP 800-12 and SP 800-30, ISO/IEC 13335, BITS (consortium of 100 largest financial institutions in the United States), CERT®/CC (Carnegie Mellon University reporting center for Internet security problems), The SANS Institute, FEMA (Federal Emergency Management Agency), OEM manufacturer of relevant software and systems, and potentially others when compiling a list of possible threats to consider. In Chapter 2, I leverage some of the above sources and a few others when compiling a list of potential threats for the information security assessment methodology (GISAM). A list of threats should be created for each type of assessment methodology and take into account any unique variables in the organization and target environment. Aligning threats with vulnerabilities in a specific system, environment, or application is considered to be highly subjective and highly dependent on the person or people performing the association. This part of risk assessment is considered to be the most subjective and weakest link by many professionals. A threat without a relevant vulnerability does not pose a risk to the organization. A threat that has a known vulnerability and is unknown to the organization is an unidentified risk. An unidentified risk has the potential to cause serious and adverse events, and the impact on the organization is potentially seriously negative. Unidentified risk is highly undesirable and this is the reason for the critical importance of pairing threats and vulnerabilities within the scope of each risk assessment. A list of relevant threats for each risk assessment should be generated and integrated into the analysis and final report component. Some type of classification system or groupings should be created for the various threats. The classification approach helps during the assessment methodology development.

VULNERABILITIES

Vulnerabilities are flaws or weaknesses that have the potential to be exploited by relevant threats and are unique for each type of assessment. There are technical and nontechnical vulnerabilities for each type of information security risk assessment.

Vulnerabilities should be identified as part of the information security risk assessment process. The scope of the assessment will drive the relevant types of vulnerabilities, and the evaluation methodology should attempt to match vulnerabilities with relevant threats to determine the potential impact to the organization. Analyzing threats or vulnerabilities without including both in the analysis will produce inaccurate and unreliable results.

CONTROL LEVEL OF EFFECTIVENESS

Existing controls within the scope of the risk assessment should be evaluated for their level of effectiveness. An appropriate scale should be developed to enable reporting on the control state and effectiveness within the target environment. Each mode in the scale should be defined and applicable to the controls being measured. As appropriate, the impact of each scale mode should be described and applicable to the environment being assessed. The control level of effectiveness is a key determinant in understanding the level of risk for each assessment type. An appropriately applied control should minimize the likelihood of a threat exploiting a specific vulnerability.

LIKELIHOOD

Likelihood is an important component of risk assessment because it provides decision makers and system owners with critical information on the probability that a negative event could occur. A likelihood scale and definition for each mode in the scale should be developed for each assessment methodology. The likelihood rating is considered to be subjective and highly dependent on the knowledge of the individual or group performing the risk assessment. The likelihood rating for each control should consider any relevant threats and vulnerabilities and the level of effectiveness of the control under review. The assessment methodology should be able to relate the likelihood rating to the risk level and ultimately the overall risk rating for the assessment.

IMPACT

Impact assumes that a particular vulnerability has been exploited by a threat and now the impact of this exploit must be quantified. Each type of assessment methodology should have the ability to communicate the impact significance for each control being measured. There is a direct correlation between impact and risk level. A scale should be developed in the assessment methodology and used during the assessment process to communicate the degree of impact for management.

RISK LEVEL

The level of risk communicated for any given assessment is a key indicator for organizational stakeholders and management. In fact, many managers tend to focus on the risk level (commonly referred to as the risk rating) and not center their attention on the details of how the risk level or rating was determined. The risk level should be accounted for at the control level as well as at the overall assessment level. Risk should also be determined for each threat and vulnerability pair.

Within the body of the assessment, risk should be quantified at the control level. Each assessment methodology should provide the detail and scope on how the risk level is determined. Typically, risk is a correlation of several factors, including threats, vulnerabilities, impact, likelihood, etc. Because each control is designed to address specific threats and vulnerabilities, a risk level should be able to be expressed for each control. Ultimately, the culmination of each risk assessment is the final or overall risk rating assigned by the assessor. This risk rating designation is an indication to management of the level of risk posed to their organization based on the assessment scope and methodology. The detailed findings and analysis will enable them to make informed business decisions and judgments about the reported risks.

In the management overview section, special care should be taken to explain the various elements of risks and how they relate to the overall risk level of the assessment. The assessment methodology should review each control and associate the four key components of risk (threats, vulnerabilities, likelihood, and impact).

To effectively determine risk level, the likelihood of a given threat and vulnerability being exploited must be considered, the potential impact must be calculated and assigned, and the level of effectiveness of the current controls must be analyzed. A risk level matrix should be developed within the assessment methodology that correlates these various factors and helps determine the risk level in a systematic and uniform method. Within the GISAM, these factors are accounted for and detailed.

The overall risk ratings should be described in five categories. These categories should be slight, guarded, moderate, high, and critical. Table 1.1 describes the five risk ratings and their intended meanings. A suggested color for each rating is as follows: slight (green), guarded (blue), moderate (yellow), high (orange), critical (red).

RECOMMENDATIONS

Recommendations are focused on identifying the gaps in existing controls and reporting on the deficiencies so that management can take corrective actions to close the gaps during the risk mitigation phase. The recommendations are performed by a knowledgeable and skilled subject matter expert who has the ability to correlate all the risk assessment data as well as the external variables that have the potential to shape a portion of the recommendations. The overall goal of the recommendations phase is to identify information security gaps and ultimately provide management a platform to reduce the risk to the organization. The recommendations should be communicated in a business format and in a way that the business leaders can understand and apply.

ANALYSIS AND FINAL REPORT

A business report should be prepared once the information security risk assessment is completed. The purpose of the analysis and final report is to provide decision makers with information needed to understand factors that can negatively influence organizational operations. The resulting analysis should help managers make informed judgments concerning the extent of actions needed to reduce risk. Each risk assessment methodology should include an executive overview and detailed analysis and recommendations sections. It should be noted that an information security risk assessment is not an audit; it is a structured analysis of the existing controls and potential risks to the organization.

TABLE 1.1
Risk Rating Scale

Rating	Description
Critical	There is no evidence that any controls or safeguards have been designed and implemented to protect organizational assets. Critical vulnerabilities with the presence of applicable threats exist within the environment being assessed. A compromise of vulnerabilities is possible and likely based on the current state. A compromise could cause a serious and negative impact to the organization including substantial financial loss, lack of compliance with regulatory or contractual requirements, and impact to the company brand and reputation. The organization would likely have an impaired ability to operate if the risks were realized.
High	There are a limited number of controls and safeguards that have been implemented to protect organizational assets. Vulnerabilities, including critical, still exist and are in the presence of applicable threats. A compromise of vulnerabilities is possible and could cause a serious impact to the organization, including financial loss, lack of compliance with regulatory or contractual requirements, and impact to the company brand and reputation.
Moderate	The majority of the most critical controls and safeguards have been implemented to protect organizational assets. Vulnerabilities still exist and are in the presence of applicable threats. A compromise of these less critical vulnerabilities is possible and would likely be contained to a business unit or division within the organization. Exercised vulnerabilities could cause a negative impact including financial loss.
Guarded	Critical controls and safeguards have been implemented to protect organizational assets. Noncritical vulnerabilities still exist and are in the presence of applicable threats. A compromise of these less critical vulnerabilities is possible and would likely be contained to a project, business unit, or division. Exercised vulnerabilities would have limited impact, including financial loss.
Slight	All critical controls and safeguards have been implemented to protect organizational assets, including additional compensating controls. There are no identified vulnerabilities in the presence of applicable threats at this time. Potential impact would be localized to the project level with minimal financial loss.

REFERENCES

Information Security Risk Assessment, Practices of Leading Organizations, U.S. General Accounting Office, Nov. 1999.

ISO/IEC 17799:2005 Information Technology — Security Techniques — Code of Practice for Information Security Management, International Organization for Standardization, 2005.

National Institute of Standards and Technology Special Publication 800-12, *An Introduction to Computer Security: The NIST Handbook*, U.S. Department of Commerce, 1997.

Stoneburner, G., Goguen, A, and Feringa, A., *National Institute of Standards and Technology Special Publication 800-30*, U.S. Department of Commerce, 2002.

2 Global Information Security Assessment Methodology (GISAM™)

It is important to keep in perspective the purpose and intent of these first two chapters. The first chapter presented a model that can be used for information security risk assessment. A model in this context is used to define the basic parameters that organizations should consider and implement when designing and developing information security risk assessments.

During the first step of the Information Security Risk Assessment Model (ISRAM™), the information security professional must assist management in the proper selection of the assessment methodology that is most appropriate for the environment to be evaluated. The Global Information Security Assessment Methodology (GISAM™) is the risk assessment methodology for the organizational information security risk assessment. As mentioned in the first chapter, this type of assessment is aimed at quantifying and qualifying information security risks holistically at the organizational level. Organizational risks can be identified and grouped into three major categories: operational, technical, and management. This type of information security assessment could be thought of as a comprehensive view of information security at an organizational level because it considers operational and management aspects of information security as well as the application and use of technology.

Many business professionals as well as information technology professionals tend to think of information security as a tactical and technical issue. The GISAM will help organizational leaders, and anyone exposed to the output and findings, quickly understand that information security has multiple dimensions that also include management and operational aspects. In fact, tactical technical controls are a small part of the overall GISAM as a direct result of the ISO/IEC 17799:2005 controls. It is not my intention to downplay the criticality and importance of technology in information security; rather it is to raise the awareness and understanding that management and operational disciplines are equally important and at times even more important.

An organization could deploy the industry's best technology controls such as firewalls, intrusion prevention and detection systems, audit logging, and a host of others, but without the proper policies, procedures, guidelines, and application by the appropriate staff, these controls will do very little to protect and safeguard the intended assets. To further extend the issue, if management does not support information security at the policy, cultural, enforcement, or financial level, the information security initiative is in danger. Information security is highly operational and people are at the core of the matter.

The GISAM can be applied to small companies or global organizations, making this assessment methodology very scalable. As with any information security risk assessment, the findings and analysis are highly dependent on the knowledge and skill of the assessor. In many cases there are very limited data and information about threat probability and asset value, therefore forcing a heavy reliance on the skill of the assessment professional. The GISAM will be presented in logical segments for the purpose of definition and clarity. In the third chapter I present and describe an evaluation process (ISE™) weaving together the assessment methodology for the purpose of communicating the risk assessment findings to executive management and key stakeholders.

GISAM AND ISRAM RELATIONSHIP

There probably is not a single information security risk assessment methodology that has the ability to fit every organization without modification and adjustments. This is due in large part to the unique requirements for each organization. However, this does not mean a suitable assessment methodology cannot be developed that meets the majority of organizational needs and requirements. The point of departure for a successful approach is the scalability and adoptability characteristics. The GISAM is adaptable and adoptable by organizations in any industry and can be applied to a small private firm or an international public company with tens of thousands of employees and several lines of business.

Because the majority of organizations that will be using the GISAM are already in existence and have preexisting information security policies and controls in place, the position of evaluating the existing environment and controls is taken in this book. The resulting analysis and recommendations will allow the management team to adjust their policies and controls as desired to meet their own individualized risk management requirements and objectives. Missing policies will be highlighted as will weak or missing controls and safeguards. The GISAM leverages the ISO/IEC 17799:2005 (27002) Code of Practice for Information Security Management as the controls framework to ensure a comprehensive review of controls across all aspects of information security at an operational, management, and technology level within the organization. The GISAM is a pragmatic operational interpretation of the ISRAM and defines the relationships between the information security elements of the model for the purpose of identifying risks and communicating the analysis and results to management.

Information security risk assessment can be described as a platform for management to make decisions about information security and higher-level risk management matters. There are two different perspectives for information security risk assessments: new or existing. A new assessment is described as an assessment that takes place during the design process and before the environment is made operational (analysis). An existing assessment is performed after the organization or system has been formed and made operational (assessment). The objectives of these two assessment types differ in that a new assessment is concerned with which controls and safeguards are appropriate and the existing assessment is focused on the measurement of existing controls. The GISAM is designed to measure the level of effectiveness of existing controls within an organization's environment, report to the organization the level of risk resulting from the current state of controls, and identify any missing elements within the control framework. Without formal information security risk assessments, management has no platform to base decisions on or fully understand the relationships between the elements in the risk model.

GISAM DESIGN CRITERIA

Each organization possesses its own unique characteristics. Some organizations focus more on technology-oriented risks, whereas other organizations are driven by legal, contractual, or regulatory information security requirements. This is the reason why I have created several different information security risk assessment methodologies as mentioned in the first chapter.

Independent of the exact method, an assessment methodology should be complete in its coverage of all relevant information security components. The property of completeness can be addressed by using a risk assessment model. An example of this type of model was presented in the first chapter (ISRAM). Because the GISAM is directed toward assessing information security risks at the organizational level, the ISO/IEC 17799:2005 Code of Practice for Information Security Management was chosen as the control framework to ensure that a comprehensive assessment was delivered and could scale across any size organization.

The issue of impact is very important to every organization, and this is why the GISAM delivers a comprehensive approach for assessing and reporting on the impact to the organization.

An effective assessment methodology should be adaptable and capable of scaling to the requirements of the target organization on all levels. The methodology must produce reliable and accurate results, irrespective of the organization being assessed. Furthermore, it should not rely on financial quantification to identify risks.

The assessment method should be easy to use by competent professionals and not require complicated training for a long period of time to use the method. Where possible, automation in the form of calculations and knowledge bases should be used to ensure accuracy and promote consistency and efficiency. The method should be straightforward and promote a fast implementation.

An assessment method must give clear, precise, and justified observations and recommendations to management. Managers must be able to understand the analysis included in the assessment report and be able to prioritize report recommendations into actionable remediation tasks.

Information security risk assessments are generally viewed from two different perspectives: information security and management. In some cases the criteria overlap and in other cases the objectives are clearly different.

In an attempt to design and implement a comprehensive and effective organizational information security risk assessment methodology, I created a listing of basic criteria from both perspectives. Refer to the following sections for a listing of criteria.

INFORMATION SECURITY PROFESSIONAL

The information security professional's view of information security is traditionally different from that of a senior business manager. The reasons are mostly obvious, but generally the information security professional possesses a deeper understanding of the underpinnings of information security and tends to lean toward a more comprehensive type of assessment method.

Information Security Professional Criteria

- Comprehensive and complete
- Requires expertise to perform assessment
- Quantify control effectiveness
- Adaptable
- Assign risk rating
- Valid and credible

The information security professional wants the assessment to be delivered by knowledgeable information security professionals, ensuring credible and valid analysis and results. They also want the assessment to be comprehensive in nature but also adaptable to various lines of business or departments. Information security professionals generally agree that for organizational assessments a risk rating expressed from mathematical calculations is not the best choice for expressing risk. A mixed-mode type of assessment that leverages quantitative data and expresses the risk in qualitative means is generally the most appropriate approach to ensure that management has the clearest path to create an action plan to start reducing and eliminating identified risks.

MANAGEMENT

The management team of an organization is also concerned with many of the same criteria as information security professionals. They also have some additional design criteria, and some of the overlapping criteria are modified.

Management Criteria

- Cost
- Agreement on assessment type and scope by security and management
- Adaptable
- Valid and credible
- Results are reportable to management
- Consistent
- Usable
- Automated

The management of any organization must always be concerned with costs and expenses. Information security assessments are no exception. The cost to employ as well as the cost of purchasing or developing an assessment method must be considered. Collecting and capturing the data also requires the valuable time of staff and managers. Organizational structure may also be a driver of cost concerns. With competing initiatives involving corporate compliance, the information security assessment process must be seen as a value to executive management to ensure its long-term health. Adaptive organizations may require fast and inexpensive methods, whereas more traditional organizations may prefer a well-documented and comprehensive method which typically has more time-consuming tasks associated with the assessment method.

Most managers would agree that it is important for the management and information security teams to agree on the scope and type of information security assessment. Management recognizes the need for expertise that information security professionals possess, and it is logical to conclude they would want their agreement on the assessment method.

Adaptability is a key design criterion from management's perspective. The assessment method should be able to adapt to an organization's needs and business requirements. The assessment should also be able to be applied to a wide array of system types and environments.

Managers typically want to avoid complexity if at all possible. In some cases, complexity cannot be avoided, but the overarching theme is to minimize complexity while still providing comprehensive and reliable results. Completeness is also a design criterion that management and information security professionals agree on. The assessment method must be complete and have the ability to capture the type of information security risks that it was originally designed for. A key objective for any information security assessment from management's perspective is to have accurate, credible, and reliable results that are reportable and actionable.

Automation of the method is highly desirable from management's perspective. If automation is properly implemented, most information security professionals would find it desirable as well. Automation efficiencies can be easily realized by creating a software application or business tool to deliver the assessment and standardize the reporting process. Tim Layton & Associates, LLC, has developed a risk assessment application based on the GISAM that is used when working with clients. To attempt a manual process with a complex assessment methodology is not reasonable because of the time and cost to deliver the assessment final product. Organizations will have to weigh the costs of developing a similar application versus the cost of delivery and application.

GENERAL ASSESSMENT TYPES

Fundamentally, there are two major types of risk assessments: quantitative and qualitative. GISAM leverages both assessment types within the methodology and is considered to be a mixed-mode type of assessment. For example, during the analysis phase in the final report, the quantitative scale data is analyzed and qualitatively expressed. It is much easier to create actionable items with qualitative expressions. Each assessment type will be described in the following sections.

QUANTITATIVE

A quantitative approach suggests a correlation between the value of the asset that needs protection and the cost of the controls required to effectively mitigate the associated risks to an acceptable level according to management. Some managers attempt to use the quantitative method to help support the ROI (return on investment) calculations. The concept of ROI has not fared very well in the information security discipline, and some individuals and groups have created variations of the ROI concept in an attempt to capture the true meaning and relationship between ROI and information security. I do not know of any organization that bases its information security controls solely on a ROI strategy.

Typically within a quantitative or ROI approach, a complex statistical analysis is performed in an attempt to predict risk and the associated impact on the organization. For this approach to work, a monetary value must be assigned to the assets being protected. The resulting analysis attempts to estimate the likelihood of a threat occurring and matches a ROI against the suggested controls and safeguards that are required to reduce the risk to an acceptable level. The ISO (information security officer) or CISO (chief information security officer) might have better luck herding cats as opposed to developing and rolling out a program based on these concepts.

A quantitative assessment requires a ratio or interval type scale because this type of scale is numerical-based. A ratio scale measures in terms of intervals and an absolute zero point of origin. The use of a ratio scale allows virtually any inferential statistical analysis. An interval scale measures in terms of equal intervals or degrees of difference, but its zero point, or point of beginning, is arbitrarily established. The use of this type of scale enables one to determine the mean, standard deviation, and Pearson product moment correlations. Because of the lack of information required to successfully perform a quantitative assessment, many organizations use a qualitative approach as the overall method and leverage quantitative approaches as appropriate.

The quantitative method attempts to assign numerical values to risk and to mathematically combine all identified risks in a way that demonstrates their absolute or relative effects. The resulting numerical-based expressions are typically converted into costs or expenses to the organization.

Depending on the assessment method being used, the culture of the organization and the business requirements will help determine if a quantitative method is appropriate or not. Report results would be expressed in terms of numbers on a scale. For example, if the risk assessment process is expected to provide management with a measure of risk for the organization being reviewed, the rating would be expressed with a number and corresponding scale. The left end of the scale would indicate low risk and numbers falling to the right end of the scale would indicate more risk, independent of ratio or interval scales.

Organizational information security assessments such as GISAM would be very difficult to report solely in quantitative terms. It would be extremely difficult to create an action plan for management to lower the risks to their organization solely with this type of information and data. They may be able to express a projected annual loss estimate as a result of weak controls, but they would not be able to communicate a plan of how to address the identified deficiencies. This is one reason why a mixed-mode approach is very effective for many organizations.

QUALITATIVE

The qualitative method uses terms and phrases to express risk. For example, "low risk," "medium risk," and "high risk" are common terms within this method. The qualitative method eliminates complex calculations, does not employ a cost-benefit analysis, and is typically easier to understand than a quantitative approach. Descriptive language is provided for each risk type that helps management and readers of the assessment findings understand the risk ratings. Risk in a qualitative method is considered to be more subjective than risk in a quantitative method. Qualitative information requires a nominal or ordinal scale as opposed to a cardinal or rational scale for quantitative data. Nominal scales measure in terms of names or designations of discrete units or categories. For statistical calculation purposes, the mode, the percentage values, or the chi-square can be figured. An ordinal scale measures in terms of values such as "more" or "less" but does not specify the size of the intervals. Ordinal scales allow the calculation of the median, percentile rank, and rank correlation.

Whether a quantitative, qualitative, or mixed-mode approach is used, risk is always the measure of the expected loss in the absence of controls, countermeasures, or mitigation actions. The assessment of information security risk is considered by most to be more difficult than others because the threat probability and asset values are often limited or reliable data do not exist. Risk factors are constantly changing and risk assessments are only as good as the last one performed.

GISAM COMPONENTS

The GISAM is composed of the following elements: controls, key risk indicators, assessment scale, rating rationale, likelihood, impact, control risk level, threats, threat ranking, vulnerabilities, risk rating, weighting, recommendations, and reporting. The next chapter takes the GISAM components and creates a formal organizational information security risk assessment process known as ISE. The following sections describe each component of the GISAM methodology.

THREATS

The topic of threats as it relates to the GISAM assessment methodology is complex and on the bleeding edge. To date I have no knowledge of any source publishing threat sources and threat actions for all 133 of the ISO/IEC 17799:2005 (27002) body of controls. The closest solution that I am aware of is the "BITS Kalculator: Key Risk Management Tools for Information Security Operational Risks" published in July 2004 by BITS. This tool is based on the ISO/IEC 17799:2000 standard and

Basel I. The tool may still be available via its Web site at www.bitsinfo.org. Although I believe this was a very good attempt, and a step in the right direction, this tool and process is not comprehensive enough to account for the many variables that exist with the current and diverse business landscape. The tool is also focused exclusively on the banking industry and therefore much less usable by other industries. Furthermore, there are many different ways and methods to express threat statements with no one commonly accepted method. Public sources such as BITS, ISO/IEC 17799, NIST, CERT, and the ISF (Information Security Forum) methodology all describe and express threats in different formats, causing more confusion about establishing an industry norm.

Aligning threats with vulnerabilities is a key component to assessing risk. Threats may exist, but if the system or organization does not have a relevant vulnerability that can be exploited by the threat, then theoretically there should not be any measurable risk at that point in time. Threats, vulnerabilities, and the assessment of their existence are a dynamic and never-ending process. The most sensible approach that management can take today is to assess their information security risks to include threat and vulnerability pairs as often as they can afford to conduct the process.

The task of producing a finite list of threats that are mapped to the ISO/IEC 17799:2005 (27002) Code of Practice for Information Security Management is time-intensive and likely will produce arguable results no matter the quality or depth of the output. The threat categories and threats published within the GISAM assessment methodology should be used as reference and considered a starting point by information security professionals. The threat information should be modified as necessary and additional threats meeting specific organizational requirements should be added as required.

After careful review of the most current threat information from industry-relevant sources, I have created threat categories and assigned appropriate threats to each category for application within the GISAM. Within the GISAM the source of threats are broken down into four major categories: Human Malicious, Human Non-malicious, Accidental, and Other (natural or other unplanned disruptions or disasters). The threats that I list within each of the four threat categories are sourced from professional experience, NIST, BITS, and other publicly available industry and trade information. Refer to the following Listings A, B, C, and D for the threats separated by category.

Listing A: Human Malicious

- Bombing (attacks or threats)
- Physical attacks
- Remote access control software
- Sabotage
- Terrorists
- Social engineering
- Surveillance
- Trojan horses
- War dialing

- Vulnerability scanning tools and software
- Customers/vendors/business partners
- Denial-of-service attacks
- Dumpster diving
- Computer viruses and worms
- Virus hoax
- Black-hat hackers and crackers
- Password crackers
- Web crawlers
- Impersonation or spoofing
- Employee or management malicious actions
- Fraud
- Corporate espionage
- Embezzlement
- Biological attack
- Network spoofing
- Network or application backdoors
- Network or application time bomb
- Web defacement
- Extortion
- Stolen laptop computer
- Vandalism, robbery
- Malicious code
- Shoulder surfing
- Tailgating to gain unauthorized access
- Unauthorized scans
- Unauthorized network or systems access

Listing B: Human Non-malicious

- Discussion of sensitive matters in open
- Human error
- Leave computer screen unlocked
- Leave door unlocked
- Leave sensitive document exposed
- Lost laptop computer
- Unintentional denial of service
- Lawsuit/litigation
- Inadequate access controls
- Inadequate training
- Inadequate corporate policies
- Inadequate program testing
- Inadequate risk analysis undertaken
- Inadequate supervision
- Lack of ethics
- Poor management philosophy

- Unlocked trash containers
- Weak internal controls
- Update of wrong file
- Damage to computer disk

Listing C: Accidental

- Airplane crash
- Automobile crash
- Building collapse
- Application software failure
- CPU malfunction/failure
- DNS failure
- Fire
- Gas leaks
- Hardware failure
- HVAC failure
- Telecommunications failure
- Software defects
- Destruction of data, documents, reports, disks
- Failure of fire and smoke alarms

Listing D: Other (natural or other unplanned disruptions or disasters)

- Dust/sand
- Snow/ice storms
- Chemical spill
- Civil disorder
- Epidemic
- Floods
- Typhoon, tidal wave
- Tornadoes, wind damage, high winds
- Hurricane
- Volcanic disruption
- Heat
- Hazardous waste exposure
- War
- Work stoppage/strike
- Seismic activity
- Lightning
- Power failure
- Power fluctuation
- Radiation contamination

The four threat categories and various threats must be mapped to each of the 133 ISO/IEC 17799:2005 (27002) controls to include them in your assessment.

Chapter 7, "Security Policy," presents a detailed example of how to create threat and vulnerability mappings for each control within the standard. The exercise of mapping threat statements to each of the 133 controls is complex and extremely time-consuming but very necessary. These mappings should be created with consensus and not in a silo. It is important to get as many qualified resources involved or reviewing the threat and vulnerability mappings as possible. It is unlikely that any single person possesses the depth of knowledge and skills within all 11 security clauses to effectively develop or review the threat and vulnerability maps. Focus on finding subject matter experts within each security clause and leverage their knowledge and skill. Also, continue looking for help and resources via the Internet in this area. Be sure to check my Web site at www.timlayton.com for additional information as well.

THREAT RANKING

In the "Threat" section, the concept of threats and how they relate to vulnerabilities and risk was established. The critical point of departure for threats can be further quantified by the following attributes: likelihood, speed of onset, existing control level of effectiveness, and impact. The likelihood and impact ratings are determined as part of the assessment process, as is the control level of effectiveness. Likelihood, impact, and control level of effectiveness are presented and described in detail in forthcoming sections later in this chapter.

The only input variable that needs to be determined by the information security professional during the assessment is the speed of onset (slow or sudden without warning). Furthermore, opportunity, motivation, and capability will be dynamically factored into the threat ranking by the information security assessment professional at the time of assessment.

A corresponding number must be assigned to each of the four variables to allow proper calculation. For the purpose of the threat ranking calculation, a value of 1, 10, or 20 will be assigned for likelihood ratings of low, medium, or high, respectively. The control level-of-effectiveness (LOE) rating ranges from 1 to 5 and will assume whatever value the information security professional assigned during the assessment. Within the LOE scale there is a possibility of a rating level 0. For the purpose of the threat ranking calculation, any control that received a level 0 rating will be calculated as the number 1. The impact rating as assigned during the assessment can range from a low of 0 to a high of 5. The 0 rating for impact will be treated the same as the control level-of-effectiveness rating. The input variable for threat ranking that will be assigned by the information security professional during the risk assessment will be "speed of onset." A value of 1 represents slow and 2 represents sudden without warning. These four variables (likelihood, control LOE, impact, and speed of onset) are used to determine the numerical score for the threat ranking.

For example, if a control received a value of 10 for likelihood (medium), 3 for control level of effectiveness (level 3 LOE), 4 for impact (high), and 1 for speed of onset (slow), it would yield a numerical score of 120. The information security professional or automated application would reference Table 2.1 to determine the threat ranking calculation qualitative expression.

TABLE 2.1
Threat Ranking Chart

Rating	Expression
Low	Less than 500
Medium	500 to 750
High	751 to 1000

Note: Threat ranking score for each control is calculated as follows: likelihood (LMH = 1, 10, 20) × speed of onset (slow 1, sudden 2) × existing control LOE (1, 2, 3, 4, 5) × impact (1, 2, 3, 4, 5).

After the threat ranking score is calculated, three variables (opportunity, motivation, and capability) must be qualitatively analyzed and factored in by the assessor before assigning the final threat ranking rating. The combination of the threat ranking score and the three threat ranking variables is used by the information security professional as guidance when assigning the threat ranking rating. As a general rule, the three variables should not increase the threat ranking to be greater than the threat ranking score. There is a strong possibility they could suggest the assignment of a lower threat ranking rating. For example, if the threat ranking score was medium, the theoretical maximum threat ranking rating is medium. The three variables (opportunity, motivation, and capability) are then factored in at the time of the assessment to determine if the assigned threat ranking rating should be lower than medium.

Table 2.2 illustrates some of the most common scenarios that will likely be discovered during most assessments. This table is intended as general guidance and not as the rule. All assessment factors and variables must be considered at the time of the assessment to effectively assign the proper threat ranking rating.

TABLE 2.2
Threat Rank Rating Guidance

Threat Ranking Score	Opportunity	Motivation	Capability	Suggested Threat Ranking Rating
High	Y	Y	Y	High
High	Y	N	N	Medium
High	N	N	N	Low
Medium	Y	Y	Y	Medium
Medium	Y	N	N	Low
Medium	N	Y	N	Low
Low	Y	Y	Y	Low

In addition to selecting and presenting the threat ranking rating, the information security professional should include a section for rating rationale to help justify or explain a threat ranking rating.

VULNERABILITIES

Vulnerabilities are weaknesses or a lack of controls which allow a threat to be exploited and realized. There may be multiple vulnerabilities for each threat. To produce meaningful data and analysis for management, a comprehensive information security risk assessment is required. The various elements within the ISRAM must be integrated and analyzed in a cohesive fashion to produce an accurate depiction of risk for management. Information security professionals must be concerned with the lower-level details such as threats, vulnerabilities, control level of effectiveness, and likelihood, whereas management wants to understand the impact to their organization and what exposures may exist. The GISAM is developed for business leaders and focuses on producing meaningful analysis and results so that management can implement an action plan to minimize or eliminate identified exposures and risks.

The GISAM or any other information security risk assessment process must account for vulnerabilities when reviewing controls and safeguards. Because the GISAM uses the ISO/IEC 17799:2005 (27002) controls as the control framework, a list of vulnerabilities must be developed for each of the 133 controls and then matched to appropriate threat statements. As with threats, it is up to the organizations and information security professionals to create this mapping and relationship between threats and each control.

In the future I hope to see some collaborative work by information security professionals or other organizations that is publicly available to review and adopt into their own information security risk assessments. The process of identifying potential vulnerabilities for each threat for all 133 controls is an enormous effort. Chapter 7, "Security Policy," presents a list of vulnerabilities mapped to a threat statement in an effort to help you get started with creating your own statements and mappings. Over time I will likely publish new and additional information on my Web site at www.timlayton.com.

CONTROLS

The information security controls for the GISAM are the 133 controls of the ISO/IEC 17799:2005 (27002). A complete listing of these controls is provided in Chapters 7 through 17. The selection of the ISO/IEC 17799:2005 (27002) Code of Practice for Information Security Management was a logical and easy process. It is the most widely accepted code of practice for information security in the world today and the controls are focused at the management, operational, and technology levels, making it a holistic business-minded best practice for information security. Using the GISAM in conjunction with the standard assures organizations that a comprehensive assessment and approach is being taken to identify information security–related risks. It also ensures that industry best-practice principles are being applied within their organization.

Key Risk Indicator (KRI) Controls

Based on several years of experience, I generally group controls into two categories: key risk indicators and compensating. Key risk indicator (KRI) controls are those controls that are paramount and required to uphold the integrity of the organization's information security posture, independent of environment or industry. Compensating controls are the controls that provide additional assurance and support for the key risk indicator controls. There are a total of 133 controls in the ISO/IEC 17799:2005 (27002) Code of Practice for Information Security Management. The concept of key risk indicators is a sound risk management concept that has roots in many different assessment frameworks. KRI controls have the ability to help management identify serious risks very quickly as well as identify shifts in established patterns within the organization. More information on KRIs is becoming available from industry sources and institutions. This can be helpful when an organization is attempting to establish initial thresholds and baselines for organization within a particular industry.

Key risk indicators can help an organization, division, or line-of-business take a proactive approach to managing information security risk. If management believes the selected KRI controls honestly reflect major risk indicators within their organization, then this is a platform for higher-quality decision making. Because the total number of KRI controls is much less than the number of controls used to measure and identify risks, it is much easier to work with the data, establish trends, and gain consensus among peers and management.

There is no formal guidance from the International Organization for Standardization (ISO) on which of the 133 controls are considered to be key risk indicators. I have created a list of KRI controls based on several years of direct experience with the ISO/IEC 17799 and assessing many different organizations. I have assessed and evaluated a host of organizations within the United States and internationally using the ISO/IEC 17799 standard as the general controls framework. I have also gained peer acceptance of the KRI list of controls by several other information security professionals who possess detailed knowledge and have extensive working experience with the ISO/IEC 17799:2005 standard.

There is a total of 35 key risk indicator controls, leaving 98 compensating controls. Table 2.3 provides a listing of the selected KRI controls. Every KRI control and why these controls create a security baseline that all modern organizations should consider are detailed in a later chapter.

In the first column of Table 2.3, the reference number for every KRI control is listed. In the second column, a designation of M (management), T (technical), or O (operational) is provided. Management controls require management's approval, support, or direct actions. Operational controls are controls that are action- or task-oriented and typically nontechnical in nature. Technical controls require the modification, configuration, or verification of information processing facilities.

Controls can possess any combination to include all three of these properties. The second column in Table 2.3 designates the dominant characteristics of each control that are required to deliver the scope and intent of the control. In the third column, the title of the control is provided.

TABLE 2.3
KRI Controls and Impact Area Designations

Control #	Class	Title of Control
5.1.1	MO	Information Security Policy Document
6.1.1	M	Management Commitment to Information Security
6.1.3	M	Allocation of Information Security Responsibilities
6.1.8	MO	Independent Review of Information Security
6.2.1	M	Identification of Risks Related to External Parties
7.1.1	O	Inventory of Assets
7.2.1	M	Classification Guideline
8.1.2	MO	Screening
8.2.2	MO	Information Security Awareness, Education, and Training
8.3.3	MTO	Removal of Access Rights
9.1.1	O	Physical Security Perimeter
9.1.4	MO	Protecting Against External and Environmental Threats
9.2.6	O	Secure Disposal or Reuse of Equipment
10.1.1	M	Documented Operating Procedures
10.1.2	O	Change Management
10.1.3	MO	Segregation of Duties
10.3.2	MTO	System Acceptance
10.4.1	MTO	Controls Against Malicious Code
10.7.1	MO	Management of Removable Media
10.7.3	MTO	Information Handling Procedures
10.8.3	O	Physical Media in Transit
10.9.1	TO	Electronic Commerce
11.1.1	MO	Access Control Policy
11.2.1	MTO	User Registration
11.4.5	TO	Segregation in Networks
11.7.2	MO	Teleworking
12.1.1	M	Security Requirements Analysis and Specification
12.3.1	MO	Policy on the Use of Cryptographic Controls
12.4.2	TO	Protection of System Test Data
12.6.1	MTO	Control of Technical Vulnerabilities
13.1.1	MO	Reporting Information Security Events
14.1.1	MO	Including Information Security in the Business Continuity Management Process
15.1.1	M	Identification of Applicable Legislation
15.1.4	MTO	Data Protection and Privacy of Personal Information
15.2.2	TO	Technical Compliance Checking

A detailed explanation for each of the KRI and compensating controls can be found in Chapters 7 through 17.

Control Assessment Scale

The assessment scale is designed to capture each control's level of effectiveness (LOE) within the organization's operations and environment. The assessment scale I have designed for the GISAM is action-oriented and provides management with a clear indication of what has been accomplished up to the time of the assessment in regard to each control. Because the scale is action-oriented, it is fairly easy for managers and executives to formulate an action plan to improve the level of effectiveness of any control. The lowest rating on the scale (level 0) indicates that the control under review applies to the organization but that nothing has been done to evaluate or implement the control within the organization. The next five levels of the scale (i.e., level 1 through level 5) are graduating steps ranging from awareness of a need for the control (though the organization has implemented the control within their environment) to a comprehensive level within the context and scope of the control objective.

The LOE scale provides a quantitative means to evaluate and assess each control while formulating a qualitative response. Each of the 133 controls within the ISO/IEC 17799 (27002) should be reviewed for each GISAM, ensuring that a best-practice and comprehensive review of information security controls and safeguards is being performed.

The seven-mode LOE scale is provided and described in Table 2.4. A short description for each mode of the scale is provided in the last column to help readers understand the intent of the scale mode. Additional information is provided in forthcoming sections later in this chapter.

A more detailed account of each LOE scale mode is described in the LOE Mode Description table (Table 2.5). This table should be used as reference and guidance by information security professionals when assigning control level-of-effectiveness ratings for each of the 133 controls.

Understanding the relationship between the various LOE scale modes and potential implications is a critical component for crafting successful solutions. The text in Table 2.6 provides a breakdown of the implications by control LOE mode.

TABLE 2.4
Level of Effectiveness (LOE) Scale

Rating	Description
Level 0	Nonexistent, but control applies
Level 1	Aware, but no action
Level 2	Partially implemented
Level 3	Defined process or program
Level 4	Managed and measurable
Level 5	Comprehensive
N/A	The control is not applicable at this time

TABLE 2.5
LOE Mode Description

Rating	LOE Mode Description
Level 0	There is no evidence that the control has been applied and there is no related documentation or procedures. At a management level, the organization has not recognized the need for this control at this time. It is determined by the assessment team that this control should apply to the organization.
Level 1	Management is aware that this control applies to their organization but no formal effort has been made to implement the control. There are no official policies, procedures, or written procedures at this time. This control may have been previously cited in an audit finding in the past but has not been fully addressed at this time. Employees are generally not aware of their specific responsibilities as they relate to this control.
Level 2	Management recognizes that this control does apply to their organization and they have made some type of attempt to implement. There may be partial documentation in the form of policy or procedures in place and some employees may be aware of their related responsibilities. This control is not reviewed on a regular basis to ensure its effectiveness.
Level 3	Management has documented the need for this control as well as the related policy and procedures. Most employees are aware of their responsibilities as they relate to this control. This control is reviewed at least annually, but the process and results are not always fully documented.
Level 4	Management has established and documented the appropriate policies and procedures. Employees are aware of their responsibilities as they relate to this control. This control is reviewed on a regular basis, at least semiannually, and the process and results are adequately documented. The control addresses the risks it was designed to address and lowers the associated risks.
Level 5	Management has established and documented the appropriate policies and procedures. Employees are aware of their responsibilities as they relate to this control. This control is reviewed on a continual basis and the process and results are completely documented. The control fully addresses the risks it was designed to address and effectively lowers the associated risks.

LIKELIHOOD

A likelihood rating is assigned by the information security assessment professional for each control in the GISAM that does not receive a N/A rating. The likelihood rating choices include low, medium, and high. This rating represents the probability that a negative event will occur based on the current state of the control and any potential vulnerability that has the potential to be exercised within the construct of applicable threats. Each control is implemented to minimize or eliminate identified or potential threat and vulnerability pairs. No default value is set within this assessment because each environment is unique, and therefore there is no reasonable way to establish a baseline based on unknown threats and vulnerabilities for each environment being reviewed.

To derive the most appropriate likelihood rating, the information security professional must consider four primary elements: control level of effectiveness, threats, vulnerabilities, and local environment.

TABLE 2.6
LOE Rating Implications

Rating	Implications
Level 0	Management has not addressed this control on any level; therefore, the organization is open and susceptible to unidentified risks.
Level 1	Management has not developed or implemented appropriate policies, procedures, and documentation. There is a major effort and investment required to produce this documentation.
Level 2	Management has produced some portion of the required policies, procedures, and associated documentation. There is potentially a significant effort required to develop and produce the required documentation.
Level 3	Management has documented and published the required policies, procedures, and related documentation. The review process, with its resulting documentation, is performed annually at best. The level of effort for management to shorten this gap can be significant depending on specific organizational circumstances.
Level 4	Management has documented all relevant policies, procedures, and related documentation. The review process is performed at least twice per year and the level of effort to shorten this gap should be minimal unless specific extenuating circumstances exist.
Level 5	There are no serious implications known at this time because management has effectively and efficiently implemented appropriate controls and safeguards for the identified risks.

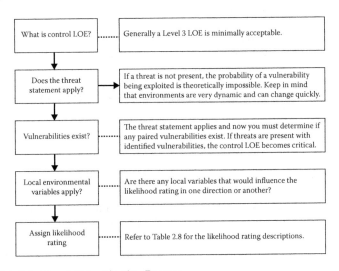

FIGURE 2.1 Likelihood Determination Process

A basic decision-based process can be developed to help the assessor determine the best possible likelihood rating. Refer to Figure 2.1 for an example.

First, the control level of effectiveness is critical to understand. If the control is not as effective as required to address an existing threat and vulnerability pair, the likelihood rating would probably be selected as high. If the control level of

TABLE 2.7
Likelihood Rating Guidance

Control LOE at L4 or L5	Vulnerabilities	Threats	Environmental Factors	Likelihood Rating Suggestion
N	Y	Y	Y	High
N	Y	N	Y	High
N	N	Y	Y	High
N	N	N	Y	High
Y	Y	Y	Y	High
Y	Y	N	Y	High
N	Y	Y	N	High
N	N	N	Y	Medium
Y	Y	N	N	Medium
Y	N	Y	N	Medium
Y	N	N	Y	Medium
Y	N	N	N	Low

effectiveness was rated very high, the likelihood rating would probably be lower. Next, vulnerabilities and threats must be assessed for the control under review. If vulnerabilities exist, but no applicable threats are present at this time, then the likelihood rating would likely be low or medium, depending on the other variables. Lastly, any local environmental variables must be accounted for and factored into the likelihood rating selection. The text in Table 2.7 depicts some of the most common combinations that information security professionals will likely encounter during the assessment process. Not all possible combinations are listed, as this would be too lengthy and it is not necessary. It is important to remember that all four components must be considered when selecting the likelihood rating. As a general rule of thumb, if a threat or vulnerability is present, then the default rating is medium unless there are local or environmental variables that cause enough concern to raise the rating to high. The text and information in Table 2.7 should be used as a training mechanism or guidance for the assessment professional.

The likelihood ratings (high, medium, low) are qualitative expressions representing how likely vulnerabilities will be exercised by applicable threats. Table 2.8 provides a definition and expression for each of the three ratings.

As mentioned in the first chapter, likelihood is an important component of risk assessment because it provides decision makers and system owners with critical information on the probability that a negative event could occur. The likelihood rating is considered to be subjective by many people. The subjective concerns can be minimized by developing and using a documented process to determine likelihood. It is critical to provide clear definitions for each likelihood rating and straightforward guidance on the selection criteria.

TABLE 2.8
Likelihood Rating

Rating	Description
High	Known threats and vulnerabilities exist and the control level of effectiveness is very low and not acceptable; other environmental variables may also exist that would increase the likelihood rating.
Medium	Threats and vulnerabilities exist, but the control level of effectiveness is considered to be borderline acceptable or other environmental variables may also exist causing the likelihood rating to be less than high but more than low.
Low	Threats or vulnerabilities may exist, control level of effectiveness is rated at level 4 or level 5, and no environmental variables exist at this time that would increase the possibility that vulnerabilities could be exploited and exercised.

IMPACT

The impact rating in the GISAM is a critical piece of information for stakeholders to understand. Independent of all the technical jargon, management wants to understand the risks, exposures, and potential impact to the organization. When impact is determined during the assessment of controls, it is assumed that vulnerabilities have been exploited by threats and now the potential impact to the organization has to be determined and communicated to management. Keep in mind that impact is only one part of the control risk level calculation. Risk level is determined by the likelihood and impact ratings. In the forthcoming risk level section, a detailed risk level rating system and matrix will be described and detailed to further explain this concept.

Assessing and assigning the overall impact rating (OIR) for each control is not an easy task. There are many variables that must be taken into consideration. An impact scale and detailed guidance for scale selection will be described in the next sections.

The impact scale is composed of four components: impact expression (low, medium, high), numeric rating (0 to 5), qualitative rating (no impact to significant), and rating description (no measurable impact, etc.). The impact scale, including the rating elements and rating descriptions, is presented and described in Table 2.9.

Each control has the ability to impact one or more areas (management, technical, operations) as previously described in the "Key Risk Indicator Controls" section. The impact rating for each of these areas can vary for each impact area depending on an unlimited number of internal or external variables. In Chapters 7 through 17 I have assigned impact area designations (M = management, T = technical, O = operations) for each of the 133 ISO/IEC 17799:2005 (27002) controls. I have assigned the impact area designations that most accurately capture the dominant characteristics required to deliver the true scope and intent of the control objective.

During the GISAM, it is up to the information security professional to assign a control area impact rating (IR) ranging from 0 (no impact) to 9 (extensive impact) for each impact area per applicable control. The ratings in the IR scale are intended

TABLE 2.9
Impact Rating Scale

Rating	#	Impact Value	Description
Low	0	No impact	No measurable impact at this time
Low	1	Minor	No revenue losses; minimal cost and effort required to make repairs
Med	2	Tangible	Some revenue loss, but not considered significant by management; potentially days of unplanned effort for recovery and repairs
Med	3	Significant	Substantial revenue loss and expenses; many weeks of unplanned effort will be required for recovery and repair; it is possible that the organization could experience damage to its reputation and be exposed to litigation; a breach of sensitive data is likely
High	4	Serious	Extensive revenue losses and unplanned expenses; loss of network operations resulting in activation of DR or BCP plans; integrity of data or services was compromised and there is likely a temporary loss of facilities; there will be damage to the organization's reputation; legal or regulatory requirements are likely in question
High	5	Grave	Complete loss of business and operations is very likely; loss of human life is possible

to communicate the level of financial exposure (revenues losses, costs, etc.) and effort (time, human capital, etc.) that is required as a result of the vulnerability being exploited by the identified threat(s).

A table describing the possible impact rating scale choices is described and illustrated in Table 2.10. This table should be used as guidance by the assessing information security professional.

To determine the OIR for each control, the IRs are summed and the calculated average represents the control's overall impact rating. During the reporting process, this rating is expressed qualitatively as low, medium, or high along with a numeric subcategory of 0 through 3 for the low and medium ratings. For example, a low rating could be described as "Low 0" or "Low 1" and a medium impact rating as "Medium 2" or "Medium 3," respectively. Using the numeric subcategory within the qualitative expression of impact provides additional information to management to help them better assess the potential impact to the organization.

This process of summing and calculating the average of the various impact area ratings is referred to as CIF or Calculated Impact Factor. Once the impact values are calculated, a table is used to determine the qualitative impact expression. Refer to Table 2.11 for the scale.

RATING RATIONALE

The rating rationale section is a free-form area where the information security assessment professional justifies the selected ratings for each applicable control and includes his or her working notes. The information in this section should include

TABLE 2.10
Impact Rating (IR) Scale

Impact Rating (IR)	Qualitative Description
0	No measurable impact
1	Measurable, but marginal impact
2	Acceptable level of impact to the organization
3	Low level of impact; there will likely be some level of financial loss
4	Moderate level of impact; some financial losses are inevitable, and a minimal level of unplanned effort for organizational resources will be required
5	Medium level of impact; financial loss will be unplanned and interrupt normal operations; a substantial level of unplanned effort on organizational resources will be required
6	Substantial level of impact; financial loss would be considered considerable, as would the effort required to recover
7	High level of impact; financial loss is significant and highly undesirable by management, likely causing adverse impact on the organization's ability to operate; the effort required to recover is significant and likely has long-term effects on the organization
8	Very high level of impact; financial loss is extensive and has the potential to shut down the organization if not managed properly; the effort required to recover is extensive and will have long-term impact on the organization's ability to operate or to operate in a profitable manner; human resources are likely in danger
9	Extensive level of impact; financial loss and effort required to recover are devastating; the organization will not likely be able to recover; human life is threatened and may result in death to one or more.
10	Reserved for KRI controls

TABLE 2.11
CIF Numeric Scale

Rating	Value
Low	0 to 3.0
Medium	3.1 through 6.0
High	6.1 and higher

supporting points regarding threats, vulnerabilities, controls, likelihood, impact, or any other topic as appropriate.

Another information security professional with the appropriate knowledge and skills should be able to make the same general conclusions as stated in this section based on the information provided. This text is considered to be confidential in nature and not for public viewing. Only those with a business need-to-know should have access to this text. There could potentially be specific information about an organization or system under review that should not be viewed without the proper authorization.

CONTROL RISK LEVEL

The risk level for each control is determined by the culmination of the likelihood rating and the impact rating. The likelihood rating is the result of qualitative analysis by the information security professional and is assigned by him or her at the time of the assessment. The impact rating is the summed calculated average of the impact area ratings for each control.

The Numeric Matrix and Risk Level Matrix are used to determine the risk level rating for each applicable control except for KRI controls. KRI controls are assumed critical and therefore always receive a "high" risk level rating because of the potential impact and exposure to the organization. Each risk assessment is intended to be an accurate depiction of risks for the point in time at which the assessment was conducted. Because of the high volatility of threats, vulnerabilities, and environmental factors, the position of "high risk" is taken with KRI controls.

Refer to the Numeric Matrix and the Risk Level Matrix (Table 2.12 and Table 2.13) to understand their relationship with the risk level rating. After the control has

TABLE 2.12
Numeric Matrix

Impact	Low	Medium	High
High	6	8	9
Medium	3	5	7
Low	1	2	4
	Low	Medium	High
		Likelihood	

TABLE 2.13
Risk Level Matrix

Impact	Likelihood	Rating	Matrix
High	High	High	9
High	Medium	High	8
Medium	High	High	7
High	Low	Medium	6
Medium	Medium	Medium	5
Low	High	Medium	4
Medium	Low	Low	3
Low	Medium	Low	2
Low	Low	Low	1

been reviewed for its level of effectiveness and rated, the threats and vulnerabilities are reviewed and analyzed. Next, the likelihood and impact ratings are assigned and calculated. Once the impact and likelihood ratings have been determined, the Numeric Matrix and Risk Level Matrix are used to determine the risk level for each control.

For example, if a control was rated medium for impact and low for likelihood, the intersection of the two ratings in the Numeric Matrix would produce the number 3. By locating 3 in the Risk Level Matrix, one can determine that a low risk level will be assigned for this control.

NETWORK SECURITY ARCHITECTURE EVALUATION

Even though the focus of the GISAM is controls-based, a review of the network architecture and who has access to the organization's applications, information services, and data are critical components to account for and understand from a risk management perspective. The overarching principle is to evaluate and understand if the organization's network was designed with the defense-in-depth principle and the objective to contain risks. This type of assessment and evaluation requires an in-depth knowledge and understanding of network architecture and design as well as a comprehensive understanding and knowledge of network-based controls. Examples of network-based controls would include packet filtering, access control lists, stateful filtering and inspection, proxy firewalls, application firewalls, router hardening, host and network intrusion detection, intrusion prevention, virtual LANs, virtual private networks, PKI, time-sync, logging, SNMP traps, encryption, IPSec, anti-virus solutions, the concept of security zones, and many more.

Many information security professionals have a technical background, but this does not mean that all information technology professionals possess the skills required to effectively evaluate and assess network architecture information security risks. Selecting the right person to conduct this portion of the review is critical. Several training courses are available from The SANS Institute to help professionals develop these types of skills. Visit www.sans.org for more information.

The network architecture review and evaluation has the potential to impact the overall risk rating as described in the next section. It is possible that an organization could have implemented the majority of the ISO/IEC 17799:2005 (27002) controls to an acceptable level of effectiveness, but because of network architecture and infrastructure risks, they might introduce an unacceptable level of risk; therefore, the overall risk rating may be increased to a higher level, indicating more risk.

In an effort to provide guidance on the typical type of controls and elements to be reviewed during this part of the assessment, a basic outline is presented in the next section as an example. This list is intended not to set the scope for this part of the assessment but rather to present a sampling of topics and concepts that are likely applicable for a large number of organizations. The main point to remember about this part of the assessment is to not turn this into a full-blown network security assessment. The rationale for including network architecture and security within the GISAM is that this area has the ability to allow or cause significant impact on an organization's overall security posture. Depending on your organization's needs and requirements, a stand-alone network architecture and security assessment might need to be developed and implemented in conjunction with the GISAM. By including the network architecture and security element within the GISAM, management will have an indication of the risks posed to their organization from this area of the business and whether a more thorough review of network architecture and network-based controls is appropriate and warranted.

Example Network Security Architecture Criteria List

Network Architecture Design

- Defense-in-depth principle applied to network architecture as a whole
- Containment of risk implemented into the network design and architecture
- The network is auditable
- Physical and logical controls for routing and switching devices, firewall screening and protection afforded the hosts, separation and logical location of application, data and presentation servers
- Routing controls—implementation of static routing as appropriate, access control lists
- Implementation of non-broadcast IP addresses as appropriate
- Protection controls for DMZ hosts concerning remote accessibility—modems, remote control software
- Implementation of IP spoofing controls on routers and firewalls
- Separation of servers containing confidential data and application code
- Identification and protection controls for usable and unused server ports for remote access, administration and defined services

Physical and Environmental Security

- Appropriate facilities and perimeter security controls exist
- Computer room/data center physical and environmental security controls

Encryption

- Ensure protection of confidential data in transit and at rest
- The type of encryption algorithms used to protect the data is appropriate
- Key length for symmetric and asymmetric encryption is acceptable
- System administration techniques and processes are secured
- Encryption of end-to-end network sessions
- Web client authentication

Firewall and ACL Configuration/Administration

- Identification of server ports and services by firewall connection rules for secured and unsecured services

- Firewall's default rule base and configuration should deny all
- Validation of firewall rules to ensure they are in alignment with security policy
- Firewall logging must be enabled and preferably part of centralized logging system
- Firewall rule inspection to ensure rules operate as designed

Network Monitoring and Logging

- Network tools used by third-party vendor must be inspected, monitored, and logged
- Retention of network audit logs as per business requirements
- Logging enabled on appropriate devices, systems, and hosts
- Log management in centralized system
- Time synchronization enabled on all network devices

System Administration

- Hardened operating systems, hosts, and applications as per industry best practice and specific business requirements
- Remote administration of hosts, systems, and devices must be secure
- Default user accounts are disabled or properly secured
- User account management must exist for all users
- Host and system access rights should be role based and based on least-privilege principle
- User account permissions
- Web application server configuration is secured for environment
- Host tampering must be controlled
- Separation of duties is critical

Change Control/Software Updates/Patching

- Patch management of all hosts, systems, and devices
- Change control system and management should exist

Incident Management

- Information security incident management program and process must exist

Business Continuity Management

- Business continuity planning and testing

Intrusion Detection and Prevention

- Intrusion detection or prevention solutions as appropriate
- IDS/IPS management

It is important to define the scope of the network security architecture portion of the GISAM before the assessment begins. There is no possible way that I can universally define that within the context of this book and have it blindly scale and fit every organization.

The best way to accomplish this is to focus on the data. If confidential or restricted data is processed, accessed, or transported over a network path, it is very likely that the information security professional should extend the scope of the GISAM to review the network controls for these network subnets, paths, and routes. Following the data path will naturally define the scope and boundaries of your assessment.

OVERALL RISK RATING

The overall risk rating is the culmination of all assessment findings and analysis. The overall risk rating is assigned and not calculated in the GISAM. The underlying rationale for this position is that people are uniquely qualified to understand and determine risk and no mathematical formula or software program can accurately determine the overall risk rating for this type of information security assessment. Calculations and quantitative data can serve as guidance and indicators, but the risk rating is too dynamic to be calculated. The overall risk rating is assigned based on three major elements: control level of effectiveness, risk level, and network security.

The information security assessment professional must consider the level of effectiveness of the 133 controls and, in particular, focus on the 35 key risk indicator controls. Theoretically, if a key risk indicator control is rated at a low level (i.e., level 0, level 1, etc.), then the overall risk rating is escalated to indicate more risk. From a risk management perspective, the first action to take to lower identified risks would be to address the KRI controls that received a low level-of-effectiveness rating. After all 35 of the KRI controls have been implemented to an acceptable level of effectiveness, the remaining 98 supporting controls should be addressed to further reduce the identified risks.

The control risk level is a calculated expression based on the impact (calculated impact factor for the three major control categories) and likelihood ratings as described in the "Control Risk Level" section earlier in this chapter. Management is always concerned with potential impact to the organization and operations. By applying the logic of the control risk level rating to each specific control within the body of the assessment, management has a credible platform on which to base business and risk management decisions. The role of the information security assessment professional is to correlate all of the various control risk level ratings with organizational requirements and qualitatively factor this into the overall risk rating assignment.

TABLE 2.14
Overall Risk Ratings

Critical	There is limited evidence that controls and safeguards, including key risk indicator controls, have been designed and implemented to protect organizational assets. Critical vulnerabilities with the presence of applicable threats exist within the environment being assessed. A compromise of vulnerabilities is possible and likely based on the current state. A compromise could cause a serious and negative impact to the organization, including substantial financial loss, lack of compliance with regulatory or contractual requirements, and impact to the company brand and reputation. The organization would likely have an impaired ability to operate if the risks were realized.
High	A limited number of controls and safeguards have been implemented to protect organizational assets. Vulnerabilities, including critical ones, still exist and are in the presence of applicable threats. A compromise of vulnerabilities is possible and could cause a serious impact to the organization, including financial loss, lack of compliance with regulatory or contractual requirements, and impact to the company brand and reputation.
Moderate	The majority of the most critical controls and safeguards have been implemented to protect organizational assets. Vulnerabilities still exist and are in the presence of applicable threats. A compromise of these less critical vulnerabilities is possible and would likely be contained to a business unit or division within the organization. Exercised vulnerabilities could cause a negative impact including financial loss.
Guarded	Critical controls and safeguards have been implemented to protect organizational assets. Noncritical vulnerabilities still exist and are in the presence of applicable threats. A compromise of these less critical vulnerabilities is possible and would likely be contained to a project, business unit, or division. Exercised vulnerabilities would have limited impact, including financial loss.
Slight	All critical controls and safeguards have been implemented to protect organizational assets including additional compensating controls. There are no identified vulnerabilities in the presence of applicable threats at this time. Potential impact would be localized to the project level with minimal financial loss.

The final element to consider before assigning the overall risk rating for the GISAM assessment is network security architecture as described in the previous section. Network architecture and network security have the potential to negatively impact the information security posture of any organization, so this is why these are included in the scope of the GISAM. Guidance was provided in the "Network Security Architecture Evaluation" section in an effort to help define the types of elements and controls an organization would typically consider including in the assessment scope.

The overall risk rating scale is composed of five modes, as per the ISRAM model. The rating elements include slight, guarded, moderate, high, and critical. Table 2.14, presents and describes the five risk ratings and their intended meanings. A suggested color for each rating is as follows: slight (green), guarded (blue), moderate (yellow), high (orange), critical (red).

A "critical" rating indicates there is limited evidence that controls or safeguards have been designed and implemented to protect organizational assets. A "critical" rating is still possible if a large portion of compensating controls were rated as acceptable, but KRI controls receive a low level of effectiveness coupled with a high likelihood and unacceptable risk level. In general, there is no awareness by stakeholders or executive management about the need for the control under review. Critical vulnerabilities with the presence of applicable threats exist within the environment being assessed, and if this is coupled with a high likelihood rating, it could have devastating consequences for the organization. A compromise of vulnerabilities is possible and likely based on the current state of the control. A compromise could cause a serious and negative impact to the organization, such as substantial financial loss, lack of compliance with regulatory or contractual requirements, and impact to the company brand and reputation. The organization would likely have an impaired ability to operate if the risks were exercised. A "critical" rating should gain the immediate attention of executive management.

A "high" rating indicates that a limited number of controls and safeguards have been implemented to protect organizational assets and it is very likely that KRI controls are implemented to a low level of effectiveness. Vulnerabilities, including critical ones, still exist and are in the presence of applicable threats. A compromise of vulnerabilities is possible and could cause a serious impact to the organization, including financial loss, lack of compliance with regulatory or contractual requirements, and impact to the company brand and reputation.

A "moderate" rating indicates that the majority of the compensating and KRI controls and safeguards have been implemented to protect organizational assets. Vulnerabilities still exist and are in the presence of applicable threats. A compromise of these less critical vulnerabilities is possible and would likely be contained to a business unit or division within the organization. Exercised vulnerabilities could cause a negative impact, including financial loss.

A "guarded" rating indicates that KRI and compensating controls and safeguards have been implemented to an acceptable level of effectiveness for all KRI controls, as well as most compensating controls. Noncritical vulnerabilities still exist and are in the presence of applicable threats. A compromise of these less critical vulnerabilities is possible and would likely be contained to a project, business unit, or division. Exercised vulnerabilities would have limited impact, including financial loss.

A "slight" rating indicates that all KRI controls and safeguards have been implemented to protect organizational assets including additional compensating controls. There are no identified vulnerabilities in the presence of applicable threats at this time. Potential impact would be localized to the project level with minimal financial loss.

There is no such concept as a risk-free environment. The concept of managing risk implies that risk is dynamic and ever changing. There are no silver bullets in information security. The closest thing to this would be a highly active executive management team that truly understands the importance and requirement for a cohesive information security program that supports the business goals, objectives, and requirements of their organization. Nothing replaces knowledgeable and motivated people.

WEIGHTING

The topic and issue of weighting seems to always surface among managers and information security professionals when discussing assessments like GISAM, and this is why it is included with the methodology scope. The concept of weighting is intended to create or allow some type of credit or allowance for specific circumstances. It has always been my stance that when an individual or organization is assessing risk, why would you want to provide allowances to offset the true risk? I believe that it is the responsibility of the information security professional to accurately identify and describe the risks within the boundaries of the assessment scope and allow management to make informed decisions about these risks without any filters.

Some people could argue that the GISAM process is weighted in that each assessment is unique and the information security professional has full control over assigning various ratings and factors that directly impact the overall risk rating. Some might argue that the impact rating is weighted because it is a calculated average of the impact ratings for the applicable impact areas (technical, management, operations). This is simply a method to quantify impact for management and not a means to provide any type of weighting or credit for the purpose of rating the control risk level or overall risk rating.

I argue that there is not a piece of software or automated application that has the ability to effectively analyze and qualify risks within the scope of a GISAM. In other words, there is not a replacement for a skilled and trained information security professional. An application based on the GISAM could help reduce the delivery and operating costs as well as ensure consistency across all information security assessments. Because of the complexity and the number of variables within the GISAM, it is reasonable to assume that a manual delivery of this assessment would be time-intensive and complex.

RECOMMENDATIONS

The recommendations for the GISAM must be based directly on the ISO/IEC 17799:2005 (27002) control objectives and the network security architecture analysis. It would be difficult for management to support an action plan to reduce identified risks if recommendations were not provided. The GISAM or any other information security risk assessment must include a clear and precise set of recommendations at the control level.

One challenge for information security professionals as well as for management is the time required to perform a true gap analysis. Each of the 133 controls must be compared to the full scope of the control objective, and any other required variables must be taken into account. The quandary is that detailed recommendations are critical for business stakeholders and the time and associated costs required to provide these types of recommendations exponentially increase the overall cost of each assessment. One approach to offset the time and costs would be to develop a set of canned recommendations for each of the 133 controls covering the entire scope of each individual control. The recommendations would cover every aspect of the control and could easily be leveraged from a database or application. The obvious downside would be that the generalized approach to providing recommendations leaves the true gap analysis to each stakeholder. In some environments and organizations, this might be acceptable; in others, it would lead to chaos.

It is up to each organization to implement the most appropriate approach for providing recommendations within the scope of the GISAM. The old saying "You get what you pay for" directly applies in this case. I do not know of any shortcuts to having an educated and knowledgeable information security professional performing the analysis and creating recommendations that are unique for each assessment.

REPORTING

The GISAM final report is the final output of the assessment methodology and the only output management and stakeholders will see. This is the only portion of the method that is tangible and meaningful to management and other stakeholders. A standardized format should be developed and used to ensure consistency and promote a clear understanding of the findings and analysis. The GISAM final report must be a self-contained product and written specifically for its target audience or audiences as appropriate.

Each final report should include the following elements and sections:

- Name of assessor, date of assessment, company address, etc.
- Executive overview
- Target company profile and overview
- Executive overview of GISAM
- Overview of risk rating scale
- Overview of scale to rate controls (LOE scale)
- Summed total of applicable controls
- Organizational responsibility table by ISO/IEC 17799 domain area
- Listing of documents reviewed during assessment
- Overview of KRI controls
- Detailed analysis for KRI controls not rated at LOE level 4 or higher
- Overview of assessment findings and recommendations
- Guidance on reading and interpreting detailed findings
- Detailed listing for each control rated level 0 through level 3, including applicable threats, vulnerabilities, threat ranking rating, impact rating, likelihood rating, risk level, rating rationale, and control objective
- Detailed or canned recommendations for each applicable control

REFERENCES

BITS Kalculator Narrative, http://www.bitsinfo.org/downloads/Publications%20Page/BITS%20Kalculator/bitskalcnarrative.pdf

BITS KRI Program document, http://www.bitsinfo.org/downloads/Publications%20Page/bitskriprog.doc.

ISO/IEC 17799:2005 Information Technology — Security Techniques — Code of Practice for Information Security Management, International Organization for Standardization, 2005.

IT Control Objectives for Sarbanes–Oxley, http://www.isaca.org/Content/ContentGroups/Research1/Deliverables/IT_Contro_Objectives_for_Sarbanes-Oxley_7July04.pdf.

Microsoft Risk Assessment Booklet, http://www.microsoft.com/technet/security/topics/policiesandprocedures/secrisk/default.mspx

Stoneburner, G., Goguen, A., and Feringa, A., *National Institute of Standards and Technology Special Publication 800-30*, U.S. Department of Commerce, 2002.

3 Developing an Information Security Evaluation (ISE™) Process

The information security evaluation (ISE™) process is a marriage between the ISRAM™ (Information Security Risk Assessment Model) and the GISAM™ (Global Information Security Assessment Methodology) into a cohesive business process delivering an accurate and reliable assessment of an organization's information security program.

The rationale for developing a formal business process is to ensure that a repeatable process is delivered for each GISAM assessment, ensuring accuracy and reliability of risk management information. In a large organization this can have tremendous impact on the success of the assessment process. By having a formal and documented process, the business has an opportunity to train information security professionals as well as the business stakeholders who will be reviewing the GISAM reports. These concepts hold true whether the assessments are delivered internally or a professional services or consulting company offers this type of assessment as a service.

Supporting documentation and systems can be developed to help business managers interpret information security findings and analysis because this type of information can be complex and overwhelming to non-information security or non-risk management professionals. I have personally developed several helper documents targeting various groups in an effort to help the target audience understand and apply the information and report data more effectively. As you begin developing your own material and assessments, the development of these types of documents will naturally unfold.

THE CULMINATION OF ISRAM AND GISAM

The ISRAM and GISAM are only one part of the equation when developing and implementing formal information security risk assessments. The model provides the context for a suitable assessment methodology to be designed and developed. The assessment method must accurately reflect all of the organizational requirements and still adhere to the principles of the model. The system or environment being assessed is the key driver for the type and scope of information security risk assessment method. The assessment method should adhere to the model but still factor in specific organizational requests and requirements.

One of the best ways to accomplish this is to ensure that there is an executive sponsor on board and that all of the necessary resources and business elements are involved in the scope statement. Representatives from human resources, legal, compliance, internal audit, risk management, and business heads are all logical choices for involvement.

BUSINESS PROCESS

Independent of business process mechanics and technology, a professional still must deliver the GISAM, and he or she will be communicating and interacting with a wide array of people within the organization. By having a well-documented assessment delivery process, management can be assured of the assessment scope and expected output results.

STEP 1: DOCUMENTATION

Documentation describing the scope and intent of the pending information security risk assessment should be developed and presented to target representatives well in advance of the assessment date. This should be included in an introduction type document and capable of standing on its own. Special care should be taken to write the document in straightforward business language and explain at a reasonable level of detail what is involved in the assessment process.

I am not sure anyone is happy and anxious to have their organization evaluated by an outsider, much less by internal audit. This is a key thought to keep in mind when setting up meetings for the assessment. Typically executive management has secured a firm to conduct the assessment, or it could be a function of internal audit in larger organizations. Whether you call it a review, an assessment, or the nasty audit word, people in general have their guards up and would rather go to the dentist than talk with you. One method that usually helps calm everyone's nerves is to have a well-documented process and provide the target audience with a concise and streamlined account of the upcoming process, activities, and expectations.

A sample meeting agenda should be developed and provided to the main point of contact within the target group. The sample agenda should be fully documented with times, meeting topics, and resource names. They should be instructed to replace the fictitious names with the actual names of company representatives who will be attending the assessment. The GISAM is logically broken up into 11 topical areas because of the security clauses in the ISO/IEC 17799:2005 (27002). Most U.S. organizations do not have a working knowledge of the security clause domains within the standard and the terms will likely sound very foreign to them. Special care should be taken to develop an overview of the 11 domains and give them some working examples to help them apply these terms and phrases to their organization. The meeting agenda should track with the flow of the GISAM. One easy way to accomplish this is to simply follow the flow of the 11 ISO/IEC 17799:2005 (27002) main security clauses.

The information security assessment professional will have a much easier time on site conducting the assessment and interviews if everyone has a predisclosed understanding of the topics, time requirements, and level of resources required to attend the personal interviews.

A separate document could be developed providing an overview of the 11 main security clauses and the type of resources normally responsible for these areas. Whether the information security assessment is internal or external, nothing is more damaging than having the wrong people available during the assessment process. A good approach to help minimize this type of error is to have the target group assign responsible parties for each of the 11 main security clauses in addition to having them assign resources to the areas within the meeting agenda. The responsible party could be potentially different from the people who will be interviewed during the assessment process.

A short questionnaire should be developed and delivered to the target group along with the rest of the assessment documents. A few select key questions in the 11 main security clause areas can go a long way toward helping the information security professional understand where the organization stands before being surprised once the assessment process begins. You can refer to Chapters 7 through 17 and use some of the questions presented for each of the 133 controls in your questionnaire. Also, you may want to align your questions around the KRI or security baseline controls to help give you a perspective on the target organization's information security program. It is not advisable that you list these controls as the security baseline or KRI controls until the time of the review. It is possible that an organization could use this knowledge to skew the outcome of the assessment.

Step 2: Documentation Review

Once the target resources have completed the initial documentation, they should be asked to send it back to a point of contact on the risk assessment team. From there the information security assessment professional should receive and ultimately review all of the returned documentation to ensure the validity of the information provided and verify that enough information was provided to ensure a successful on-site assessment. If the documentation does not meet the information security professional's expectation, action should be taken to help close this gap as quickly as possible. A careful review should be performed on the meeting agenda to ensure that all of the correct resources will be available for the upcoming meetings.

Step 3: Negotiate Meeting Agenda

The meeting agenda is one of the most critical documents in the entire assessment process. It has the potential to make the assessment painless and straightforward as well as the potential to derail the process to the point of creating gaps or even failure. Special care should be taken to ensure that all vested parties have the appropriate expectations about the upcoming meetings and that the correct resources will be available during the assessment.

Step 4: Perform GISAM

The assessment actually beings when the information security assessment professional shows up on site and begins the meeting process with the target resources. Typically it is a good idea to hold a kickoff meeting to make introductions and set expectations for the upcoming interviews and activities. After the initial meeting it is important to only meet with the responsible parties for each of the 11 main security clauses and keep the number of people in the meetings to a minimum. It can be very distracting and produce inaccurate results if multiple people are attempting to answer the same question.

The GISAM is broken down into five main activities: introduction, network architecture review, tour of data center and facilities, controls review, and control validation.

The introduction was described in the above paragraph. The other thing to note is that this is a critical time of the assessment because first impressions are critical and perceptions will likely be difficult to change after this time. It is always a good idea to make the target group feel comfortable and at ease.

Next, the network architecture review should be conducted with the appropriate network resources. In Chapter 2 in the "Network Security Architecture Evaluation" section, the scope of this portion of the assessment was reviewed and discussed. This is a critical part of the review because every organization is concerned about how confidential data is stored, processed, and transported. The local and wide area network is the vehicle most often used for these activities. If the assessing organization has control standards or security policies to be enforced around data protection, this section of the assessment becomes even more important and potentially critical. The time required to perform the network architecture review varies based on the complexity of the network and the amount of confidential data being transported, processed, or stored in the network.

Taking a tour of the facilities and data center is a key component to understanding the state of the physical and environmental controls that will be assessed in the upcoming controls review. During this walkthrough, the information security professional should be taking written and mental notes to discuss later in the assessment as appropriate. This portion of the assessment can take as little as 30 minutes or, depending on the size of the facilities and data center, it can take substantially longer.

Next, the individual interviews should occur for each of the 11 main security clauses as agreed on in the meeting agenda. For most organizations, reviewing the 133 controls can be accomplished in about one day, or possibly a little longer depending on a number of variables. At this point, a total of one and a half days have expired and the remaining on-site activities involve the validation of controls.

The process of validation is up to the assessing organization, but it is highly recommended for a select number of controls. A good foundation for validation is the 35 KRI controls. It is important that KRI controls are validated to the level of effectiveness that they were rated during the assessment. The KRI controls have the ability to impact the overall risk rating for the assessment, and it is logical to assume that executive management would want confirmation on the state of these critical controls. This is something that will have to be decided on in the scope of each assessment. Typically, the enterprise compliance or corporate information security function will have strong feelings about this one way or the other. Be sure to include all appropriate people and roles within the organization before making any decisions on this.

Step 5: Analysis and Findings

After the on-site portion of the assessment is complete, the information security professional must analyze all of his or her notes and assessment data before assigning the overall risk rating. Each control is reviewed very closely with special attention on the KRI controls and the network architecture portions of the review. Special care should be taken for any control that is rated as a level 3 or below because management must be able to understand the identified risks and create an action plan to eliminate or reduce the gap to an acceptable level. This part of the assessment can take several days to complete depending on the complexity of the data and the amount of controls that received a low rating. The information security assessment professional must keep in mind that business leaders were not present during the assessment and the only information they receive on the cited risks is the information provided in the final report. The analysis, findings, and recommendations should be written in a business type format and targeted at non-security professionals.

Step 6: Peer Review

The last recommended step before providing the final report to the target group, or to the management of the target group, is to have a peer review the findings and analysis. Having a peer review the assessment adds one more layer of assurance that the information and analysis included in the report are accurate, understandable, and credible. It is highly advisable for organizations to include a peer review process for these types of assessments.

Step 7: Submit GISAM Final Report

The GISAM final report is the culmination of everyone's effort and the only portion of the product that executive management and key stakeholders will see. In the second chapter in the "Reporting" section, a listing of suggested report elements was described and provided for consideration. Whatever the final report sections turn out to be, it is important that the reports are consistent and delivered in the same way to ensure consistency. The information included in the GISAM final report is highly sensitive and considered confidential by most. Therefore, it is critical that the reports are provided to only the appropriate parties and that any copies of them are protected by appropriate controls. Information and data in these reports could lead to devastating events for the organization if the noted vulnerabilities were exploited.

It is a good idea to hold a postreview meeting with all of the appropriate stakeholders and the information security assessment professional to discuss the key points and findings of the assessment. The information security assessment professional is closest to the review and has the most comprehensive knowledge about the identified risks. It is highly likely that management may want or need more information to help prioritize risk management activities. Readers of the GISAM report should have read through the report and taken notes on key topics requiring more information before the group meeting is scheduled and held.

Step 8: Remediation

At this point, the appropriate management personnel and key stakeholders should have a current copy of the GISAM report and have read through the entire report. After the postreview meeting, it is up to executive management and key stakeholders to address the findings and analysis of the GISAM report according to their risk management strategy. For obvious reasons, the information security assessment professional should not be included in the remediation or risk management process.

4 A Security Baseline

The security baseline proposed in this chapter is built on the key risk indicator (KRI) controls identified in Chapter 2. Of the possible 133 controls in the ISO/IEC 17799:2005 (27002), I have identified 35 controls as KRI controls. These controls are critical and paramount to every information security program, independent of organization or industry. Each of the 35 controls will be listed in the forthcoming sections. The rationale of why they should be considered as a security baseline is described and included within the text. Requirements for implementation and assessment are beyond the scope of this chapter, and if additional guidance is required, refer to Chapters 7 through 17 as needed as well as the official standard itself.

KRI SECURITY BASELINE CONTROLS

Any organization, independent of industry, could benefit from having the 35 KRI controls implemented to a high degree of effectiveness within their organization and operation. Furthermore, the absence or lack of effectiveness of the KRI controls would likely result in a weakened security posture and introduce unnecessary risks into the organization. A listing of these 35 controls is provided in Listing E.

Listing E: KRI Security Baseline Controls

- Information Security Policy Document
- Management Commitment to Information Security
- Allocation of Information Security Responsibilities
- Independent Review of Information Security
- Identification of Risks Related to External Parties
- Inventory of Assets
- Classification Guidelines
- Screening
- Information Security Awareness, Education, and Training
- Removal of Access Rights
- Physical Security Perimeter
- Protecting Against External and Environmental Threats
- Secure Disposal or Reuse of Equipment
- Documented Operating Procedures
- Change Management
- Segregation of Duties
- System Acceptance
- Controls Against Malicious Code
- Management of Removable Media

- Information Handling Procedures
- Physical Media in Transit
- Electronic Commerce
- Access Control Policy
- User Registration
- Segregation in Networks
- Teleworking
- Security Requirements Analysis and Specification
- Policy on the Use of Cryptographic Controls
- Protection of System Test Data
- Control of Technical Vulnerabilities
- Reporting Information Security Events
- Including Information Security in the Business Continuity Management Process
- Identification of Applicable Legislation
- Data Protection and Privacy of Personal Information
- Technical Compliance Checking

SECURITY BASELINE

The concept of a security baseline is intended to establish and document a series of key controls that every organization should consider implementing to a high level of effectiveness within their operations. The scope and intent of these controls must also be documented as part of the information security program, including the information security policy. All 35 of the KRI controls will be listed and described in detail in the forthcoming sections. The controls are presented by order of their control reference number (i.e., 5.1.1, 6.1.1, etc.) in ascending order. There is no type of weighting or credit applied to one control versus another. The idea is that all 35 of the KRI controls are critical to uphold the information security program in its entirety and that the sum of controls is required to ensure program integrity.

Chapters 7 through 17 provide detailed information and guidance on all 133 of the ISO/IEC 17799:2005 (27002) controls including control purpose and scope, control class, key questions to ask for assessment purposes, and any additional information as appropriate. Implementing the KRI controls does not guarantee 100 percent security, as no balance of controls and safeguards could ever guarantee this. It is reasonable to assume that if all 35 of the KRI controls are implemented to a high level of effectiveness, an organization will have much fewer risks than the average organization. The KRI controls will need to be continually assessed, monitored, and reinforced. Organizations are dynamic, and information technology systems and environments are ever changing. New vulnerabilities can be introduced that can possibly be exploited by new threats at any given time, resulting in increased risks to the organization.

INFORMATION SECURITY POLICY DOCUMENT

The information security policy document control points out the obvious requirement of an organization developing and publishing an information security policy document. The control stresses the importance of communicating the policy to all appropriate parties including employees, consultants, contractors, and external parties. The code of practice does not give specific guidance regarding how to accomplish this, but it suggests that the policies be communicated in an effective manner that ultimately gains the acceptance and compliance of the target users. The exact mix and process for delivering information security awareness messages will likely vary for each organization, but the method to build and deliver an information security awareness program is basically the same for every organization. The ISO/IEC 27001 provides guidance on the development and maintenance of the security policy and program.

Implementation guidance provides basic instructions on some of the most obvious sections and statements that should be included in the formal information security policy document. One of the most overlooked and most critical components that should be included in every information security policy is risk assessment and its relationship to risk management. There is little guidance on exactly what should be included in the information security policy, and for good reason. There is no magic list of items, other than the basic components included in the implementation guidance section of this control, that should be a part of all information security policies.

Information security policies are developed by information security managers and ultimately approved by senior or executive management—as they should be. As an information security professional who has reviewed information security programs for many organizations, I see this one area cause information security managers the most trouble. It is a difficult task to decide what should, or should not, be included within the policy and exactly which words to use to effectively convey the intent and meaning of the policy.

A large number of information security managers have backgrounds that are rooted in information technology and not in the writing and publishing of policy documents. No matter the depth of a professional's background, writing, developing, selling, and publishing information security policy documents that meet all of the organizational requirements are complex and difficult tasks. The potential impact of having misaligned or missing information security policies is potentially devastating for an organization. There could be financial, compliance, regulatory, or other negative consequences as a result of the missing or inappropriate policies. In severe cases, it could lead to legal actions or the downfall of the company.

For public organizations, legal, federal, and regulatory compliance matters involving information security must be accounted for in the formal policy document. With the recent legislation (HIPAA, GLB, SOX), it is imperative that information security policies appropriately document the organization's requirements or there is a possibility of serious negative consequences.

It is logical to refer to the 5.1.1 control implementation guidance section for additional information about the sections and components to be included in the information security policy. The implementation guidance has limited value for information security managers seeking advice and input on what should be included in the policy. Control 5.1.1 is not intended to provide structure and advice on information security policy. The purpose of this control is to state the importance and criticality of having a documented and supported information security policy and not to state the definition of its content. Refer to the ISO/IEC 27001 for additional information and help in this area.

Information security managers should attempt to form peer relationships with organizations within their same industry. Most organizations are typically not inclined to share corporate documents, and information security policies are no exception. Most organizations are fearful of the legal consequences that might occur as a result of sharing the information contained within their policy documents.

The information security manager should be concerned first with creating a framework for the information security policies and then with creating the individual policies as needed. The framework should be approved by executive management and be realized by a formal process that ultimately produces an approved policy. The structure of the ISO/IEC 17799:2005 (27002) is one option for the structure of the information security policies. There are a number of resources available via the Internet that can assist in the creation of an ISO/IEC 17799:2005 (27002)–compliant framework. There are a number of professional consulting firms specializing in the creation and development of ISO/IEC 17799–aligned information security policy documents. Information security managers and executive management should leverage every resource available to them and not be afraid to involve external experts for guidance or confirmation.

It is theoretically impossible for an organization to have a cohesive information security program that will appropriately protect the organization's assets without having a written and approved information security policy. It is easy to understand that if an organization has a written and approved policy as described in this section, many other actions are required by several other organizational resources to formally publish the policy. The benefits gained from involving the correct resources in the policy development process are invaluable to the overall security posture for an organization.

MANAGEMENT COMMITMENT TO INFORMATION SECURITY

Control 6.1.1 (Management Commitment to Information Security) outlines the importance of senior management supporting and sponsoring the information security program. This control suggests that management involvement goes all the way to the board of directors and requires that executive management and the board of directors take an active role in information security.

For example, it is the responsibility of the information security officer, or the highest-level position for information security within the organization, to develop, sponsor, and publish the information security policy documents, but it is the responsibility of the executive management team to ensure that the policies meet organizational, legal, contractual, and regulatory requirements.

The information security officer or manager should seek out the help and advice of an executive management sponsor and leverage this relationship to carry a number of information security issues forward to the board of directors.

The implementation guidance section within this control gives practical and relevant advice on how management can actively support the information security program. Without the clear and active support of executive management, the information security program will not be as effective as it should be and will likely fail at some level. The reason this control is considered a key risk indicator is that without executive management support, the information security posture of the organization would be at significant risk and likely lead to devastating consequences for the organization at some point in the future. Management commitment for information security could be thought of as a key element that absolutely must exist at the core of every information security program if it is going to be effective and successful in controlling information security risks.

ALLOCATION OF INFORMATION SECURITY RESPONSIBILITIES

Information security roles and responsibilities must be defined by management; otherwise, it is unreasonable to assume that employees and users of the organization's assets clearly understand their responsibilities for information security. Confusion or lack of understanding is the recipe for disaster.

The issue of information security responsibility should be clearly defined and described within the information security policy document. The standard suggests that organizations anchor responsibilities to assets. Assets must have owners, and if the owners are aware of their information security responsibilities, this objective is executed. It is logical to conclude that the identification of assets would have numerous benefits throughout the organization and specifically within the information security program. The definition of an asset in traditional terms typically indicates some type of tangible item located on the balance sheet. Risk management and information security have challenged this traditional view of assets and suggest that assets are also intangible. Examples of these types of assets would include company goodwill, employee morale, brand, etc.

The overall assumption is that if an asset has an assigned owner, the owner can be responsible for its protection and security. The spirit of this control is a good candidate to include in the information security awareness and education program as well. People are very busy and tend to forget some of the most obvious requirements about information security. For example, it seems very logical to lock your workstation or computer when leaving your desk, but in the heat of the moment it is very easy to simply forget and leave the computer unprotected. How many people have you passed within your organization whom you did not know, allowing them to pass you because you assumed they were legitimate?

INDEPENDENT REVIEW OF
INFORMATION SECURITY

The regular and independent review of an organization's information security policies and program is one of the best investments the organization can make. Having trained and knowledgeable information security subject matter experts review an organization's policies and security practices will expose any shortcoming and deficiencies before they are exploited and possibly turned into a negative or devastating event. The code of practice suggests that this type of review be led by senior management and not by the system owners. The analysis and report should be shared with executive management and information security management to produce the most desirable results. There is no such concept of a completely secure organization, but the goal is to ensure that the security program is in alignment with the business goals and various requirements including legal, contractual, and regulations. An independent review of the information security policies and program has the potential to help the organization avoid potentially serious and negative consequences.

IDENTIFICATION OF RISKS RELATED TO
EXTERNAL PARTIES

One of the easiest areas for the information security program and strategy to break down is the area involving business activities and processes beyond their direct control. An example of this is when an organization utilizes a third party to fulfill a business requirement. It is very difficult to control what you do not have access to or knowledge of. Information security management should develop a series of information security risk assessment processes to evaluate and assess information security risks of third parties. This process should begin during the third-party selection process and be included in the criteria for their selection. The scope of the assessment should be driven by the amount of risk or potential loss. Control 6.2.1 provides a number of very good examples of what an organization should consider including for the review of external parties.

INVENTORY OF ASSETS

Besides the obvious accounting requirements, an inventory of information technology and systems is a logical and critical task for information security and assurance. In the event of a business interruption, for whatever reason, how would the organization know what to include in the disaster recovery or business continuance plan unless a detailed and systematic inventory is maintained? Example of critical assets would include hardware, software, applications, application data, data files, hard and soft copies of legal and contractual agreements, security and support procedures, human resource data, financial records, etc. The inventory of assets may be critical for some organizations to understand and evaluate the potential impact to their organization in the event of their loss or interruption.

consider performing additional checks upon promotion or increased responsibilities. The background and risks associated with an employee can change drastically over time. It is possible for employees to commit fraudulent actions, experience financial distress, or develop other conditions that could possibly alter their normal behaviors. This is why it is critical for organizations to create a process that is in alignment with the risks of their organization. The actions of a single bad person can compromise the integrity of the actions of the entire organization. People, without doubt, are an organization's greatest assets—but also one of its greatest risks.

INFORMATION SECURITY AWARENESS, EDUCATION, AND TRAINING

Information security awareness, education, and training are overarching principles that must be implemented in every organization. There is a clear difference between awareness, education, and training. Awareness is typically directed at all users and tends to focus their attention on global security principles. Training, on the other hand, is much more in-depth and the message is directed at a specific group or audience with an expected outcome. Education is another step beyond training where concepts and topics are covered in depth for the purpose of developing new skills and altering the outcome in some way. Education answers the question "why" and focuses on theory and research. Education is understood to continue over a period of time to master the concepts and theories.

REMOVAL OF ACCESS RIGHTS

Without a formal process and diligent actions on the part of the network administration staff, access rights for terminated employees, consultants, contractors, and third parties could lead to a negative and significant security-related event. All access rights should be removed and recorded immediately upon termination of the relationship. The removal process could also include logical and physical access such as keys, identification badge/card, access badge, etc. Depending on company policy, collection of these types of items could be handled by the human resources department or the reporting manager. Either way, a clear and documented process and procedure should be developed and executed as required. Failure to do so could result in a security-related breach or exploit of systems or assets.

PHYSICAL SECURITY PERIMETER

Physical perimeters are obvious but often overlooked by many. Walls, gates, manned parking lots, and alarm and fire systems are all commonly thought of by many organizations. Card-controlled access to every entry into the organization's facilities is becoming more common, as is a manned reception desk. Physical security perimeter controls should undergo the same due diligence and risk assessment process as other controls. The controls and safeguards should be implemented because of the result of analysis and consideration, not because they are obvious and customary.

CLASSIFICATION GUIDELINES

Organizations operating in current times leverage the advantages and effi afforded them by information processing systems and applications. It is imagine even a small organization operating without the help and assista computing systems. Even if an organization operates without the help of infori systems, it does not eliminate or reduce the potential impact of operating w information classification. An organization must create and publish inforn classification guidelines if it expects users to appropriately handle informatioi data. This topic should be one of the primary elements included in every inform; security awareness and education program. The classification guidelines shoul clearly documented within the information security policy as well.

An information classification scheme should be developed by managemen terms of its importance, value, sensitivity, and legal requirements for the organi tion. Typical classification labels would include public, internal use, confidenti and restricted. Clear definitions for each of these classifications must be documenti and communicated to every user within the organization. Supporting procedures ar guidelines must be developed and published so that users understand the requiremer for appropriately protecting each class of information and the correct procedure ensuring its protection. Management should refer to control 7.2.1 for additional help and work with their peers within their same industry to possibly provide additional help and guidance.

It is logical to conclude that if an organization does not create and publish classification guidelines for all information and data types within their organization, they are making themselves and their organization vulnerable to unnecessary risks and dangers. For many industries, this is required by law or regulation. Even if information classification is not required by law or regulation, it is considered to be an industry best practice for information security.

SCREENING

The act and process of screening employees, contractors, and third-party users is critical to uphold the integrity of the information security policy. The scope and degree of the screening should be in alignment with organizational requirements. For example, the scope of the screening process for a manufacturing firm that manufactures widgets and does not store or process information that is governed by laws or regulations would likely be different from the scope of the screening process for a financial institution that must comply with numerous regulations and laws. However, the manufacturing firm may elect to screen employees, consultants, and third parties just as aggressively as financial or government organizations do because their data is critical to the long-term success of their organization.

Typical screening activities would include past employment dates and references, personal references, identity check (driver's license, social security cards, etc.), college education verification, confirmation of professional certifications, personal credit check, criminal background investigation, etc. Many organizations perform this type of check only at the beginning of the employment process and do not

This approach can create a false sense of security because management believes that all of the appropriate physical perimeter controls have been implemented to protect and safeguard the organization. If an organization has implemented a card-controlled access system for all entry and exit points to the organization's facilities but does not have a cohesive business process to monitor and audit the logs, the control has not been implemented properly and there is unnecessary risk for the organization. This control and other closely related information should be included in the information security awareness initiative. Several examples for implementation guidance are provided in the body of the code of practice.

PROTECTING AGAINST EXTERNAL AND ENVIRONMENTAL THREATS

Protecting against external and environmental threats is a continuation of the same philosophy from the physical perimeter security control. Protecting your organization from natural or man-made disasters should be considered a primary and critical concern by any organization. Implementation guidance and examples are reviewed and described in the standard. The scope of this control should be part of the annual risk assessment an organization undergoes to evaluate the appropriate controls and safeguards required to uphold the integrity of the security policy and associated business requirements.

SECURE DISPOSAL OR REUSE OF EQUIPMENT

Computers and all types of devices house sensitive company data and information. Special care should be taken to properly remove all data before disposal or reuse in another capacity. There are many sources available to organizations to help them understand how to properly destroy data on media. This control must be part of the formal information security policy, and written procedures and supporting guidelines should also be developed and published.

DOCUMENTED OPERATING PROCEDURES

Having a clear set of operating procedures for all critical systems and applications within an organization is a huge task, even for smaller organizations. The intent of this control is to set the expectation that information security-related tasks and operations must also be included in the operating procedures. Special care must be taken to ensure that only authorized personnel have access to this information, as failure to do so could lead to a system or application compromise. In the implementation guidance section of the standard, several examples are provided that anyone can reference and use as a baseline to get started. The examples provided in the standard should not be used as the benchmark, only as a representative example of what should be included.

CHANGE MANAGEMENT

Controlling changes to information processing facilities is a logical request within any sized organization. The potential negative impact, regardless of the information security consequences, should drive the need and requirement for a formal change management process and system. A documented change management process can also serve as an audit log for information security in the event an unauthorized change is suspected. Part of change management is the assessment of potential impact to the organization. Information security representatives should be included in this assessment to ensure that a comprehensive impact analysis was conducted. As a general rule, the person requesting a change cannot approve the request.

SEGREGATION OF DUTIES

Segregation of duties has long been a recognized control to help minimize unauthorized changes or misuse of company assets. For organizations where segregation of duties is not possible or feasible, detailed audit logs should be designed and implemented and only audit personnel should have the ability to view or access the logs. Segregation of duties is a fundamental concept that should be applied across the board whenever possible, and compensating controls such as audit logging should be implemented in addition to, or in lieu of, this concept, as appropriate.

SYSTEM ACCEPTANCE

The concept of system acceptance as it relates to information security is critical, because it ensures that information security controls have been assessed and designed during the development phase of a new system or upgrade project before the system or application is implemented and promoted to production. System acceptance should be a part of normal business operations and not a stand-alone process. The most effective way to ensure that system acceptance occurs is to integrate it into existing processes and controls. Current research is beginning to validate that people rarely read stand-alone policies, procedures, or guidelines. This is why the approach of integrating the scope of this control into existing business operations is highly effective. The implementation guidance within the standard provides numerous examples of the types of elements to consider for formal acceptance prior to implementation.

CONTROLS AGAINST MALICIOUS CODE

With the proliferation of information systems and enterprise applications, it is logical to include controls against malicious code as a key risk indicator control. If an exploit was exercised in a networked environment with the deployment of the appropriate controls, rapid proliferation of the exploit is very possible and would likely devastate the operations of an organization. Guidance within the body of this control suggests that the focus be placed on detection and repair, and couple the scope of this control within the information security awareness training program. A detailed list of items to consider within the malicious code area is presented and described in the implementation guidance section of the standard. Information security professionals and management should refer to these items to ensure that a holistic approach has been taken with the scope of their unique operations.

MANAGEMENT OF REMOVABLE MEDIA

Unsecured removable media has the potential to create significant risk for any organization. Because the media is likely small and transportable and often houses a large amount of data and information, a proper balance of controls must be implemented that is in alignment with the organization's business requirements. Removable media typically includes backup tapes, CD-ROMs, DVDs, removable hard disks, USB flash drives, PCMCIA hard disks, etc. Controls ranging from technical safeguards (encryption, etc.) to management controls (authorization for movement process, etc.) should be developed and monitored to ensure compliance.

INFORMATION HANDLING PROCEDURES

Properly handling information is one of the best controls an organization can deploy to help protect unauthorized disclosure or authorization. This control states that organizations should develop formal procedures for handling and storing information. These procedures should be developed in alignment with the classification guideline (7.2.1) and be integrated into normal business operations. Information can be housed and transported in many different forms including logical and physical media (paper, voice, network, tape, etc.). All of the appropriate transport media should be identified and addressed within the operating procedures to ensure that the scope of the control is effectively implemented.

PHYSICAL MEDIA IN TRANSIT

In many cases, a breach of data and information occurs outside the direct control of the owner and organization. While media is in transit, for whatever purpose, controls should be designed, implemented, and monitored to ensure that the data and information is not misused, corrupted, or improperly accessed in any way. Several examples are provided in the implementation guidance section of the control.

ELECTRONIC COMMERCE

Data and information transported and transmitted over public networks require special controls to ensure the confidentiality, integrity, and availability of the data to its authorized users. These controls should involve all three types of controls (management, technical, operations), and each organization based on a risk assessment should develop and implement the appropriate balance of controls. Several examples ranging from encryption to data verification are included in the implementation guidance section of the standard. The examples provided within the standard should be considered not a holistic criteria but rather typical examples that likely apply to most organizations. A formalized information security risk assessment will always yield the correct balance of controls for each unique environment and organization.

ACCESS CONTROL POLICY

Controlling access to data and information is one of the most difficult and critical series of controls an organization with sensitive data and information must design, implement, and monitor. The development of a formal policy is the framework for the development of associated procedures and guidelines. Controlling access to data, information, applications, and systems is a difficult task for any sized organization. The scope of how to accomplish this is out of context for this section, but several examples and guidelines are provided within the standard for review and consideration. Information security professionals and management should review the standard in detail to ensure that their risk assessment process contains all of the elements and variables that apply to their organization.

USER REGISTRATION

Having a formal and documented process for registering and deleting new user accounts for all information systems and applications is critical to uphold the integrity of the organization's information security posture. To ensure complete auditability, each user account must be unique and not shared by multiple resources. Accounts should only have access and rights as appropriate for their role and function. An external party should audit and review system accounts on a regular basis to ensure that the integrity of this control is completely implemented.

SEGREGATION IN NETWORKS

One of the primary objectives in the defense-in-depth principle is to contain risks and separate as many risk elements as possible. Within the high-tech world of inter-networks, it is increasingly difficult to separate systems, applications, networks, resources, etc. into small and manageable segments. The scope and intent of this control is to separate networks into smaller segments and apply a graduated set of controls within each domain. Whenever possible, an organization should design and support the segregation of its networks, and have a clear distinction and separation between its public and private networks.

TELEWORKING

Remote or mobile working and telecommuting is becoming more common for many organizations. For those organizations that deploy and support mobile workers, a clear policy and set of procedures should be developed and implemented to ensure that the integrity of the organization's security posture is maintained. Issues ranging from theft of remote equipment to system or identity spoofing are a concern for executive management. A series of technical and operational controls must be considered and ultimately implemented to protect the organization and its assets. Several examples and guidance are provided in the standard, and a risk assessment should guide the design and deployment of controls.

SECURITY REQUIREMENTS ANALYSIS AND SPECIFICATION

Within the initial planning or upgrade of information systems and planning, control 12.1.1 outlines the need to specify information security requirements and controls during this stage as opposed to including information security as a postprocess. Incorporating information security into existing business processes is a timely task and could take years for large organizations. It is difficult to change environments, behaviors, and attitudes even in the smallest organizations. The onslaught of reported information security incidents in 2005 should help provide the leverage and motivation some organizations need to start implementing information security now as opposed to later.

POLICY ON THE USE OF CRYPTOGRAPHIC CONTROLS

The use of cryptography as a technical control is mandatory in some industries and considered best practice for others. Encryption is the type of control that has no other replacement. In other words, if it is needed or required, compensating controls will not likely address the requirement.

Defining the requirement or understanding when the use of this type of control is necessary can be difficult in some cases, but in others it is easy and straightforward. For example, if a publicly traded financial institution is using a third-party vendor to process and transmit confidential client data over the Internet, the requirement for encryption is mandated by law and by regulation. The information security policy should provide clear direction in this area, and it should be a part of the information security awareness and training program. A set of procedures and guidelines would help staff and stakeholders implement encryption within the intended scope.

PROTECTION OF SYSTEM TEST DATA

Test data must be treated with the same rigor as production data. The same controls implemented to protect and safeguard production data should be implemented for test data. Control 12.4.2 points out that the selection of test data should be a careful and diligent process. Using production data containing personal or private information should be avoided at all costs. If this is not possible, a series of procedures and guidelines should be developed and used by applicable users to ensure the protection and integrity of the data and information. The implementation guidance provided in the standard has a series of elements to consider if sensitive data is used as test data.

CONTROL OF TECHNICAL VULNERABILITIES

Technical vulnerabilities exist in literally every system, application, and host. The process of applying security patches to eliminate identified vulnerabilities should be a top priority for organizations. If the vulnerability does not exist, the threat of this vulnerability being exploited has been eliminated. All assets must be identified to know if they require patching or updating. Detailed guidance and procedures should be developed and provided to all staff members responsible for system maintenance and updating. Several items should be considered to be implemented within the scope of this control. They are included in the implementation guidance security of the standard.

REPORTING INFORMATION SECURITY EVENTS

Information security events have the potential to be information security incidents if not handled properly and appropriately. Organizations should develop and publish procedures and processes to enable quick reporting and containment of potential incidents. All users should know who to contact in the event of a suspicious or obvious security incident. Information security event identification and reporting procedures are good candidates to include in the information security awareness and training program. The Reporting Information Security Events implementation guidance provides a series of very good examples that every organization should consider when developing the scope of its security reporting and incident management program. Depending on the organization, industry, and possible unique requirements, reporting information security events can take on many different meanings and directions. For some organizations, reporting security events is simply good business practice; in other organizations, it can have serious legal or regulatory implications.

INCLUDING INFORMATION SECURITY IN THE BUSINESS CONTINUITY PROCESS

In a time of crisis, it is very easy for professionals and organizations to cut corners and overlook prudent information security controls and safeguards. After an organization has activated its disaster recovery plan and recovered or relocated its information systems, the business continuity plan must be enabled and activated. It is critical that information security controls are carried over from the production system's environment to the recovered environment. These controls can range the entire scope of the ISO/IEC 17799:2005 (27002) Code of Practice for Information Security Management. Information security personnel should be included in the planning and testing of disaster recovery and business continuity processes and plans. The implementation guidance section within the standard provides a lot of good information and guidance that should be considered by almost every organization.

IDENTIFICATION OF APPLICABLE LEGISLATION

It is the responsibility of executive management to identify all statutory, regulatory, legal, and contractual requirements and their approach for compliance. In many cases, information security is an integral part of compliance. At a minimum, a complete and thorough assessment and review of the 133 ISO/IEC 17799:2005 (27002) controls provides a platform for information security and executive management to understand the scope of their information security controls and the state of their controls. The information security policy should document and account for the entire scope of an organization's requirements. Information security policy statements should clearly define the scope of requirements.

DATA PROTECTION AND PRIVACY OF PERSONAL INFORMATION

The protection and safeguarding of personal information is required by legislation and regulation for many organizations. For organizations not bound by regulations and laws, it is considered best practice and ethically a good business decision to safeguard and protect personal information. A documented data protection and privacy policy should be developed, published, and communicated throughout the organization. The compromise of personal or private information can have serious and negative consequences leading to the complete downfall of an organization. Many different resources from executive management, legal, human resources, information security, and other areas within the organization should be involved in the identification of data protection and privacy requirement to ensure accuracy and applicability.

TECHNICAL COMPLIANCE CHECKING

Information systems, including hardware, operating systems, and applications, possess a wide array of vulnerabilities. It becomes dangerous when these vulnerabilities are matched with relevant threats. These information systems should be tested for known vulnerabilities, and appropriate actions should be taken to reduce or eliminate the identified vulnerabilities as quickly as possible. Compliance checking should be carried out by unbiased technical experts to help ensure accuracy and a full report.

REFERENCES

ISO/IEC 17799:2005 Information Technology — Security Techniques — Code of Practice for Information Security Management, International Organization for Standardization, 2005.

5 Background of the ISO/IEC 17799 Standard

In simple terms, the ISO/IEC 17799:2005(E) Code of Practice for Information Security Management is a comprehensive business-minded international best practice for information security independent of industry or geography.

HISTORY OF THE STANDARD

There are actually two parts to the standard: the code of practice or the controls, commonly referred to as the ISO/IEC 17799:2005(E), and a specification for an information security management system, commonly referred to as part 2 or ISO/IEC 27001. The code of practice was updated on June 15, 2005, five long years after the publication of the first edition. It is expected that within the next couple of years this standard will be renamed to ISO 27002 to be in alignment with a new numbering scheme. Part 2 of the standard has recently been renumbered to fit into this new scheme (27001). There were not any significant changes to this part of the standard other than the reference number.

In essence, the ISO/IEC 17799:2005 standard is intended to serve as a single point of reference to information security controls for organizations. The primary goal is to identify a range of controls needed for most situations where information systems are used by organizations in industry and commerce.

The standard was first published as a DTI (Department of Trade and Industry) code of practice in the United Kingdom and then shortly thereafter rebranded as version 1 of the BS7799 in 1995 (BS 7799:1995). A major revision was released in 1999 and labeled as version 2 (BS 7799:1999). Later that year, a formal certification scheme and accreditation was launched, and then a series of supporting tools started to appear in the marketplace.

The International Organization for Standardization (ISO) and the International Electrotechnical Commission (IEC) formed a joint technical committee (JTC 1) to adopt the British Standard 7799 or BS 7799:1999 as the ISO/IEC 17799 Information Technology — Code of Practice for Information Security Management. The ISO/IEC 17799:2000(E) was published in 2000 as the first edition on December 1. The current version is ISO/IEC 17799:2005(E) and was released on June 15, 2005. The international standard for information security is referred to as "ISO/IEC 17799" throughout this book and within the information security industry to reference the aforementioned standard.

INTERNALS OF THE STANDARD

Within the ISO/IEC 17799 there are a total of 133 controls contained in 39 control areas within the 11 major security clauses. Each clause has anywhere from 1 to 32 controls and 1 or more control objectives.

A control is understood to mean an action, process, or technology that, when implemented, is intended to lower the risk to an organization, and controls may be any combination of the three.

It is beyond the scope of this section to discuss the process and methodology of selecting controls for identified risks and vulnerabilities for a specific environment. It should be noted, however, that controls should be implemented as the result of a series of risk mitigation activities that includes a formal risk assessment as detailed in the first section of this book.

Such activities typically include understanding the information system, identifying threats, identifying potential vulnerabilities, discussing potential controls including cost-benefit analysis, evaluating the likelihood of an exploit or compromise, reviewing the potential impact to the business or organization, etc.

GUIDANCE FOR USE

Through professional experience and industry consensus, each control can be identified by type. In Chapters 7 through 17, I have assigned a control category to each of the 133 controls for your reference in an effort to help management and information security professionals assign resources for each of the respective controls. The three types of controls as outlined in this book are management, operational, and technical. Within the control area, a number of controls will exist and may have a combination of control types.

A *management control* is any control that requires management approval, support, or activities. An *operational control* is any control that is action- or task-oriented and nontechnical in nature. A *technical control* is any control that requires modification, configuration, or verification of information processing facilities. The 133 controls that are referenced throughout the ISO/IEC 17799 standard can effectively be associated with one or more of these categories. The standard does not provide any type of direction or support for this type of classification, but I have found it very useful through practical experience to associate each of the controls with each of the three types. Doing this provides a high-level grouping of the controls, and typically organizations have resources assigned to each of the classes.

I associated each of the controls with their respective types based on the dominant characteristics of the control. For example, if the control primarily required management attention and support, it would have been labeled a management control.

For each control, the information security scope is presented first. This scope is focused on the spirit of the control objective. The scope is outcome based, and an organization can use this as a reference to determine what needs to be accomplished at a high level. Next, a series of key questions have been developed and provided to help the reader determine the state of the control objective within the operations of the organization. An external reference section is provided to note any links or references to external information to include applicable laws, regulations, or other standards that you might want to investigate further. Next, a reference to "security baseline" is provided with a yes or no response after each control. Those controls that should be considered as industry best practice would apply to the majority of organizations that would receive the "yes" indicator. Special attention should be paid to these controls to ensure to what degree they apply to your organization. An area is also included for additional information that might be helpful to promote a better understanding of the control or other relevant information that would be useful.

The best technology in the world cannot be truly effective unless it is supported operationally and with management sponsorship. Each control throughout the book will be broken down and identified with its respective type and class.

HIGH-LEVEL OBJECTIVES

As mentioned, the 133 ISO/IEC 17799:2005 controls are separated into 11 main security clauses and 39 control objectives. The high-level objectives for the 11 main security clauses are presented in the following section to help provide a management level overview for each main clause.

SECURITY POLICY

- Provide management direction and support for information security

ORGANIZATION OF INFORMATION SECURITY

- Manage information security within the organization
- Maintain the security of information and processing facilities with respect to external parties

ASSET MANAGEMENT

- Achieve and maintain appropriate protection of organizational assets
- Ensure that information receives an appropriate level of protection

HUMAN RESOURCES SECURITY

- Ensure that employees, contractors, and third parties are suitable for the jobs they are considered for, understand their responsibilities, and reduce the risk of abuse (theft, misuse, etc.)
- Ensure that the above are aware of IS threats and their responsibilities and are able to support the organization's security policies
- Ensure that the above exit the organization in an orderly and controlled manner

PHYSICAL AND ENVIRONMENTAL SECURITY

- Prevent unauthorized physical access, interference, and damage to the organization's information and premises
- Prevent loss, theft, and damage of assets
- Prevent interruption to the organization's activities

COMMUNICATIONS AND OPERATIONS MANAGEMENT

- Ensure the secure operation of information processing facilities
- Maintain the appropriate level of information security and service delivery, aligned with third-party agreements
- Minimize the risk of systems failures
- Protect the integrity of information and software
- Maintain the availability and integrity of information and processing facilities
- Ensure the protection of information in networks and of the supporting infrastructure
- Prevent unauthorized disclosure, modification, removal, or destruction of assets
- Prevent unauthorized disruption of business activities
- Maintain the security of information or software exchanged internally and externally
- Ensure the security of E-commerce services
- Detect unauthorized information processing activities

ACCESS CONTROL

- Control access to information
- Ensure authorized user access
- Prevent unauthorized access to information systems
- Prevent unauthorized user access and compromise of information and processing facilities
- Prevent unauthorized access to networked services
- Prevent unauthorized access to operating systems
- Prevent unauthorized access to information within application systems
- Ensure information security with respect to mobile computing and teleworking facilities

INFORMATION SYSTEMS ACQUISITION, DEVELOPMENT, AND MAINTENANCE

- Ensure that security is an integral part of information systems
- Prevent loss, errors, or unauthorized modification/use of information within applications

- Protect the confidentiality, integrity, or authenticity of information via cryptography
- Ensure the security of system files
- Maintain the security of application system information and software
- Reduce/manage risks resulting from exploitation of published vulnerabilities

INFORMATION SECURITY INCIDENT MANAGEMENT

- Ensure that security information is communicated in a manner allowing corrective action to be taken in a timely fashion
- Ensure that a consistent and effective approach is applied to the management of IS issues

BUSINESS CONTINUITY MANAGEMENT

- Counteract interruptions to business activities and protect critical processes from the effects of major failures/disasters
- Ensure timely resumption of the above

COMPLIANCE

- Avoid the breach of any law, regulatory or contractual obligation, and of any security requirement
- Ensure that systems comply with internal security policies/standards
- Maximize the effectiveness of and minimize associated interference from and to the system's audit process

ISO/IEC DEFINED

ISO (International Organization for Standardization) is the world's largest standards developer and probably the one most recognized and trusted by the business and corporate community. ISO understands the social and economic importance of its work and takes the publication and distribution of standards seriously. ISO is a comprehensive network of national standards institutes of 151 countries with one member per country and the central coordinator located in Switzerland.

You may have noticed IEC (International Electrotechnical Commission) in the name of the standard and wondered what it represented. The ISO/IEC 17799:2005(E) is a product of a joint venture between both entities. Together they form a specialized body of members known as the ISO/IEC JTC 1. The ISO/IEC JTC 1 is a joint technical committee that specifically focuses on the field of information technology. For the ISO/IEC 17799:2005 there is a special subcommittee that focuses on security techniques. This SC 27 subcommittee focuses on the ISO/IEC 17799.

Organizations around the world have been using the information and best practices contained in the ISO/IEC 17799 for over ten years. With the release of the second edition, organizations will be able to continue to benefit from the standard provided by ISO. The updated standard took nearly five years to complete. This is a result of a diligent effort by the global community and the JTC 1 SC 27.

REFERENCES

ISO/IEC 17799:2005 Information Technology — Security Techniques — Code of Practice for Information Security Management, International Organization for Standardization, 2005.

6 ISO/IEC 17799:2005 Gap Analysis

The first edition of the 17799 standard, also known as ISO/IEC 17799:2000(E), was published in December 2000 and the second edition (ISO/IEC 17799:2005[E]) was released in June 2005. Several changes—including formatting changes, extensive rearrangement, deletion and merger of controls, and addition of new controls and new control areas—are part of the 2005 update. This update was nearly five years in the making and many professionals from around the world contributed to the updates, revisions, and modernization of the standard.

Also, within the last five years several new regulations and laws have been passed and made effective. For example, heavily regulated organizations within the finance and banking industry must address several new regulations and guidance placed on them from an information security perspective. This can range from the FFIEC (Federal Financial Institutions Examination Council) to the OCC (Office of the Comptroller of the Currency) to FDIC (Federal Deposit Insurance Corporation) guidance. Publicly traded organizations are exposed to a host of legislation such as Sarbanes–Oxley (SOX), Gramm–Leach–Bliley (GLB), or the Health Insurance Portability and Accountability Act (HIPAA). Information security and its association with corporate governance is quickly becoming a complex business responsibility. This is made obvious by the creation of many new roles such as chief risk officers and chief privacy officers. Through January 2006, there were over 22 states with security breach notification laws and several others in the process of passing similar laws. California was the first state to blaze this path in 2002 with the country's first notification law via SB1386.

Many organizations have discovered the business benefits in aligning their information security programs with the ISO/IEC 17799 Code of Practice for Information Security Management. By implementing and aligning an organization's information security programs and policy with the ISO/IEC 17799 standard, they will naturally address most legal and compliance requirements. This is because the ISO/IEC 17799 is a holistic business-oriented approach to information security, independent of industry or organization. The standard can be applied to organizations in just about any industry or setting. It is one of the few standards today in this category and the only standard within the information security discipline.

OVERVIEW

The ISO/IEC 17799:2005(E) international information security standard is the most widely accepted best-practice standard for information security around the world—independent of industry. The long-awaited second edition improved several parts of the standard. A new section on implementation guidance provides an action-oriented approach to each control, making it easier for organizations to adopt the framework to their operations. Much of the text in the "implementation guidance" section existed in the first edition, but with the repackaging and added text, it is much easier to read and understand.

Upon its release in June 2005, the second edition superseded the first edition. One of the most notable changes was the chapter on risk assessment. I felt this was the missing link in the first edition. Any practicing information security professional understands the importance and requirement of performing a risk assessment before applying controls and safeguards. The inferred use of a risk assessment methodology and framework was not obvious to many organizations trying to use or apply the standard during the span of the first edition. I hope this new chapter will help organizations to understand the importance and place for risk assessment and eventually seek out a way to adopt and apply a framework to their overall information security strategy and program.

In the second edition there is a new chapter and main security clause for information security incident management. This was one of the biggest structural changes to the second edition. Most of the controls existed in the first edition, and in other control areas, but they were out-of-date for current times. The extended incident management and handling scope in the second edition has a new control objective to help provide more clarity and packaging of the respective controls.

The second edition of the standard expands on third-party and business partner relationships and extends the scope and guidance text in this area. The new scope goes well beyond the obvious perimeter and border security issues by tackling topics such as business processes, relationships, and legal agreements. This series of changes will prove to be very useful for most organizations.

The main security clause for asset classification has been renamed to asset management. This changed clause significantly expands on the scope and guidance from the first edition. These new updates scale well for regulated and publicly traded industries because the controls and ideas within this control area are fundamental to current laws and regulations. At the same time, the security clause is applicable to any organization, independent of industry, because asset management is a fundamental concept to information security.

The new human resources security clause includes the three phases of employment (before, during, after). This is a logical and straightforward series of controls that any organization should and could adopt and apply within their operations. The new controls and control objectives make for a more complete standard.

Many other topics and controls have been extended in the second edition. The most notable include mobile technology, audit and logging, and vulnerability management. These changes, as well as an already solid code of practice, make this current version of the standard the best code of practice for information security management in the world today. With ten years of history and its wide acceptance, it is unlikely that any other standard will have the impact or applicability of the ISO/IEC 17799 information security standard.

GUIDANCE FOR USE

The information provided in this chapter is pragmatic and to the point. The intent of this section is to provide information security professionals who possess a working knowledge of the ISO/IEC 17799:2000 with a concise analysis of the changes in the second edition. The section preceding the gap should be read by managers and anyone who is interested in gaining a general understanding of the updates and modifications in the second edition. The gap analysis for each of the controls and control objectives should be used as a reference on an as-needed basis.

GENERAL CHANGES

TERMINOLOGY

In the 2005 update, there is a fluid and consistent use of terminology throughout the standard to help lessen misunderstandings or misinterpretations. There is an existing ISO standard that defines many of the terms and phrases utilized in information security management. The second edition uses many of the definitions and terms from the ISO Guide 73 on risk management vocabulary and ISO/IEC Technical Reports 13335 and 18044, respectively. The ISO/IEC 13335 is a guideline for managing IT security and the 18044 focuses on information security incident management. Many new definitions were added to support the new section on risk assessment, which is discussed below. For more information on either of these standards, refer to the ISO Web site at www.iso.org.

NEW SECTIONS/CLAUSES

In the new edition, the following new clauses were added: "Structure of this standard," "Risk assessment and treatment," and "Information security incident management," with the latter being the only clause that directly impacts controls and control objectives.

NEW CONTROL AREA: RISK ASSESSMENT

One of the first things you will probably notice is the new section on risk assessment. I believe this was a missing link from the first edition. Most information security professionals understand that risk assessment is a compulsory part of the information security management process. By including this as part of the standard, senior management will be more aware of the importance and critical role that it plays. The one-and-a-half-page section on risk assessment included in the second edition was originally written in the ISO/IEC TR 13335 standards documents. If your organization would like to review your existing risk assessment process or methodology, the 13335 series would be a great investment. A free alternative for a formal risk assessment model is the NIST Special Publication 800-30. Similar but varying views on the risk assessment and risk management processes can also be found in the NIST SP 800-30 Special Publication. It may make sense to review both models for risk assessment and create a new model that best fits your organization's requirements and objectives. The Information Security Risk Assessment Model (ISRAM™) presented in this book should also be referenced.

CONTROL LAYOUT AND FORMAT

The layout and format for each of the 133 controls are new and improved in the second edition. The new layout is as follows: security clause, control objective, control, implementation guidance, other information.

Please note that in the second edition of the standard, the control reference numbers (e.g., 5.1.1, 7.1.1) do not indicate their order of importance and each control and control objective is assigned a number for reference purposes only.

Each security category contains a control objective and one or more controls. Please note that it is up to each organization to conduct a risk assessment and analysis to determine which of the controls are applicable for their environment. The ISO/IEC 17799 is a true standard, and it needs to be adopted and integrated into an organization's environment based on several considerations. These considerations typically include but are not limited to business requirements and goals, legal and regulatory requirements, contractual or statutory requirements, and the industry of the organization.

In both editions, there is a control objective for each of the main security objectives in the main security clauses. In the second edition the format of each control is slightly different. This new format will promote a better understanding of the true intent of each control. In the first edition, under the main security objective, each control was listed followed by a series of information detailing and explaining the control. In the second edition, a new area is added under each control. The implementation guidance area is now included for each control. This area will assist organizations in understanding the control, as well as implementing it into their environment as appropriate. Following the "implementation guidance" section, a new area is also included for "other information." Information provided in this area can range from links to other documents and standards to sources where more information can be located. Also, in some controls, supplemental guidance and insight is provided within a situational context to provide additional help to organizations.

THE NUMBERS

A total of nine controls were deleted and 17 new controls were added, leaving a net result of 133 controls is the second edition (Figure 6.1). Table 6.1 illustrates the deleted controls, and the new controls are presented in Table 6.2.

In the first edition there were 36 control objectives in total, contained in ten control areas or control clauses as referenced in the second edition. The control objectives are also referenced as main security clauses or categories. Their uses and meanings are synonymous. In the second edition there are a total of 133 controls in 39 control areas in 11 main security clauses.

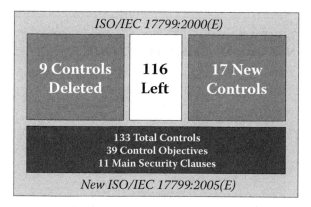

FIGURE 6.1 ISO/IEC 17799:2000(E) and ISO/IEC 17799:2005(E)

TABLE 6.1
Deleted Controls from ISO/IEC 17799:2005

The nine deleted controls for ISO/IEC 17799:2005 include the following:
- 4.1.1 — Management Information Security Forum
- 4.1.5 — Specialist Information Security Advice
- 8.1.6 — External Facilities Management
- 9.4.2 — Enforced Path
- 9.4.4 — Node Authentication
- 9.5.6 — Duress Alarm to Safeguard Users
- 10.3.2 — Encryption
- 10.3.3 — Digital Signatures
- 10.3.4 — Non-repudiation Services

There were a total of 17 new controls added to the second edition of the ISO/IEC 17799:2005. These controls are the "official" controls that are considered new. This is a little bit misleading because many other controls appear to be new, but they were simply created based on existing controls or were the culmination of several controls. Refer to Table 6.2 for the complete list.

MAIN CLAUSE DIFFERENCES

In the ISO/IEC 17799:2000 edition of the standard, there were ten main security clauses. In the current edition there are 11 main clauses. There was a slight rewording of a few of the clauses and the addition of one clause for information security incident management. Refer to Table 6.3 for the modifications to the main clause titles. The ISO/IEC 17799:2000 is referenced as "first edition," and the ISO/IEC 17799:2005 is referenced as "second edition."

TABLE 6.2
New Controls for ISO/IEC 17799:2005

6.1.1 — Management commitment to information security
6.1.7 — Contact with special interest groups
6.2.2 — Addressing security when dealing with customers
7.1.2 — Ownership of assets
7.1.3 — Acceptable use of assets
8.2.1 — Management responsibilities
8.3.1 — Termination responsibilities
8.3.2 — Return of assets
8.3.3 — Removal of access rights
9.1.4 — Protecting against external and environmental threats
10.2.1 — Service delivery
10.2.2 — Monitoring and review of third-party services
10.2.3 — Managing changes to third-party services
10.4.2 — Controls against mobile code
10.9.2 — Online transactions
10.10.3 — Protection of log information
12.6.1 — Control of technical vulnerabilities

TABLE 6.3
Main Security Clause Updates and Modifications

The main clauses will be listed with the first edition description first, followed by the second edition.

Clause 3 — Security Policy; Clause 5 — Security Policy
Clause 4 — Organizational Security; Clause 6 — Organization of Information Security
Clause 5 — Asset Classification and Control; Clause 7 — Asset Management
Clause 6 — Personnel Security; Clause 8 — Human Resources Security
Clause 7 — Physical and Environmental Security; Clause 9 — Physical and Environmental Security
Clause 8 — Communications and Operations Management; Clause 10 — Communications and Operations Management
Clause 9 — Access Control; Clause 11 — Access Control
Clause 10 — Systems Development and Maintenance; Clause 12 — Information Systems Acquisition, Development, and Maintenance
Clause 11 — Did not exist in first edition; Clause 13 — Information Security Incident Management
Clause 12 — Business Continuity Management; Clause 14 — Business Continuity Management
Clause 13 — Compliance; Clause 15 — Compliance

NEW CONTROL OBJECTIVES

There are nine new control objectives in the second edition. A listing of the new controls is provided in Table 6.4. Other controls are listed as new or revised in the text, but these controls were revised or derived from previous controls in the first edition.

TABLE 6.4
ISO/IEC 17799:2005 New Control Objectives

8.1 — Prior Employment
8.2 — During Employment
8.3 — Termination or Change of Employment
10.2 — Third-Party Service Delivery Management
10.8 — Exchange of Information
10.9 — Electronic Commerce Services
10.10 — Monitoring
12.6 — Technical Vulnerability Management
13.2 — Management of Information Security Incidents and Improvements

The listings in the previous section cannot fully capture all the modifications and deletions to the current version of the standard. Viewing the information in these listings can give the reader a perspective on the high-level structural changes. The following sections will provide more information for each of the existing ten main security clauses as well as the new clause on incident management. These sections can be read in sequence or used independently as a reference for each main security clause or control area.

SECURITY POLICY

The "Security Policy" clause still has one control objective and two controls. The control objective was modified, extending the scope to include relevant legal and regulatory aspects of an organization's business model. The spirit of these two controls is basically the same, but additional input and implementation guidance was added, making the controls easier to understand. The second control (3.1.2) was revised to be in synchronization with the 7799-2:2002 (27001) standard. The final draft of the 27001 standard was released in Q3 2005, and the final version was published on October 15, 2005.

These two controls only account for less than 1 percent of the total number of controls. It might be possible to assume that these controls carry a proportionate level of impact on the information security posture of an organization. Without question, these two controls are considered to be some of the most important controls within the standard. In particular, the information security policy document (5.1.1) is considered to be the focal point of the program and has a dramatic effect on the overall security posture of any organization. The information security policy can be directly modeled after the main security clauses in the ISO/IEC 17799:2005 (27002).

ISO/IEC 17799:2000 for the remainder of this chapter will be referred to as "first edition" and the ISO/IEC 17799:2005 will be referred to as "second edition." Each main security clause, control objective, and control will be presented and a short description will be provided on the gap between the two editions. The second edition controls will be listed as the section headings, and reference will be made to the first edition control; any meaningful changes or updates will be outlined and described.

In the first edition the clause name was the same as in the second edition. The title remained the same, but it was referenced as clause 3 in the first edition. Refer to the following sections to gain a high-level understanding of the recent modifications.

5.1 — INFORMATION SECURITY POLICY

The reference name of the information security policy objective remained the same in the second edition. The objective in the second edition was modified and extended to include business requirements and objectives as well as any relevant law or regulation. Since 2000, when the first edition was released, the importance of compliance surrounding legislative and regulatory concerns has increased exponentially. Now we are seeing this trend move from the federal level down to the state level. As of January 2006 there are over 20 states with security-related notification legislation similar to the California SB-1386.

5.1.1 — INFORMATION SECURITY POLICY DOCUMENT

The control name remains the same in both editions and continues to be a focal point of the standard. Implementation guidance was added, as it was for all controls in the second edition, specifically calling out the recommendation for risk assessment, risk management, and the selection of safeguards and controls. The concept of risk management and risk assessment was not as evident in the first edition, and even in the second edition, little more than the suggestion to include and incorporate it within the information security policy and program is provided. Another set of ISO/IEC documents cover these concepts, and this is probably why it is not described or illustrated beyond reference and best practice.

Another key point in the second edition is the suggestion for organizations to communicate their information security policies and requirements outside their organization to relevant external parties. This concept is integrated throughout the second edition in several controls, and most would agree that this is a best-practice approach to helping ensure the integrity of the organization's security policies.

5.1.2 — REVIEW OF THE INFORMATION SECURITY POLICY

The title in the second edition has been modified from "Review and evaluation" to "Review of the information security policy." The title is a little more descriptive and is a better descriptor for the intent of this control. The control text has been updated to help managers and organizations understand that the information security policy should be subject to review and lists some of the reasons and methods to employ this concept. The "implementation guidance" section includes some very specific input and output elements that management should consider as part of the information security policy review process.

ORGANIZATION OF INFORMATION SECURITY

Six new controls were added to the "Organization of Information Security" control area clause, three were deleted, one control was modified and split into two new controls, and one control objective was deleted. There are a total of eleven controls and two control objectives within this control area, constituting approximately 8 percent of the total controls.

The title for this main security clause has been modified in the second edition from "Organizational Security" to "Organization of Information Security." This title revision should be more descriptive and supportive of the intent of this clause.

6.1 — INTERNAL ORGANIZATION

The title for this control objective has been modified in the second edition from "Information Security Infrastructure" to "Internal Organization." The title is more representative of the intent of the control objective, and the use of "infrastructure" was misinterpreted by many in the first edition. The focus of this objective is management-based. The overall theme is that management must embrace and support information security throughout the organization or the information security program is at risk. It also sets the expectation of external review and why management must continually assess information security to remain effective.

6.1.1 — MANAGEMENT COMMITMENT TO INFORMATION SECURITY

This is considered to be a new control in the second edition. Part of the first edition 4.1.1 control is included in this new control, but it has been modified to reflect the scope of this control. Most felt that small organizations would not have the depth of resources or possibly the need for a formal information security forum. This is addressed in 6.1.1 and reworded to reflect the size of the organization. Also, part of the first edition 4.1.5 control (Specialist information security advice) is also included in this new control. Guidance is provided to help managers and organizations understand how to leverage external information security advice.

6.1.2 — INFORMATION SECURITY COORDINATION

The control name remained the same in both editions. There is additional guidance in the second edition to help managers and practitioners decide who should be included and involved in the coordination of information security activities. A listing of seven activities is included in the "implementation guidance" section, helping managers quantify the range of activities suggested by the control objective.

6.1.3 — ALLOCATION OF INFORMATION SECURITY RESPONSIBILITIES

The title of the control name is the same in both editions of the standard. The text of this control is more descriptive in nature and more clearly communicates the scope of the control for the second edition. Callouts to other controls (7.1.2) and clauses (clause 4) is included in the "implementation guidance" section of this control. In general, the control is easier to read and understand.

6.1.4 — AUTHORIZATION PROCESS FOR INFORMATION PROCESSING FACILITIES

The control title remained the same in the second edition. Only minor revisions to the text have been made to this control. With the new structure (control, implementation guidance, other information), this new control is easier to read and understand. Although the scope and intent of this control remained the same between the two editions, a manager or practitioner could more easily evaluate and implement the intent of this control in the second edition as opposed to the original version. This is due in large part to the clarity of the text.

6.1.5 — CONFIDENTIALITY AGREEMENTS

This control is considered to be a new control in the second edition. The origin of this control from the first edition control is 6.1.3 in the personnel security clause. This new control provides some specific guidance regarding what should be included in confidentiality agreements as well as business contracts that should prove to be useful for management. In the past, many organizations have overlooked the need to extend their information security policies to business and contractual agreements. This is becoming more of a common practice and in some cases required because of the legal and regulatory requirements placed on the organization. Data classification is a key component to the creation of risk assessment strategies because there should be different approaches based on the class of data and information.

6.1.6 — CONTACT WITH AUTHORITIES

The first edition control (4.1.6 — Cooperation between organizations) has been split between two controls in the second edition (6.1.6 and 6.1.7). The title for 6.1.1 was revised to "Contact with authorities" and reflects the elements from the first edition control. In addition to the mechanical changes to this control, the scope has been modified to help managers and organizations deal with Internet-based attacks and determine which authorities are most appropriate to contact and communicate with. Linkage to security clause 13 (Information Security Incident Management) and clause 14 (Business Continuity Management) is established in the body of the control text.

6.1.7 — CONTACT WITH SPECIAL INTEREST GROUPS

Contact with special interest groups is considered to be a new control in the second edition, and, as described in the preceding section, this control was created from a section in the original 4.1.6 (Cooperation between organizations) control. Examples of interest groups are provided along with a rationale of why this is important.

6.1.8 — INDEPENDENT REVIEW OF INFORMATION SECURITY

The title for this control remains the same in both editions, but the scope has been edited to help provide more clarity of the control scope and to delineate its difference between similar concepts in controls 5.1.2 (Review of the information security policy) and 15.2.1 (Compliance with security policies and standards). Clear guidance is provided to help managers understand what should be included in an independent review of information security and why this is important to information security and risk management.

6.2 — EXTERNAL PARTIES

The title in the second edition was modified from "Security of Third-Party Access" in the first edition, and the scope was also edited and modified. This modified scope helps managers and organizations interact and communicate with external parties more securely.

6.2.1 — IDENTIFICATION OF RISKS RELATED TO EXTERNAL PARTIES

The control title was modified from "Identification of risks from third-party access" in the first edition, and the scope has also been extended to include communications and activities with external parties in addition to the access components.

Special guidance is included that should be included in a risk assessment process when partnering with external resources or entities. Detailed information on risk identification is provided in the "implementation guidance" section, and this should prove to be very useful for security-minded organizations.

6.2.2 — ADDRESSING SECURITY WHEN DEALING WITH CUSTOMERS

Addressing security when dealing with customers is a new control in the second edition. This new control helps managers and practitioners interact and deal with clients and customers in a secure method. The focus and scope of this control is around the security-related controls and activities that are appropriate before giving clients and customers access to the organization's assets and resources.

6.2.3 — ADDRESSING SECURITY IN THIRD-PARTY AGREEMENTS

The title in the second edition has been modified from "Security requirements in third-party controls," and the scope and intent of the control has been updated. The scope has been broadened to include all of the various types of agreements between organizations, not just contracts. A comprehensive and detailed list of items and elements is provided in the "implementation guidance" section for consideration by management. These items should be reviewed by legal or human resource teams as well to help strengthen external agreements with external parties. The issue and requirement of information security has clearly moved into third-party agreements, and this control will prove to be very useful for security managers and executives when developing risk assessment processes and agreements with any external party or entity.

ASSET MANAGEMENT

Two new controls were added to the "Asset Management" clause. There are a total of two control objectives and five controls within this control area. The asset management controls account for 3 percent of the total controls. Although there are not a great number of controls in this area, asset management is considered a critical component of an effective information security strategy, and special attention and care should be taken when reviewing these controls. It is theoretically impossible to assess risk if you cannot identify the assets to be protected and safeguarded.

The main clause title was revised from "Asset Classification and Control" in the first edition to "Asset Management." As described above, new controls (7.1.2, 7.1.3) were added to this clause as well.

7.1 — RESPONSIBILITY FOR ASSETS

The title for this control objective was revised from "Accountability for Assets" in the first edition. The key words "accountability" and "responsibility" were exchanged to be in alignment with this revised objective and flow of the text with this clause.

7.1.1 — INVENTORY OF ASSETS

The title name remained the same between both editions, and only minor edits were made to the control text. Language was included in the implementation guidance to display linkage to a new control (7.1.2) and explain why this is important for information security. Several very good examples of asset types are included in the "other information" section that should help organizations identify asset types.

7.1.2 — OWNERSHIP OF ASSETS

Ownership of assets is also considered to be a new control in the second edition. This control illustrates the importance of assets and information ownership and its relationship with information security. Asset owners are provided guidance on responsibilities, and direction is described for ownership allocation. Ownership of assets and asset management and its relationship to information security is typically overlooked in smaller organizations.

7.1.3 — ACCEPTABLE USE OF ASSETS

Acceptable use of assets is the second new control in the second edition. This control extends the concept of information security and asset management by establishing the importance of acceptable use. Specific guidance is included for policy development for key technologies such as electronic mail, Internet usage, and mobile devices. The relationship to control objective 10.8 and control 11.7.1 was presented.

7.2 — Information Classification

The title control objective remained the same in the second edition. Only editorial changes were made to the text and the scope basically remained the same.

7.2.1 — Classification guidelines

The control title remained the same in both editions, as did the overall scope objective. No real changes were made, only minor editorial edits to the text. This control is the key to many other areas within the standard. Without establishing appropriate and proper classification guidelines, organizations cannot implement many other key controls.

7.2.2 — Information labeling and handling

The title for this control remained the same in both editions, and the scope also remained the same with only minor editorial updates. Detailed implementation guidance is provided in the control text to help managers and organizations understand how and where to apply this control. It would be impossible to implement this control without a proper classification guideline (7.2.1).

HUMAN RESOURCES SECURITY

The "Human Resources Security" clause was one of the most reworked sections in the new edition of the standard. Three new control objectives were added to address the three stages of employment (prior, during, post). This was a very logical rearrangement and modification to this control area. There are a total of three control objectives and nine controls within this control area, and they account for approximately 6 percent of the total controls within the standard. In environments where people are critical to the security posture, special attention should be taken when assessing these controls.

The title in the second edition has been revised from "Personnel Security" in the first edition. New control objectives and controls in this section were implemented in the second edition to more directly deal with information security matters as they relate to the various stages of employment. The new arrangement and controls should make it much easier for managers to develop and implement these controls. The update or creation of policy statements should be much easier as well.

8.1 — Prior to Employment

"Prior to Employment" is a new control objective in the second edition. This control objective is one of three stages for employment as outlined in the standard. The controls for this section are supportive of this multistage approach and are easy and straightforward to implement.

8.1.1 — ROLES AND RESPONSIBILITIES

The "Roles and responsibilities" control title was revised in the second edition from "Including security in job responsibilities" in the first edition. This control was created based on the first edition 6.1.1 control. As outlined in this control, roles and responsibilities of all users, including employees, consultants, third-party contractors, etc., should be developed and documented in alignment with the information security policy. Several examples outlining requirements are included in the "implementation guidance" section.

8.1.2 — SCREENING

The "Screening" control used the core text from the first edition 6.1.2 control (Personnel screening and policy) and focuses on aligning screening activities with regulations, laws, etc. This control includes the screening of consultants, contractors, and third-party users. This is a new trend in information security as a result of the recent laws and regulations. Also, a large number of security-related breaches over the last two years have occurred at third-party or vendor locations, making this control more applicable than ever before.

8.1.3 — TERMS AND CONDITIONS OF EMPLOYMENT

The control title remained the same in both editions, and the new control was created based on the first edition 6.1.4 control. The scope of this control has been modified and extended to include terms and conditions of all users including third parties, vendors, contractors, and consultants. The "implementation guidance" section illustrates linkage to several other controls (e.g., 15.1.1, 15.1.2, 7.2.1, 10.7.3) within the standard, and several examples are provided to help managers apply this control within their own environment.

8.2 — DURING EMPLOYMENT

"During Employment" is a new control objective for this human resources security main clause, and it addresses three main concepts: information security awareness and training, the scope of management responsibilities, and the development and establishment of a disciplinary process.

8.2.1 — MANAGEMENT RESPONSIBILITIES

"Management responsibilities" is a new control for the second edition, helping managers quantify the actions required to define information security requirements for employees, consultants, contractors, and appropriate third-party users. The "implementation guidance" section describes several scenarios that should help managers assess and apply the control within their organization.

8.2.2 — INFORMATION SECURITY AWARENESS, EDUCATION, AND TRAINING

The control title has been slightly edited from "Information security education and training" to "Information security awareness, education, and training" to better reflect the true intent of this control. The scope of the original control 6.2.1 still exists within the second edition, and the new title raises the awareness and importance of awareness, no pun intended. The control points out that awareness, education, or training should be directed at the correct target audience and be suitable for its role and responsibility level within the organization. There are distinct differences between awareness, education, and training, and managers must understand these differences when designing and implementing these concepts into the organization.

8.2.3 — DISCIPLINARY PROCESS

The control title remains the same in both editions of the standard. The scope and intent of the control basically remains the same as well. The "implementation guidance" section helps managers qualify the disciplinary process and determine when it should be implemented.

8.3 — TERMINATION OR CHANGE OF EMPLOYMENT

"Termination or Change of Employment" is a new control objective in the second edition. The controls within this area address how to effectively and securely deal with termination and changes of employment status and the various issues surrounding these activities. Three new controls were created for this control objective.

8.3.1 — TERMINATION RESPONSIBILITIES

"Termination responsibilities" is a new control in the second edition that helps managers understand the full scope of their duties surrounding termination and its relationship to information security. The relationship to human resources and legal is described in this control, and linkage to other controls such as 6.1.5 (Confidentiality agreements) and 8.1.3 (Terms and conditions of employment) is communicated.

8.3.2 — RETURN OF ASSETS

"Return of assets" is also a new control in the second edition and deals with the proper return of organizational assets in the event of termination. Termination can occur at the employment, consultant, contractor, or business partner level and must be dealt with accordingly. Several, often overlooked items are presented and described, helping management ensure that they have a holistic asset return process.

8.3.3 — REMOVAL OF ACCESS RIGHTS

"Removal of access rights" is the third new control within the "Termination or Change of Employment" control objective. This control illustrates the importance of removing access, logical or physical, in the event of a change in employment or relationship status, such as termination or modification of employment status, contract, or agreement. A great deal of information is provided in the "implementation guidance" section covering issues such as information system access removal to card key access.

PHYSICAL AND ENVIRONMENTAL SECURITY

The "Physical and Environmental Security" main security clause largely remained the same, but with a few minor modifications including one control that was split into two controls, one new control, one new control objective, and one deleted control that was turned into a new control. There are a total of two control objectives and thirteen controls within this control area, making this section represent a little over 9 percent of the total controls within the standard. A large percentage of security incidents happen as a result of weak physical controls, so these controls should be taken very seriously by information security and management. The main security clause title remained the same in both editions.

9.1 — SECURE AREAS

The title for the control objective remains unchanged in the second edition, but the scope has been revised. For example, the clear desk and clear screen policy was deleted from this area and moved to another clause.

9.1.1 — PHYSICAL SECURITY PERIMETER

The title for this control remains unchanged, and only minor editorial changes were made to the text. The scope was modified to use elements from the first edition control 7.1.3 (Securing offices, rooms, and facilities). The implementation guidance was also extended for this version of the control and provides numerous examples of physical security perimeter controls that should be considered and evaluated by managers and security professionals. Additional guidance and valuable information was added to the "other information" section of the control text.

9.1.2 — PHYSICAL ENTRY CONTROLS

The title of this control remains unchanged in the second edition. Minor editorial changes were made to the control text to help align the language with the flow of the new version of the standard. Key points from the first edition 7.1.4 (Working in secure areas) control were added to the "implementation guidance" section. Additional points were added in the implementation guidance text to continue the theme of including all relevant external parties within the scope of the control. This inclusion of all relevant external parties throughout the second edition was one of the best updates to this edition, in my professional opinion. It is very easy to overlook or not extend the scope of controls to partners, vendors, consultants, or contractors and therefore to not account for a potentially large degree of risk.

9.1.3 — Securing offices, rooms, and facilities

The control title remains the same, but significant changes occurred within the text and scope. The original control was split into two controls in the second edition (9.1.3, 9.1.4), and some of the control text was moved to 9.1.1 (Physical security perimeter). The new scope of this control is largely focused on the securing of offices, rooms, and facilities and stops there. The other areas that were previously present within the scope were moved as outlined above or deleted.

9.1.4 — Protecting against external and environmental threats

"Protecting against external and environmental threats" is a new control in the second edition that is based on portions of the first edition 7.1.3 control (Securing offices, rooms, and facilities). Minor editorial modifications were made to the text, but the control scope is basically unchanged.

9.1.5 — Working in secure areas

The title of this control remained the same in both editions, but modifications were made to the body of the text to make it fit better with the logic and flow of the second edition. The text relating to third-party access was deleted from this control and moved to 9.1.2 (Physical entry controls).

9.1.6 — Public access, delivery, and loading areas

The title of the "Public access, delivery, and loading areas" control was originally "Isolated delivery and loading areas" (7.1.5) in the first edition. The scope of this control has been modified to include public access in addition to delivery and loading areas. Minor editorial changes were made to the text within the control to make it sync up with the flow of the second edition as well. In the old 7.1.5 control, risk assessment was included and is now considered redundant in the second edition, so that portion of the control was deleted from the text. The "implementation guidance" section has also been modified and extended to include public access.

9.2 — Equipment Security

The title for this control objective remained the same in both editions, and only minor editorial changes have been made to the scope.

9.2.1 — Equipment siting and protection

The title for this control remains the same in the second edition, and only minor revisions were made to the text to make it more compatible with the second edition. The text regarding disasters was moved to 9.1.4 (Protecting against external and environmental threats). The implementation guidance text was extended to include information leakage and fire protection.

9.2.2 — Supporting utilities

The control title was modified from "Power supplies" in the first edition to "Supporting utilities." The scope of the control has been modified to include utilities in general and not just power supplies. Minor editorial changes were made to the existing text to allow better flow with the second edition framework. The "implementation guidance" section was expanded to include additional utility items in addition to power supplies.

9.2.3 — Cabling security

The title for this control remains unchanged in the second edition, and only minor editorial changes were made to the body of the text. The "implementation guidance" section was extended to include information about protecting sensitive and critical systems (item f).

9.2.4 — Equipment maintenance

The control title remained the same in both editions, and only minor editorial changes were made to the text in the control. The scope of the control remained the same as well.

9.2.5 — Security of equipment off-premises

The title for this control remains unchanged in the second edition, and only minor text-related edits were made to the control to make it in sync with the language and structure of the second edition.

9.2.6 — Secure disposal or reuse of equipment

The title for this control remains unchanged in the second edition. Minor edits were made to the control to make it in sync with the language of the second edition.

9.2.7 — Removal of property

The title for this control remains unchanged in the second edition, and only minor text-related edits were made to the control to make it in sync with the language and structure of the second edition.

COMMUNICATIONS AND OPERATIONS MANAGEMENT

There are a total of ten control objectives and thirty-two controls within the "Communications and Operations Management" security clause, making this by far the largest security clause within the standard. This section makes up a little over 24 percent of the total number of controls within the standard. It stands to reason why this section is so large. In effect, information security is highly operational in nature, and therefore many of the controls must address this aspect of information security. It is highly critical that organizations implement the appropriate controls within this security clause to a high degree of effectiveness. Undervaluing just one of these controls could lead to seriously negative consequences. The title for the main clause remains unchanged in the second edition. A host of controls were modified, added, and deleted, and the following sections will detail these changes.

10.1 — Operational Procedures and Responsibilities

The title for the "Operational Procedures and Responsibilities" control objective was unchanged in the second edition. The incident management controls and text were deleted from this area and were moved to clause 13 as a new and stand-alone security clause.

10.1.1 — Documented operating procedures

The control title was not changed in the second edition, but edits were made to the body of the text to be in alignment with the new structure. The "implementation guidance" section was extended to include more operating procedures.

10.1.2 — Change management

The "Change management" control title was originally "Operational change control" in the first edition. The focus of this control is narrower and emphasizes the importance and relevance of change management to information security. Some updates have been made to the text of the control to support the new structure of the second edition. Additional guidance is provided in the "implementation guidance" section, and the relationship to other controls (e.g., 11.5.4, 10.7.2, 10.7.3) is included.

10.1.3 — Segregation of duties

The control title remains unchanged in the second edition. Editorial changes were made to the text to facilitate the new structure and flow of the second edition. Options were provided for small organizations where it is not suitable to perform the full intent of this control.

10.1.4 — Separation of development, test, and operational facilities

The "Separation of development, test, and operational facilities" control was originally "Separation of development and operational facilities" in the first edition. The control in the second edition includes test systems and environments, and the text was also updated to reflect the structure of the new release. Information in the "implementation guidance" and "other information" sections was rewritten to be clearer for the reader.

10.2 — THIRD-PARTY SERVICE DELIVERY MANAGEMENT

The "Third-Party Service Delivery Management" control objective is new for the second edition. The controls in this section deal with the implementation and maintenance of information security and service delivery to be in line with third-party service delivery agreements, if they exist.

10.2.1 — SERVICE DELIVERY

"Service delivery" is a new control in the second edition and deals with delivering, operating, and maintaining security controls in regard to a third party as per any agreements.

10.2.2 — MONITORING AND REVIEW OF THIRD-PARTY SERVICES

"Monitoring and review of third-party services" is a new control in the second edition. The scope of this control includes the review, monitoring, and auditing of services, reports, and records provided by a third party. Detailed implementation guidance is provided to help managers include the critical components of this control within their operations.

10.2.3 — MANAGING AND REVIEW OF THIRD-PARTY SERVICES

"Managing and review of third-party services" is a new control for the second edition. The spirit of this control deals with the monitoring, assessment, and update to controls and safeguards as a result of the services offered or provided to or for third parties.

10.3 — SYSTEM PLANNING AND ACCEPTANCE

The control objective title remained the same, and only minor editorial changes were made to the text.

10.3.1 — CAPACITY MANAGEMENT

"Capacity management" was originally "Capacity planning" in the first edition. The text of this control was extended to embrace the management aspect as opposed to the planning objective. Edits to the text were required to bring the revised control into alignment with the title change.

10.3.2 — SYSTEM ACCEPTANCE

The "System acceptance" title remained the same in the second edition. Only minor text edits were performed to bring the control into alignment with the new structure of the second edition. The implementation guidance section was extended to include ease of use and migration elements.

10.4 — Protection Against Malicious and Mobile Code

The control objective title was revised from "Protection Against Malicious Software" in the first edition. The title and the scope of the control was extended to include mobile code. The issue of mobile code is addressed in control 10.4.2.

10.4.1 — Controls against malicious code

The title for this control remained unchanged in both editions of the standard. Minor edits and rephrasing of a few keywords were carried out to make the control be in alignment with the new control structure. The implementation guidance was extended to include malicious code and Web pages and how to protect against the various scenarios of malicious code. The issue of conducting regular reviews of software and data was expressed as well.

10.4.2 — Controls against mobile code

"Controls against mobile code" is a new control in the second edition. The issue of mobile code operating in accordance with the information security policy is presented, and only authorized code should be allowed to execute.

10.5 — Backup

The title for this control objective was originally "Housekeeping" in the first edition. Several changes have been made to this section, including the removal of controls on operator logs and fault logging to the "Monitoring" (10.10) control objective. Only one control remains in this section for the second edition.

10.5.1 — Information backup

The title for this control remained the same in the second edition. Only minor editorial changes have been made to the text in this control to make it more suitable for the logic and flow of the second edition. Additional implementation guidance has been added in this version to help managers and practitioners with security matters as they relate to information backup.

10.6 — Network Security Management

The control objective title was slightly revised from "Network Management" in the first edition to "Network Security Management" in the second edition. The title helps provide the necessary focus on information security as opposed to network management, which is a different topic. The two controls in this section relate directly to information security.

10.6.1 — Network controls

The title for this control remained the same in both editions. Some editorial changes were made to the text within the control, and implementation guidance on monitoring and logging was added.

10.6.2 — Security of network services

"Security of network services" is a revised control in the second edition that is based on the first edition 9.4.9 (Security of network services) control. The bulk of this control focuses on including security features, service levels, and management requirements in network security services agreements.

10.7 — Media Handling

The title of the "Media Handling" control objective was "Media Handling and Security" in the first edition. Some changes have been made to the scope in regard to threats and risks as these concepts relate specifically to handling media.

10.7.1 — Management of removable computer media

The title for this control remained the same in both editions. Only minor editorial updates have been made to the body of the text to support the language and format of the second edition. The "implementation guidance" section has been extended to include guidance on media drives, media registration, and media degradation.

10.7.2 — Disposal of media

The title remains unchanged for this control in the second edition, and only minor editorial changes were made to the text to make it more suitable for the language and structure of the second edition.

10.7.3 — Information handling procedures

The title remains unchanged for the "Information handling procedures" control in the second edition, and only minor editorial changes were made to the text to make it more suitable for the language and structure of the second edition.

10.7.4 — Security of system documentation

The title remains unchanged for this control in the second edition, and only minor editorial changes were made to the text to make it more suitable for the language and structure of the second edition.

10.8 — Exchange of Information

The title for this control objective was originally "Exchanges of Information and Software" in the first edition, and the full scope of the objective was split between

10.8 (Exchange of Information) and 10.9 (Electronic Commerce Services). Controls with each of these objectives have been modified and some new controls have been added to address the scope changes.

10.8.1 — INFORMATION EXCHANGE POLICIES AND PROCEDURES

The "Information exchange policies and procedures" control was created based on two controls from the first edition: 8.7.4.2 (Policy on electronic mail) and 8.7.7 (Other forms of information exchange).

10.8.2 — EXCHANGE AGREEMENTS

The original title for this control was "Information and software exchange agreements" in the first edition, and minor edits have been made to the text within the control to bring it into alignment with the second edition. Implementation guidance has been added to this control for escrow agreements, traceability, and non-repudiation.

10.8.3 — PHYSICAL MEDIA IN TRANSIT

The title was revised from "Security of media in transit" to "Physical media in transit" in the second edition. Editorial changes were made to the text of the control and additional text was added to the "implementation guidance" section to help managers and information security professionals better understand the intent and spirit of this control.

10.8.4 — ELECTRONIC MESSAGING

"Security of electronic mail" in the first edition has been revised to "Electronic messaging" in the second edition. The origin of this control was the old 8.7.4.1 and 8.7.4.2 controls. These two old controls were split into new controls in the second edition. The basis for this control came from 8.7.4.1.

10.8.5 — BUSINESS INFORMATION SYSTEMS

This control title was revised from "Security of electronic office systems" in the first edition, and the text has been revised and extended to include business systems interconnection. The implementation guidance text has been modified to address the issue of vulnerabilities.

10.9 — ELECTRONIC COMMERCE SERVICES

The "Electronic Commerce Services" control objective was originally part of 8.7 (Exchanges of Information and Software) in the first edition. As previously discussed, two new control objectives were created (10.8 and 10.9) in the second edition.

10.9.1 — Electronic commerce

The "Electronic commerce" control is based on a related control in the first edition but has been extended to include fraud, insurance, confidentiality, and authorization. Several edits were made to the text in the control to make it more suitable for the second edition framework.

10.9.2 — Online transactions

"Online transactions" is a new control for the second edition and deals with the security and protection of data and information involved in network transactions.

10.9.3 — Publicly available systems

The title for this control remained the same in the second edition, and only minor editorial changes were made to the text to ensure its alignment with the framework of the second edition.

10.10 — Monitoring

"Monitoring" is considered to be a new control objective in the second edition, but it is based on existing concepts contained in the first edition. The core of this control objective is based on the old 9.7 (Monitoring System Access and Use) objective. The objective has been moved to the "Communications and Operations Management" main security clause, and this rearrangement makes much more sense.

10.10.1 — Audit logging

The "Audit logging" control is based on the first edition 9.7.1 (Event logging) control. This newly revised control has been extended to include additional operational-related elements.

10.10.2 — Monitoring system use

The "Monitoring system use" control is based on 9.7.2.1 and 9.7.2.2 in the first edition. There were several edits to the texts to bring the new control into alignment with the framework of the second edition.

10.10.3 — Protection of log information

The "Protection of log information" was created based on parts of the old 9.7.2 and 9.2.7.3 controls. The scope of this control is more narrow and focused on the security and protection of log data and information. The "implementation guidance" section has been extended to address the concerns of protecting this data and information.

10.10.4 — ADMINISTRATOR AND OPERATOR LOGS

The "Administrator and operator logs" control was created based on the old 8.4.2 (Operator logs) control. The text in the control has been revised to adapt to the framework of the second edition.

10.10.5 — FAULT LOGGING

The "Fault logging" control was created based on the first edition 8.4.3 control. The concept of fault logging is straightforward, but the importance is often overlooked. Operational examples and ideas are provided in the "implementation guidance" section to help managers and security professionals.

10.10.6 — CLOCK SYNCHRONIZATION

The "Clock synchronization" control in the second edition is based on the first edition 9.7.3 control. Additional implementation guidance has been added to time format and why it is important within information security.

ACCESS CONTROL

There are a total of 25 controls and 7 control objectives within the "Access Control" security clause, making this the second largest control area within the standard, accounting for approximately 19 percent of the total controls. Access control is critical to an effective information security strategy. I personally urge organizations to continually reassess themselves for these controls and base their controls and safeguards on a formal risk assessment process. The main security clause title remains the same in the second edition. Several modifications to control objectives and controls were made in the new edition, and they will all be described and presented in the forthcoming sections.

11.1 — BUSINESS REQUIREMENTS FOR ACCESS CONTROL

Only minor text-related updates have been made to the "Business Requirements for Access Control" objective to make it more suitable and in alignment with the framework of the second edition.

11.1.1 — ACCESS CONTROL POLICY

The "Access control policy" title remains unchanged in the second edition. Minor text updates were performed, and additional implementation guidance on access rights, periodic review of access controls, formal authorization, and segregation was added.

11.2 — USER ACCESS MANAGEMENT

The "User Access Management" control objective title did not change in the second edition, and no real content changes occurred; only minor editorial changes were made to the text to bring the objective into alignment with the second edition framework.

11.2.1 — USER REGISTRATION

The "User registration" control title remained unchanged in the second edition, and the scope has been extended to include deregistration. Minor editorial updates were made to the text.

11.2.2 — PRIVILEGE MANAGEMENT

The "Privilege management" control title did not change in the second edition. No structural or scope changes occurred, but additional implementation guidance was added about use of privileges.

11.2.3 — USER PASSWORD MANAGEMENT

The title for this control was not changed in the second edition. New implementation guidance was added to address temporary and default passwords. Minor edits were made to the text to bring it into alignment with the second edition.

11.2.4 — REVIEW OF USER ACCESS RIGHTS

The title for "Review of user access rights" did not change in the second edition. Implementation guidance on logging and access rights was added and minor changes to the text were made to adapt the text to the second edition framework.

11.3 — USER RESPONSIBILITIES

The title for the "User Responsibilities" control objective was not changed in the second edition, but the scope was modified to include the clear desk and clear screen policy.

11.3.1 — PASSWORD USE

The title for this control did not change in the second edition, and implementation guidance on dictionary attacks and using passwords in a business environment was added. Minor updates to the text were made to bring the text into alignment with the second edition.

11.3.2 — UNATTENDED USER EQUIPMENT

The title and scope for this control did not change in the second edition. Only minor text changes were made to the control.

11.4 — NETWORK ACCESS CONTROL

The title and scope for this control objective remains unchanged in the second edition. Only minor edits to the text were made.

11.4.1 — POLICY ON USE OF NETWORK SERVICES

The title for "Policy on use of network services" did not change in the second edition, and minor editorial changes were made to the text within the control.

11.4.2 — USER AUTHENTICATION FOR EXTERNAL CONNECTIONS

The 9.4.3 (User authentication for external connections) and 9.4.4 (Node authentication) controls were merged together to form the "User authentication for external connections" control. The text of these two old controls was slightly modified to conform to the framework of the second edition, and new implementation guidance on virtual private networks and wireless communications was added.

11.4.3 — EQUIPMENT IDENTIFICATION IN THE NETWORK

The "Equipment identification in the network" control was created based on the first edition 9.5.1 (Automatic terminal identification) control. The text within the control was extended to include equipment identification in addition to terminals.

11.4.4 — REMOTE DIAGNOSTIC PORT AND CONFIGURATION PROTECTION

The title for this control has been slightly revised from "Remote diagnostic port protection" in the first edition and modified to include both diagnostic and configuration port security.

11.4.5 — SEGREGATION IN NETWORKS

The title for this control remains the same in the second edition. A lot of text has been edited and rearranged to fit within the structure of the second edition. New implementation guidance has been added on virtual private networks, wireless networks, routing, and switching technologies.

11.4.6 — NETWORK CONNECTION CONTROL

The title remains unchanged in the second edition, and only minor edits were made to the text. Additional guidance has been added on access rights. Linkage to the 11.1.1 "Access control policy" was added.

11.4.7 — NETWORK ROUTING CONTROL

The title of the "Network routing control" did not change in the second edition. Some minor edits were made to the control text to bring it into alignment with the framework of the second edition. The text that was moved to the "implementation guidance" section was also edited, but the objective and spirit of this control remained the same in the second edition.

11.5 — OPERATING SYSTEM ACCESS CONTROL

The title for this control objective did not change in the second edition, but the scope did. This objective focuses on the unauthorized access to operating systems now.

11.5.1 — SECURE LOG-ON PROCEDURES

The original title for this control was "Terminal log-on procedures." Editorial changes were made to the body of the text to bring it into alignment with the second edition.

11.5.2 — USER IDENTIFICATION AND AUTHENTICATION

The title for this control was not modified for the second edition. However, the text was modified to focus on authentication technologies as a result of a formal risk assessment. New guidance was added to cover generic user and privileged accounts.

11.5.3 — PASSWORD MANAGEMENT SYSTEM

The title did not change in the second edition, and only minor editorial changes were made to the body of the text. The implementation guidance section provides several good examples of why security passwords, and their management, is important to the overall information security posture for an organization.

11.5.4 — USE OF SYSTEM UTILITIES

The title remained the same in the second edition, and only minor edits were made to the text within the control. Some new implementation guidance was added regarding segregation of duties.

11.5.5 — SESSION TIME-OUT

The title in the second edition was modified from "Terminal time-out" in the first edition. The title change tells most of the story. The control was reworded to address the issues of sessions as opposed to a physical terminal.

11.5.6 — LIMITATION OF CONNECTION TIME

The title for "Limitation of connection time" did not change in the second edition. The text basically remained the same except for some edits to bring the text into alignment with the structure of the second edition. Additional implementation guidance on reauthentication was added as well.

11.6 — APPLICATION AND INFORMATION ACCESS CONTROL

The control title was extended to include information. The original title for this control was "Application Access Control." Along with the title revision, the objective was extended to also cover both dimensions (application and information) access control.

11.6.1 — INFORMATION ACCESS RESTRICTION

The title for this control did not change in the second edition. The text of the control was edited and revised to be in alignment with the structure of the second edition. The consideration for controlling access rights of other applications was added to the "implementation guidance" section.

11.6.2 — SENSITIVE SYSTEM ISOLATION

The title for the control remained the same in the second edition. Minor updates to the text were made and the control basically remained the same.

11.7 — MOBILE COMPUTING AND TELEWORKING

The title and the control objective remained the same in the second edition. No other notable changes were made to this objective.

11.7.1 — MOBILE COMPUTING AND COMMUNICATIONS

The title was extended from "Mobile computing" in the first edition to include communications. New guidance was added on insurance and legal considerations. References to other control objectives were stated to help readers understand the relationship and interconnection between this control and other parts of the standard.

11.7.2 — TELEWORKING

The title for this control did not change in the second edition. Wireless networking, software licensing, anti-virus protection, and others were added to the implementation guidance section of this control.

INFORMATION SYSTEMS ACQUISITION, DEVELOPMENT, AND MAINTENANCE

There are a total of sixteen controls within six control objectives for the "Information Systems Acquisition, Development, and Maintenance" security clause. This section makes up about 12 percent of the total controls for the entire standard. This security clause received a much-needed update and revision. The titles of the controls and control objectives have been reviewed and updated. I personally witnessed many organizations overlooking or discounting this section in the first edition because they did not develop their own software or applications. The updates and revisions to this main security clause dramatically help illustrate the importance of these control objectives and controls and their relationship to other areas within the standard.

12.1 — SECURITY REQUIREMENTS OF INFORMATION SYSTEMS

The control objective title was revised to include "Information" to clarify the objective is information systems.

12.1.1 — SECURITY REQUIREMENTS ANALYSIS AND SPECIFICATION

The title for this control remains unchanged in the second edition, and minor updates were made to the text. New guidance on purchasing of products was added, and reference to the ISO/IEC 13335-3 and ISO/IEC 15408 was included in the "other information" section.

12.2 — CORRECT PROCESSING IN APPLICATIONS

The original title for this control objective was "Security in Application Systems." The scope has been extended to cover application errors.

12.2.1 — INPUT DATA VALIDATION

The title for this control did not change in the second edition, and minor edits were made to the text of the control. New information on creating logs and examination of input data was added to the "implementation guidance" section.

12.2.2 — CONTROL OF INTERNAL PROCESSING

There were no changes to the title of this control, but new information on buffer overflows was added to the "implementation guidance" section.

12.2.3 — MESSAGE INTEGRITY

Message integrity was originally "Message authentication" in the first edition. The title change indicates the scope change, which now includes the integrity of messages at the application layer.

12.2.4 — OUTPUT DATA VALIDATION

The title did not change in the second edition, and new information on log creation has been added to the "implementation guidance" section.

12.3 — CRYPTOGRAPHIC CONTROLS

The title for this control objective did not change in the second edition, but the scope has been modified to cover just policy and management aspects of cryptography. Many of the technical details for the first edition were completely deleted or refined in the second edition.

12.3.1 — POLICY ON THE USE OF CRYPTOGRAPHIC CONTROLS

The title in the second edition did not change for this control. However, several of the first edition controls (10.3.1 to 10.3.4) were modified and ultimately reworked into this control. New information about algorithms, impact of cryptographic controls, and proper protection of removable media was added to the "implementation guidance" section.

12.3.2 — KEY MANAGEMENT

The title for this control remained the same in both editions of the standard, and only minor editorial changes were made to the text. New information on the protection of cryptographic keys was added to the "implementation guidance" section.

12.4 — SECURITY OF SYSTEM FILES

The title for this control objective did not change in the second edition. The text for this objective was edited to account for the modification of the controls within this sub-clause.

12.4.1 — CONTROL OF OPERATIONAL SOFTWARE

The title was not modified in the second edition of the standard. New information on configuration control, old software, externally supplied software, and rollback strategy was added to the "implementation guidance" section.

12.4.2 — PROTECTION OF SYSTEM TEST DATA

The title remained the same in the second edition, and new text was added addressing the security-related risks that test data can pose to organizations if it is not handled properly.

12.4.3 — ACCESS CONTROL TO PROGRAM SOURCE CODE

The title did not change in the second edition, and the focus of this control is the protection of source code and how a source library is one viable option to help with this. Minor edits were made to the text to bring it into alignment with the framework of the second edition.

12.5 — SECURITY IN DEVELOPMENT AND SUPPORT PROCESSES

The title for this control objective remained unchanged in the second edition. The text for the scope was slightly modified but carried the same meaning as it did in the first edition.

12.5.1 — Change control procedures

There were no changes to the control title in the second edition, and only minor editorial changes were made to the text within the control structure. New information regarding a formal change process was added to the "implementation guidance" section, and a reference was made to the new "Technical Vulnerability Management" control objective.

12.5.2 — Technical review of applications after operating system changes

The title for this control was slightly revised from "Technical review of operating system changes" to "Technical review of applications after operating system changes." The scope of the control followed the title change and gave way to the new 12.6 control objective.

12.5.3 — Restrictions on changes to software packages

The title did not change in the second edition, and updates were made to the text within the control to adapt it to the structure of the second edition. Supporting information on independent evaluation was added to the "implementation guidance" section.

12.5.4 — Information leakage

The "Information leakage" control is based on the first edition 10.5.4 (Covert channels and Trojan code) control. This newly modified control includes much of the old content about covert channels and excludes any reference to Trojan code because it has already been addressed in control 10.4.1 (Controls against malicious code). Other various forms of information leakage are added to the structure of this control.

12.5.5 — Outsourced software development

The title remains unchanged in the second edition, and the scope is the same. Only minor edits to the style of the text were made to adapt it to the structure of the second edition.

12.6 — Technical Vulnerability Management

"Technical Vulnerability Management" is a new control objective for the second edition and addresses the topic of software patches.

12.6.1 — Control of technical vulnerabilities

Control of technical vulnerabilities is a new control in the second edition and deals with control technical vulnerabilities.

INFORMATION SECURITY INCIDENT MANAGEMENT

There are a total of five controls in two control objectives within the newly formed "Information Security Incident Management" main security clause. These controls constitute only about 3 percent of the total controls for the standard. All five of the controls were derived from existing controls within the first edition, and a new control objective was added (13.2 — Management of Information Security Incidents and Improvements). These controls, as with the majority of the others, have been reviewed and fine-tuned to more accurately reflect the control objective they support, and they are clearer and easier to understand. The implementation guidance added to these controls will significantly assist organizations within this domain.

13.1 — REPORTING INFORMATION SECURITY EVENTS AND WEAKNESSES

This control objective is based on the first edition control 6.3.1 (Reporting security incidents). There were several modifications. First 6.3.1 was a control and 13.1 is a control objective. The spirit of 6.3.1 was used to formulate the objective for this sub-clause. This sub-clause comprises two controls, one on security events and the other on security weaknesses.

13.1.1 — REPORTING INFORMATION SECURITY EVENTS

"Reporting information security events" was created based on first edition controls 6.3.1 (Reporting security incidents), 6.3.3 (Reporting software malfunctions), and 9.5.6 (Duress alarm to safeguard users). The text from the listed controls was modified and adapted to the context of incident management and the framework of the second edition.

13.1.2 — REPORTING SECURITY WEAKNESSES

"Reporting security weaknesses" is based on the first edition 6.3.2 (Reporting security weaknesses) control. The text had to be modified to adapt to the second edition framework as well as be more aligned with the concept of incident management.

13.2 — MANAGEMENT OF INFORMATION SECURITY INCIDENTS AND IMPROVEMENTS

This is a new control objective in the second edition. This objective deals with the approach to management information security incidents and provides guidance for readers.

13.2.1 — RESPONSIBILITIES AND PROCEDURES

The "Responsibilities and procedures" control is partially based on the first edition 8.1.3 (Incident management procedures) control. The body of the text had to be adapted to the framework of the second edition, and the implementation guidance was edited as well.

13.2.2 – Learning from information security incidents

"Learning from information security incidents" is based on the first edition 6.3.4 (Learning from incidents) control. The spirit of this control remains the same with only minor editorial changes to adapt it to the framework of the second edition.

13.2.3 – Collection of evidence

"Collection of evidence" is based on the first edition 12.1.7 (Collection of evidence) control. The text is adapted to the context of incident management.

BUSINESS CONTINUITY MANAGEMENT

The "Business Continuity Management" main security clause still has one control objective and five supporting controls. These controls make up approximately 3 percent of the total controls within the standard. Extensive revisions have been made to the scope of these controls, and the text has been significantly updated and revised. Information security has been overlaid as the main focus for these controls in the second edition.

14.1 – Information Security Aspects of Business Continuity Management

This control objective in the second edition is based on the first edition 11.1 (Aspects of Business Continuity Management). The business continuity scope remains the same, and the overall scope was adjusted to embrace information security aspects as they relate to business continuity management.

14.1.1 – Including information security in the business continuity management process

The control is based on the first edition 11.1.1 (Business continuity management process) control, and it is basically the same control with the addition of information security concepts.

14.1.2 – Business continuity and risk assessment

The title for this control was modified in the second edition from "Business continuity and impact analysis" in the first edition. The overall scope is basically the same but has been extended to embrace information security and a formalized risk assessment process.

14.1.3 — Developing and Implementing Continuity Plans Including Information Security

The original title of this control was "Writing and implementing continuity plans" in the first edition. The scope has been extended in the second edition to include information security matters and controls.

14.1.4 — Business Continuity Planning Framework

The title and control scope remained the same except that information security is now included within the planning process and framework.

14.1.5 — Testing, Maintaining, and Reassessing Business Continuity Plans

The title remained the same in the second edition, and the scope was extended to embrace information security in the testing and assessment processes.

COMPLIANCE

A total of three control objectives and ten controls make up the "Compliance" main security clause. A few of the key controls (e.g., 15.1.2, 15.2.1, 15.3.2) have been revised and their scopes modified and extended. The other remaining controls were updated and the text was modified to be more in alignment with the second edition of the standard.

15.1 — Compliance with Legal Requirements

The title for this control objective did not change in the second edition, and there were only minor revisions to the text to adapt it to the framework of the second edition.

15.1.1 — Identification of Applicable Legislation

The title did not change in the second edition. The scope and spirit of the control remained the same as well, but the issue of continually evaluating and identifying legal and regulatory requirements was added.

15.1.2 — Intellectual Property Rights (IPR)

The title for this control did not change in the second edition. Edits were made to the body of the text to adapt it to the new format of the second edition. New guidance was added on software acquisition and the dimension of intellectual property rights was extended.

15.1.3 — PROTECTION OF ORGANIZATIONAL RECORDS

The title for this control was slightly revised for the second edition. The original title in the first edition was "Safeguarding of organizational records." Edits were made to the text in order to adapt it to the structure and flow of the second edition. Additional information on stored record cryptology was added to the implementation guidance section.

15.1.4 — DATA PROTECTION AND PRIVACY OF PERSONAL INFORMATION

The title for this control did not change in the second edition. Edits were made to the structure and context of the text to adapt it to the second edition. The issue of legislation was introduced in this control, and the associated policy was added to the "implementation guidance" section.

15.1.5 — PREVENTION OF MISUSE OF INFORMATION PROCESSING FACILITIES

The title remained the same in the second edition, and the text for the control was modified to adapt it to the framework of the second edition.

15.1.6 — REGULATION OF CRYPTOGRAPHIC CONTROLS

The title was unchanged in the second edition, and scope of this control is basically the same except for the editorial updates that were required for the second edition. Information on the restriction of cryptography was added to the "implementation guidance" section.

15.2 — COMPLIANCE WITH SECURITY POLICIES AND STANDARDS AND TECHNICAL COMPLIANCE

The title for this control objective was originally "Reviews of Security Policy and Technical Compliance" in the first edition. Updates to the scope include compliance-related elements such as checking for compliance against documented controls and policy.

15.2.1 — COMPLIANCE WITH SECURITY POLICY AND STANDARDS

The title was modified and extended to include "standards." The original title in the first edition was "Compliance with security policy." The scope was extended to include standards as well as other possible requirements in addition to policy. New information is provided to help managers deal with noncompliance situations in the "implementation guidance" section.

15.2.2 — TECHNICAL COMPLIANCE CHECKING

The title for the control did not change in the second edition, and the text was modified to adapt to the framework of the second edition. New information was provided including guidance on how compliance checking should be carried out, and new text on penetration and vulnerability testing was added as well.

15.3 — INFORMATION SYSTEMS AUDIT CONSIDERATIONS

The original title for this control objective was "System Audit Considerations" in the first edition. The scope was not modified other than simple text edits to adapt it to the flow of the second edition.

15.3.1 — INFORMATION SYSTEMS AUDIT CONTROLS

The title was "System audit controls" in the first edition, and new information about protecting audit files and time-stamping was added to the "implementation guidance" section.

15.3.2 — PROTECTION OF INFORMATION SYSTEMS AUDIT TOOLS

The title has been slightly modified from "Protection of system audit tools" in the first edition, and new information about third parties was added in the "other information" section.

REFERENCES

ISO/IEC 17799:2000 Information Technology — Security Techniques — Code of Practice for Information Security Management, International Organization for Standardization, 2000.

ISO/IEC 17799:2005 Information Technology — Security Techniques — Code of Practice for Information Security Management, International Organization for Standardization, 2005.

Section II

Analysis of ISO/IEC 17799:2005 (27002) Controls

For each of the 133 controls of the ISO/IEC 17799:2005 (27002) Code of Practice for Information Security Management, Chapters 7 through 17 provide detailed information in the following categories:

- Scope
- Key Risk Indicator
- Control Class
- Key Questions

As available and appropriate, information is provided in two additional categories:

- External References
- Additional Information

The scope of each control is described in an effort to help readers understand the intended boundaries and the spirit of the control according to the standard.

The key risk indicator is included with each control to indicate if the control is designated as a KRI control. Details on the KRI controls can be found in Chapter 4.

As described in Chapter 2, each of the 133 controls has been assigned a control class. A designation of M for Management, T for Technical, or O for Operational is provided for each control. Management controls require management's approval, support, or direct actions. Operational controls are controls that are action- or task-oriented and typically nontechnical in nature. Technical controls require the modification, configuration, or verification of information processing facilities.

Examples of key questions are provided for each control that should help information security assessment professionals form questions to include in their own assessments. This section is not intended to be an all-inclusive questions list but rather a working example of the types of questions that are most effective when using the Global Information Security Assessment Methodology (GISAM™).

External references are provided as appropriate to help readers extend their knowledge and understanding of the control.

Additional information, as appropriate, is provided for each control. Information provided here does not fit into any of the other categories, but it is still important information and should be included with the control.

7 Security Policy

An organization's information security policy is one of the most important business documents within the organization. That's right—business document and not a technology document. The security policy should always be an extension of the organization's business environment, culture, and mission as well as account for any applicable laws and regulations. By having a formal information security policy, the organization will benefit in a number of ways.

The information security policy should be customized to reflect the business objectives of each organization. This is one of the primary reasons why using standard template-based policies is not effective for many managers. It is clear that many organizations share similar business objectives and many policies can overlap. The element that makes the information security policy effective, strangely enough, is not the policy document—it is the people. For information security to be taken seriously within any organization, there absolutely must be visible support from management at all levels. This can range from funding information security initiatives to managers and executives attending user training sessions with everyone else in the company as well as holding all users accountable for their actions.

Effective information security is about people and their actions. An organization can publish well-written documents that have all the right words on the page. If the users and employees do not internalize and accept these requirements, however, the results will likely be less than desirable for management. In a previous book, *Information Security Awareness: The Psychology Behind the Technology* (ISBN: 1-4208-5632-4), I research and describe the relationship between psychology and behavior involving users internalizing information security messages and why this process is so critical to the overall successes of every information security program.

The first control area within the ISO/IEC 17799:2005 (27002) Code of Practice for Information Security Management is about the information security policy document and management's support and direction for the information security program. There are only two controls within this area. The number of controls in this area does not represent its lack of importance. In fact, the first control is a key risk indicator control as previous described.

The overall objective for this control area could be characterized by stating that management must provide direction for the overall information security initiative and outwardly support the program. The two controls for this control area are focused on the information security policy document and the review and evaluation of the policy. The security clause and two associated controls for the information security policy control area are listed and described in the following sections.

INFORMATION SECURITY POLICY

The high-level purpose and intent of the "Information Security Policy" main security clause is to ensure that there is a management-sponsored information security policy and that all relevant users (internal, external, etc.) are aware of their responsibilities. Senior management and organizational stakeholders must provide visible support and direction for the information security initiative as a whole. All applicable laws and regulations must be accounted for in the policy documents as well as the business objectives and requirements of the organization.

The two controls within this main security clause are detailed below for your review and evaluation. Keep in mind that these controls, as well as the other 131 of them, were written as a framework for organizations to adopt and implement within their own individual organizations based on their own unique business requirements.

Through the use of a customized risk analysis and organizational evaluation, the management team must decide how to implement each of the controls within their own environments. The basic framework and guidelines are presented within the body of each control. These controls should be evaluated against the business strategy and plans of each organization before being implemented. This is exactly why the information security management team and staff must be knowledgeable and fluent with the organization's mission, business goals, and objectives.

It should be clear to everyone within the organization that the management team supports the information security mission and that the mission is linked to the overall business strategy. The reality for most organizations is that each department and manager is very busy with their own objectives and challenges. Information security at times can be viewed as another hurdle or obstacle keeping them from achieving their goals or project deadlines. The responsibility falls onto the information security team to keep this mission moving forward and in front of key organizational stakeholders to ensure that the requirements and objectives of the organization are being met. The concept of information security is gaining a wider acceptance within many organizations because of the legal and regulatory requirements.

I have met a wide array of managers in organizations that operate in various industries. Many managers do not fully understand the intended purpose of the ISO/IEC 17799 Code of Practice. Many confuse the standard with laws such as the Sarbanes–Oxley (SOX) or Gramm–Leach–Bliley (GLB) acts. The standard can be thought of as a "code of practice" that an organization can follow to implement information security best practices, independent of industry. After a close inspection of the controls within the standard, you will notice that if an organization implements the controls within the appropriate context of its environment, many, if not most, of the information security requirements by current laws and regulations will be directly or indirectly met. This holds true whether you are discussing the Data Protection Directive in Europe or SOX, GLB, or HIPAA (Health Insurance Portability and Accountability Act) in the United States.

5.1.1 — Information security policy document

As previously discussed, example threat and vulnerability statements are presented in this control in an effort to help the readers of this text develop and implement their own threat and vulnerabilities into their risk assessment process. The exercise of mapping threat statements to each of the 133 controls is complex and extremely time-consuming—but very necessary. These mappings should be created with consensus and not in a silo. It is important to get as many qualified resources involved or reviewing the threat and vulnerability mappings as possible. It is unlikely that any single person possesses the depth of knowledge and skills within all 11 security clauses to effectively develop or review the threat and vulnerability maps. Try to focus on finding subject matter experts within each security clause and leverage their knowledge and skill. Also, continue looking for help and resources via the Internet in this area, as more people will try to do very similar projects the longer this version of the standard has been published. Check my Web site at www.timlayton.com for new or additional information on threat and vulnerability statements as they develop over time.

Scope: Management should provide support in the form of funding, business process, establishment of a cultural norm, and a clear policy direction across the organization in the form of a written business document for information security. Management must communicate information security policies to all employees and relevant parties including consultants, contractors, vendors, business partners, etc.

Key Risk Indicator: Yes

Control Class: (M) Management, (O) Operations

Key Questions:

- Is there a formal information security document published by management representing the business, legal, contractual, and regulatory requirements of the organization?
- Is the information security policy document made available to all employees and users including external third parties of the organization's information systems?
- How is the policy communicated to all affected parties and what is the frequency of communication?
- How does the information security policy document support the business objectives of the organization?
- Does the information security policy document account for all applicable laws, regulations, and contractual requirements?
- Is there a documented structure for risk assessment and risk management within the body of the information security policy?
- Are all applicable 11 control areas within the standard represented in the policy?
- Does the information security policy reference other policies, standards, or control procedures as appropriate?
- Can management provide a business case as to why any of the controls or control areas does not apply to their organization?

As described in the second chapter, the GISAM provides a source of threats that are broken down into four major categories: Human Malicious, Human Non-malicious, Accidental, and Other (natural or other unplanned disruptions or disasters). The threats that I list within each of these four threat categories are sourced from professional experience, NIST, BITS, and other publicly available industry and trade information. Refer to Listings A, B, C, and D in Chapter 2 for a listing of threats separated by category.

The vulnerabilities listed in this control begin with a category and are followed by a specific vulnerability. This is a systematic approach to developing a list of associated vulnerabilities for each control. Refer to the following example as a means to develop your own threat and vulnerabilities.

> **Threat:** Users (employees, consultants, partners, etc.) do not comply with information security policies.
> **Vulnerability: Human Non-malicious—Poor Management Philosophy:** Management does not support security policy development by lack of funding. Control Class: (M) Management
> **Vulnerability: Human Non-malicious—Poor Management Philosophy:** Management does not support security awareness and education training for all users and relevant parties. Control Class: (M) Management
> **Vulnerability: Human Non-malicious—Poor Management Practices:** Management does not enforce compliance with published information security policies. Control Class: (M) Management
> **Vulnerability: Human Non-malicious—Poor Management Practices:** Users are not aware of information security policy requirements. Control Class: (M) Management
> **Vulnerability: Human Malicious—Employee or Management Malicious Actions:** Users purposely do not comply with information security policies. Control Class: (O) Operations

External References: NIST SP 800-30, ISO/IEC 13335-1:2004, SOX IT Controls, GLB

Additional Information: There are a total of 11 control areas within the ISO/IEC 17799 standard. For the purpose of a quick reminder, those areas are information security, organizing information security, asset management, human resources security, physical and environmental security, communications and operations management, access control, information systems acquisition, development and maintenance, information security incident management, business continuity management, and compliance. The challenge for each organization is to identify which of the 11 main security clauses and the respective control objectives and controls within these areas applies to their organization and therefore should be communicated within the information security policy document. A standard format and process should be developed and utilized to communicate the information security policies. Many organizations that embrace the ISO/IEC 17799:2005 (27002) structure their information security policies after the standards table of contents. This approach can be very helpful for organizations that do not have an existing approved or published format.

One of the key points about the information security policy control is that management interaction is required on a lot of different levels. It is clear from strategic and pragmatic perspectives as well as the overall intent of this control that management support is mandatory for this control to be truly effective.

Many organizations when writing and implementing their information security policy fail to realize the importance of senior management support. Most everyone understands the funding part of the support, but the visible and cultural support dimensions often get overlooked or downplayed. These dimensions are critical for helping build cultural norms within the organization and gaining the acceptance of individual users and groups.

An information security policy document is a strategic business document that to be effective must have a clear strategy and series of goals defined, just like any other business initiative. I have personally witnessed many organizations placing the development and deployment of their information security policy on their information technology department. In many cases this is a sure sign of impending failure. The information security policy is much broader than information technology. There are compliance and legal requirements that may drive a series of policies versus excluding others. Depending on the industry, the policy may by its very nature include or exclude certain aspects of the ISO/IEC 17799:2005.

Other variables such as organizational culture, geography, diversity, and business objectives and requirements factor into what the information security policy will ultimately need to communicate. By conducting a business-oriented risk analysis, an organization can determine what needs to be included within its information security policy. This is not a one-time effort. There must be a continual process designed and implemented to review and update the various security policies as appropriate. For publicly traded or regulated organizations, the process of ensuring compliance with laws and standards is a continual process that must be supported at all levels within the organization.

It is important to establish the meaning of policy. An information security policy is developed to communicate what users "must" do, and not how to accomplish the policy objective. A series of supporting procedures, guidelines, and standards should be developed to support the mission of the information security policy document. Refer to the standard for specific elements to include within the set of information security policies. In addition, the ISO/IEC 27001 should be reviewed and consulted for additional guidance in this area.

5.1.2 — REVIEW OF THE INFORMATION SECURITY POLICY

Scope: To continually monitor and update the information security policy document as required by a host of qualifying events to ensure its applicability and effectiveness.
Key Risk Indicator: No
Control Class: (M) Management
Key Questions:

- How often is the information security policy reviewed?

- Does management engage qualified external subject matter experts to review the information security policy?
- Does the policy owner operate from a defined and documented review process to revise and update the policy?
- How are qualifying events reviewed to determine if a policy revision or update is required?
- Is a formal management-approved process required for policy changes and updates?

Additional Information: A key point to consider about this control objective is the assignment of ownership. The information security policy document and process should have an owner or owners responsible for its continual review, updating, and deployment. As with any other organizational policy, the information security policy needs to be monitored and reviewed for its effectiveness and applicability.

One of the best ways to ensure the effectiveness of the information security policy is to measure it at the control level. A formal information security review and evaluation process should be developed or outsourced that measures and reports on the level of effectiveness for each of the 133 controls within the 11 main control areas. A scale and review methodology should be developed or adopted to accomplish the review and monitoring activities discussed above. A business impact analysis should be conducted to identify those controls and controls areas that, if not implemented to a high degree of effectiveness, would introduce an unacceptable amount of risk into the environment, organization, and business model.

Qualifying events as discussed earlier would include events or activities such as changes in the information systems, information technology environment, operational processes, business objectives, new well-known vulnerabilities that are known to potentially impact your systems and operations, etc. The environment, vulnerabilities, and business landscape are in a constant state of change, and this is fundamentally why it is critical to continually monitor and adjust as well as add new controls within your information security program as applicable. If you want to review the actual security program, refer to the ISO/IEC 27001 for guidance as well as my Web site at www.timlayton.com.

SUMMARY

I am routinely asked by many different people and organizations around the world, "What exactly should our information security policy contain, and how long should it be?" My response is the same every time no matter where the organization is based or their industry: "It depends." It honestly depends on several factors. For example, federal, government, legal, and regulatory factors absolutely must be factored into the information policy and strategy, as appropriate. The business objectives and requirements of the organization are equally important and must be included to ensure continuance and integrity of the organization's information systems and processes. These factors alone will shape the table of contents for the information security policy.

For example, a small privately held organization that does not engage third-party vendors simply would not include those controls that are applicable for this type of business activity, and there is no need for them to be addressed at this time in the information security policy. However, the organization should have a defined process to address this type of activity if and when it presents itself. Conversely, a publicly traded organization in the financial industry, by default, has a host of legal, federal, and regulatory requirements that must be addressed at the control level as well as within the information security policy document. The requirements for a well-documented and routinely monitored information security program is not an option; it is a federal requirement. The financial organization referenced in the example above must comply with legal requirements for information security regarding Sarbanes–Oxley and Gramm–Leach–Bliley, as well as federal and regulatory requirements from the OCC (Office of the Comptroller of the Currency), etc.

My earlier response of "It depends" is the short way of saying that each organization must assess its individual requirements. It is in the best interest of the information security management team to include as many departments and business units within the information security planning process as possible and appropriate. This is a practical way of keeping organizational stakeholders actively involved in information security matters.

REFERENCES

ISO/IEC 17799:2005 Information Technology — Security Techniques — Code of Practice for Information Security Management, International Organization for Standardization, 2005.

8 Organization of Information Security

The "Organization of Information Security" clause is particularly important to the overall information security initiative because controls within this section set the expectation for management's commitment and involvement with information security. In addition, information security as it relates to external parties is clearly defined and presented in a series of controls.

To a large degree, information security is about continually assessing risks that are applicable to the environment under review, associating threats, and determining a likelihood of a vulnerability being exploited. Any organization must implement a series of controls and safeguards to protect its assets. The balance and exact controls that are implemented should be the result of a detailed and customized risk analysis process. Management should control the design and implementation of controls within the organization.

From an organizational perspective, management should establish and provide an approval mechanism for the information security policy as discussed in the previous chapter and guide the implementation of information security across the organization. People within the organization must know and understand their responsibilities to information security.

You may be beginning to understand how each of the control areas and controls are interrelated. In the previous chapter an outline and detailed explanation was provided on the information security policy document. The "Organization of Information Security" area builds on the controls set within the security policy area by suggesting that management provide organizationwide support by providing an approval mechanism and guiding the implementation of information security across the entire organization.

Within the "Organization of Information Security" control area, another objective is for an organization to establish and maintain relationships with external information security specialists. It is impossible for anyone or any single group to be completely versed and operate at peak levels within every area of information security. The key is for an organization to establish specific relationships with external firms and subject matter experts/consultants to stay up-to-date on all applicable issues and trends that apply to their business model.

For example, an organization may be exposed or required to adhere to legal or regulatory requirements for information security. It is highly unlikely that all organizations will employ full-time subject matter experts on the associated legal and regulatory requirements and understand how to apply them within the context of the information security strategy and program. This is one of the fundamental reasons for establishing and maintaining relationships with third parties to monitor, review, and assist the organization with matters such as this.

The "Organizing Information Security" clause also suggests that organizations have a multifaceted approach to their information security program. The approach should include a wide array of organizational members including senior management, managers, system administrators, application developers, internal audit, information technology professionals, legal, system users, human resources, facilities, enterprise risk management, etc.

INTERNAL ORGANIZATION

Simply stated, management must be actively involved in the information security effort on many different levels to ensure the program's accuracy and effectiveness as it relates to the requirements of the organization.

Management should establish a methodology and framework to implement information security within the organization in a way that is conducive and effective based on organizational culture and business objectives and requirements. Visible management support and leadership should be developed and implemented to approve information security policies, procedures, guidelines, and objectives. The key to success is organizationwide deployment and acceptance of this approach. Information security should become part of the cultural norm and integrated at every stage of the business process including concept, functional specification, design, implementation, and integration.

As needed, information security subject matter experts should be utilized to assist at any level. Everyone in the organization, ranging from end users to managers to developers to information technology staff to senior and executive management, should be actively involved in the information security journey.

The associated controls for organizational security are not technology related or driven. It is about everyone in the organization taking responsibility for the information security mission and integrating it into their functional areas. This all begins with executive sponsorship and strong management support at the ground level.

6.1.1 — MANAGEMENT COMMITMENT TO INFORMATION SECURITY

Scope: The title for this control is very straightforward and captures the spirit of the control. It is clear that management must be actively involved and committed to information security or failure is inevitable. Management support has many dimensions. Some of the basic commitments include the following: review and approve information security policy; provide resources required for information security; participate and sponsor information security awareness and training programs; ensure that information security is consistent across the entire organization by actively monitoring and assessing the various elements and controls of the information security program; ensure that information security is integrated into business processes and that all users within the organization understand the relevancy and importance of information security to the overall mission of the organization.
Key Risk Indicator: Yes

Control Class: (M) Management
Key Questions:

- How does management clearly support information security within the organization?
- What formal programs exist today for information security?
- How frequently does management engage external information security resources to help with advice or to make assessments?

External References: ISO/IEC 13335-1:2004
Additional Information: It is important to remember that the level of commitment and the role of management are likely different for each organization. There are too many variables to list or quantify. The key to success is linking information security to the business model and management supporting this relationship in an active and visible manner.

6.1.2 – INFORMATION SECURITY COORDINATION

Scope: Information security requires people to take responsibility and their actions must be coordinated and driven by management.
Key Risk Indicator: No
Control Class: (O) Operations
Key Questions:

- What groups or roles are actively involved in information security within the organization?
- How does your organization identify significant threats and vulnerabilities?
- Describe how information security controls are formulated and implemented within the organization.
- How are existing information security controls and safeguards assessed for adequacy and effectiveness?
- Does your organization have a formal information security awareness and education program led by an assigned individual or group?
- Describe how information security incidents are coordinated.

Additional Information: For small organizations, it might not be possible to have clear delineation of responsibilities between individuals, and that is to be expected. The real key is ownership and responsibility. The degree of coordination is likely relative to the size of the organization.

6.1.3 – ALLOCATION OF INFORMATION SECURITY RESPONSIBILITIES

Scope: The scope of this control is very simple and clear: information security responsibilities should be defined in writing by management.
Key Risk Indicator: Yes

Control Class: (M) Management
Key Questions:

- Does the information security policy define the requirements for information security responsibilities?
- Describe and list any documented guidelines that exist today that users are required to follow when dealing with specific instances within the organization.
- Does your organization allow delegation of information security responsibilities? If so, describe the process they are required to follow when delegating.
- How does management define who is responsible for specific assets?

Additional Information: Information security responsibility definition should start within the job description and be extended into each role as appropriate.

6.1.4 — AUTHORIZATION PROCESS FOR INFORMATION PROCESSING FACILITIES

Scope: Management should develop and publish a formal process to allow new information systems into the network and environment. This will have to be accomplished all the way down to the department level.
Key Risk Indicator: No
Control Class: (M) Management, (O) Operations
Key Questions:

- Describe what actions, if any, are required to connect a new system or host to the company network.
- If an individual connected a personal laptop computer to the company network from his or her desk, would the system have access to the network?
- Describe any controls that exist to keep unidentified network systems or devices from connecting to the company network.

Additional Information: Authorization has both technical and operational dimensions.

6.1.5 — CONFIDENTIALITY AGREEMENTS

Scope: Organizations should create and require confidentiality or nondisclosure agreements to protect confidential information as defined by appropriate legal counsel. Legal resources must be consulted to ensure that the agreements are enforceable.
Key Risk Indicator: No
Control Class: (M) Management
Key Questions:

- Has management defined "confidential information"? If so, where is the information documented and who is responsible for its upkeep and maintenance?
- In the terms of the confidentiality agreement, is the duration of the agreement clearly stated?
- Has management included the right to audit and monitor external parties when confidential information is involved?
- Does the confidentiality agreement clearly state the actions required in the event of an unauthorized breach of information?

Additional Information: Confidentiality and nondisclosure agreements can be complex and must adhere to all applicable legislation and regulations. Management should employ the services of internal or external legal advisers to help ensure that these types of agreements are accurate and reflect the requirements of the organization.

6.1.6 — CONTACT WITH AUTHORITIES

Scope: Contact with local authorities (police, fire, FBI, etc.) should be developed and maintained to ensure a quick response in the event a negative or unlawful incident occurs.
Key Risk Indicator: No
Control Class: (O) Operations
Key Questions:

- What relationships does information security have with local authorities (fire, police, FBI, etc.)?
- Is the contact information for local police, fire, FBI, etc., included in the organization's security incident procedures?

Additional Information: Contact with other critical providers such as telecommunications and Internet service providers is a good idea as well.

6.1.7 — CONTACT WITH SPECIAL INTEREST GROUPS

Scope: This control strongly suggests that information security professionals within the organization establish contact with special interest groups within information security that could benefit the organization. Also, professional associations should be established and maintained.
Key Risk Indicator: No
Control Class: (O) Operations
Key Questions:

- What associations or special interest groups do information security management belong to or attend?

- Describe how your organization receives early warnings or advisories that specifically apply to your assets.
- How does the information security staff stay current on the latest technologies?
- How does your organization match common vulnerabilities in information systems with potential threats?

6.1.8 — INDEPENDENT REVIEW OF INFORMATION SECURITY

Scope: To ensure effectiveness and applicability of control and safeguards, management should engage external subject matter experts to review controls, control objectives, policies, procedures, etc., at planned intervals and when significant changes occur within the environment or operations.
Key Risk Indicator: Yes
Control Class: (M) Management, (O) Operations
Key Questions:

- When was the last time your management hired external subject matter experts to review the organization's information security posture?
- Does your organization have an internal audit department? If so, when was the last time they reviewed the organization's information security controls to ensure that they are still suitable, adequate, and effective for the organization's approach to managing information security?
- Does the information security policy require independent review of information security?

Additional Information: Depending on the size of the organization and other variables such as industry or regulatory drivers, it may be appropriate to have internal audit and external resources review the information security practices and operations. In other cases, the internal audit function may be sufficient.

EXTERNAL PARTIES

External parties, including third-party vendors and business partners, are very common today for organizations, and they are a source of unidentified risk in many cases. There are many different dimensions to identifying and managing information security risks of external parties. The controls within this sub-clause will help management identify some of the most common and most critical elements to assess within their own operations and environment.

6.2.1 — IDENTIFICATION OF RISKS RELATED TO EXTERNAL PARTIES

Scope: Information security risks should be identified before engaging into operations with external parties. Controls should be developed as a result of the risk assessment process and implemented prior to operations.
Key Risk Indicator: Yes

Control Class: (M) Management
Key Questions:

- Does your organization have a formal information security risk assessment process for external parties, third-party vendors, and business partners?
- Describe the scope of the information security risk assessment process for external parties, if one exists.
- Has management performed an impact analysis in the event the external party does not follow the information security policy and guidelines?
- Does management allow an external party, third-party vendor, or business party to connect to the network prior to a formal information security risk assessment?
- Describe how external parties and partners are made aware of their information security responsibilities as they relate to your organization.

External References: NIST 800-30, ISO/IEC 13335

6.2.2 — ADDRESSING SECURITY WHEN DEALING WITH CUSTOMERS

Scope: This control deals with addressing all of the information security risks that were identified as part of the risk assessment process before permitting client access to organizational information or resources.
Key Risk Indicator: No
Control Class: (M) Management, (O) Operations
Key Questions:

- Describe any documented procedures or guidelines that you must follow prior to allowing an external party access to organizational information or resources.
- Is the information security team required to perform a formal information security risk assessment before allowing external parties access to organizational information and resources? If so, who approves access?
- Does your organization have a formal access control policy? If so, does it include language for external parties, third-party vendors, or clients?

Additional Information: Many times a legal agreement is required between the organization and external party. It is advisable that the scope of this control be part of this agreement.

6.2.3 — ADDRESSING SECURITY IN THIRD-PARTY AGREEMENTS

Scope: Written agreements with external parties including access, processing, networking, or third-party management should include the organization's information security requirements.
Key Risk Indicator: No
Control Class: (M) Management

Key Questions:

- In third-party contracts or agreements, does your organization include requirements for information security?
- Is the organization's information security policy provided to all third-party vendors and partners?
- Is any type of information security awareness training required of third-party vendors and clients?

Additional Information: The issue of addressing information security requirements in legal agreements can be complex. In some cases it may make sense to have a separate agreement specifically addressing information security requirements for third parties and have the main agreement call out to this agreement. Consult legal counsel that has specific experience in dealing with information security matters.

SUMMARY

The "Organization of Information Security" clause helps organizations evaluate internal and external aspects of information security. Internally, the expectation that management must be directly involved and committed to information security is established, and responsibility for information security must be documented and communicated. Information security requirements should be included in internal and external agreements to ensure that the organization's information security policy is upheld. When dealing with external parties, a formal risk assessment process should be a part of normal business operations before allowing access to organizational information and resources.

REFERENCES

ISO/IEC 17799:2005 Information Technology — Security Techniques — Code of Practice for Information Security Management, International Organization for Standardization, 2005.

9 Asset Management

The "Asset Management" main clause is focused on asset assignment of ownership, inventory, and acceptable use of major assets. By having all major assets accounted for, an owner can be assigned to monitor the maintenance and update for each asset. If an asset is not properly identified, ownership will not be assigned and potentially unnecessary vulnerabilities and risks may exist within the organization. The owner of the asset should ensure that the appropriate information security controls have been developed and implemented to protect and safeguard the asset.

In the second half of this clause, information classification and handling is the focus. In practice, many organizations achieve the classification part of this control, but many struggle with the implementation of asset control. In many cases this comes in the form of labeling, etc. Although there are not many controls within this area, they are very important and are difficult for many organizations to effectively implement. A clear strategy and business plan aids in the development process for these controls.

RESPONSIBILITY FOR ASSETS

This control objective is fundamental to protecting important and critical assets within the organization. All assets should be accounted for within an organization, and because of the information security implications, each asset should have an assigned owner who is responsible for its security and maintenance.

7.1.1 — INVENTORY OF ASSETS

Scope: All assets should be accounted for and inventoried. The inventory should be maintained and updated as needed.
Key Risk Indicator: Yes
Control Class: (O) Operations
Key Questions:

- How does your organization identify new assets?
- Does your organization consider computer systems, software applications, and operating systems as assets? If so, how is this inventory maintained and updated?
- Does management require assignment of assets to a specific individual or role to ensure that the information security policy is upheld as it relates to these assets?

Additional Information: It is important that each major asset be identified and assigned an owner, as stated in the control objective. It is not enough to simply create a document or listing of assets. A security classification should be developed for each major asset, and its location and owner should also be documented and communicated. The ownership and location information will be of great help during a recovery effort. Refer to the "Classification Guidelines" control for more information on classifying the assets.

Some examples of classification categories would include software, physical, information, and services. Refer to the standard for detailed examples of assets within these categories.

By keeping a current and detailed inventory of assets, an effective protection/information security plan can be developed and monitored. Other business requirements within the organization already likely require some form of asset inventory, and this may be a very good item to research before trying to start a new project. Information security management should understand the importance of each asset to the business and organization. This is a process that should be developed with peers and management and updated over time as the business and environment changes. If you do not understand the value of an asset, it is theoretically impossible to perform an effective risk assessment for the purpose of developing proper controls and safeguards.

7.1.2 — OWNERSHIP OF ASSETS

Scope: It is important for the information security posture of an organization to assign ownership of assets within the information processing environment.
Key Risk Indicator: No
Control Class: (M) Management
Key Questions:

- Does management require that owners be assigned to assets within the information processing environment?
- Are assets owners required to ensure that access policies and restrictions are enforced at the time the new asset is brought on line?
- Does your organization consider data to be an asset? If so, does management require assigned owners for the data?

7.1.3 — ACCEPTABLE USE OF ASSETS

Scope: Management should identify, document, and implement policies, procedures, and guidelines as applicable for the acceptable use of information and assets that are associated with information systems.
Key Risk Indicator: No
Control Class: (M) Management
Key Questions:

- Does management publish an acceptable use information security policy for information process facilities and systems?

- Describe how management ensures that third parties, vendors, and business partners that have access to information processing facilities follow the organization's acceptable use policy.
- Are electronic mail, Internet services, instant messaging, and mobile devices covered in the acceptable use policy?

Additional Information: An acceptable use policy is a key information security policy, and organizations should be very clear on acceptable use as well as possess a strong awareness program around this concept.

INFORMATION CLASSIFICATION

This control objective was created to make sure that all information assets within the organization receive the appropriate level of protection based on their value and importance to the business. Smaller organizations tend to shy away from classifying information, and this can lead to very negative and serious consequences—even for smaller organizations. Information and data may be even more important to smaller organizations because there is little room for error or financial loss to sustain profitability or a quality level of service. Many other controls within the code of practice anchor on a documented information classification scheme.

7.2.1 — CLASSIFICATION OF GUIDELINES

Scope: This control was designed to help organizations classify information and data based on its value, criticality, sensitivity, and legal or business requirements to the organization.
Key Risk Indicator: Yes
Control Class: (M) Management
Key Questions:

- Does management publish written classification guidelines for data and information in the information security policy or other similar document?
- Does management publish procedures and guidelines for information classification in accordance with the associated policy?
- Does the classification policy have provisions for initial classification as well as reclassification over time?
- Describe any responsibilities that asset owners have in regard to classification.
- Does the scope of the classification policy include physical and logical information? If so, can you provide a few examples of each?

Additional Information: The responsibility for information classification definition should be the responsibility of the asset owner. Remember, information can be manifested in many forms (e.g., files/data, physical documents, media such as tapes, CD-ROM, diskette). When developing the classification scheme for your organization, it is important to not make it complicated and difficult for the intended users to understand. A benefits analysis should be considered and reviewed. One of the best litmus tests is to ask all involved parties for input and ideas. The value and information sensitivity must be considered as a part of this process.

The controls for classified information must take into account all business requirements as well as the associated impacts if the information is compromised (e.g., lost, stolen, corrupted, altered). The ultimate goal of the classification scheme is to direct users how to handle and protect the information asset.

Information in some cases may need to be reclassified after a period of time. Keeping information in a higher-level classification scheme than necessary can cause undue expenses and overhead to the organization. Care should be taken when reclassifying information, so be sure the owner is directly involved in this process. In many cases a policy can be developed for some types of data that will set the required timelines for reclassification.

In practice, I consistently see many organizations, ranging from very large corporate institutions to smaller private firms, struggle with this control. It is very difficult to implement this control and have the users adopt the process. It is a large undertaking for any size organization, and for the larger organizations it can be very costly. With any sizable business expense, a thought-out plan and strategy will have to be developed and presented to management for their support and funding. For some organizations it is easier to gain support from management due to legal or regulatory requirements. Even if your organization is not directly required by a federal law or regulation, I strongly encourage information security managers to review the creation of information classification guidelines within their organization. Information is a key asset, and without a proper classification guideline and process, unnecessary risk is being introduced into the operations of the company.

7.2.2 — INFORMATION LABELING AND HANDLING

Scope: Once information and data are classified (7.2.1), labeling and handling procedures should be developed to uphold the integrity of the data classification scheme.
Key Risk Indicator: No
Control Class: (O) Operations
Key Questions:

- Has management developed and published procedures for labeling classified data in both physical and electronic formats?
- Provide some examples of information that requires labeling (e.g., paper reports, tapes, disks, CDs, DVDs, e-mails, file transfers).
- When external parties, third-party vendors, or business partners handle classified information, are they required to follow the same policy, guidelines, and procedures as required by internal staff?

Additional Information: When developing the procedures for information labeling and handling, the focus should be on the information types that apply to your organization. Information can be stored in physical and electronic formats. Handling procedures need to be developed for each classification type. For a detailed listing of types, refer to the standard, but some basic examples should include anything on paper (copies, fax, etc.), communications via voice (phones, voicemail, etc.), and storage of information. If a physical label is not possible because of the format (e.g., electronic), some type of electronic label should be utilized.

SUMMARY

Asset management is an extremely important security clause and has a big impact on the information security posture of an organization. For assets to be protected via applicable controls and safeguards, they must first be identified and inventoried (7.1.1), and then ownership (7.1.2) must be established to ensure their assessment and application of controls. After the assets have been inventoried and owners assigned, a policy (7.1.3) must be developed and published by management to ensure their acceptable use.

Information can exist in many different forms and on many different media. Management must create and publish an information classification scheme (7.2.1) to ensure its proper handling (7.2.2).

REFERENCES

ISO/IEC 17799:2005 Information Technology — Security Techniques — Code of Practice for Information Security Management, International Organization for Standardization, 2005.

10 Human Resources Security

The "Human Resources Security" main clause deals with all three phases of employment: prior, during, and post. There are critical information security controls and safeguards within each of these three elements. This clause helps management evaluate and deploy important controls within these three dimensions of the employment life cycle. People will always be an organization's greatest asset—and its greatest risk.

PRIOR TO EMPLOYMENT

This control objective is focused on ensuring that all relevant parties, including employees, consultants, contractors, and third-party users, understand their role and responsibility to information security. Furthermore, measures should be taken on the part of management and human resources to reduce some of the most common threats by properly screening and educating all users of the organization's information systems and resources.

8.1.1 — ROLES AND RESPONSIBILITIES

Scope: For users (employees, consultants, contractors, third-party users) to understand their role and responsibilities to information security, management must document them in the information security policy and communicate them accordingly.
Key Risk Indicator: No
Control Class: (M) Management
Key Questions:

- Did management document the requirement for roles and responsibilities for all types of users as they relate to information security in the information security policy?
- Are information security responsibilities included in each job description?
- Describe how management communicates each user's role and responsibility for information security.

Additional Information: It is easy to overlook the requirement for documenting and communication information security responsibilities for nonemployee roles. Information security managers should use this control to widen their information security roles and responsibilities scope beyond the employee role.

139

8.1.2 – Screening

Scope: All candidates for employment, consultants, contractors, and third-party users should undergo a background check that is proportional to their position and the risk they pose to the organization. Typically, the more access a user has to sensitive and confidential data, the more extensive the background check should be. Background checks should be in alignment with any applicable laws or regulations as well as meet any specific business requirements.

Key Risk Indicator: Yes

Control Class: (M) Management, (O) Operations

Key Questions:

- Does management require background checks for candidate employees, consultants, contractors, and third-party users?
- Describe the elements included in each type of background check (e.g., employee in IT administration: character, criminal, driving, credit, identity, academic).
- Does management perform background checks postemployment? If so, under what conditions (e.g., promotions, role change)?

Additional Information: It is critical to verify who will have access to your organization's information systems. A bad or uninformed decision about a new employee, consultant, or contractor could be potentially devastating to your organization. A strategy should be developed to check and verify information based on workers' roles and access to systems. For example, a custodial worker with no assigned network access would likely require a different set of checks than a network systems administrator.

All employees, consultants, and contractors should provide at least one personal and one business reference that can be satisfactorily verified within a reasonable amount of time. They should also be able to supply some form of personal identification, such as a driver's license, passport, social security card, etc. If a position requires a certain level of education, their education and respective degrees should be verified appropriately. Although the standard does not specifically call out the need for a criminal background investigation or a check on their driving history, these are very good options to consider based on the target role. If the individual will have access to or will handle financial information or data, a personal credit check would be appropriate.

When temporary employees or contractors are being utilized by an outside firm, your organization should communicate the screening and verification checks within the contract between the two firms.

Before requiring some of the more in-depth checks such as personal credit or criminal history, check with the human resources department to ensure that they can accommodate these types of checks and ask for their help to implement such programs if they do not already exist. It is not the job of information security management to carry out such checks; it is their responsibility to verify the results before assigning access to systems.

8.1.3 — TERMS AND CONDITIONS OF EMPLOYMENT

Scope: Information security responsibilities should be clearly stated as part of an employee, consultant, contractor, or third-party user terms and conditions of contractual agreement.
Key Risk Indicator: No
Control Class: (M) Management, (O) Operations
Key Questions:

- Does your organization have a written terms and conditions of employment agreement?
- Specifically, who is required to sign this agreement, and when?
- Are other users of information processing facilities such as consultants, contractors, or third-party users required to sign this or a similar agreement before access is granted?
- Does the information security policy state the requirement that information security responsibilities be included in the terms and conditions of employment or similar agreement?

Additional Information: The terms and conditions of employment contract can be a complex legal document that is difficult for an employee to understand. Practically speaking, this is a business-sided document to protect the interests of the business. I have witnessed some creative individuals struggle with signing these types of documents. If it is the requirement of the business, there are no exceptions. For some critical roles where this may be a potential issue, it is probably a good idea to discuss this early on in the recruiting process to potentially save time and resources.

In all cases, the terms and conditions of employment must state the employee's responsibility for information security. In many cases I have seen these types of agreements extend for some period of time postemployment. In the event an employee disregards the information security policy and requirements, the actions taken by the company should be included in this agreement.

Cases where copyright laws or other legislation might apply should be included within the terms and conditions contract, and employees should fully understand how this applies and affects them. The responsibility for understanding is placed upon the potential employee, and if he or she is not an attorney, it is highly unlikely that the potential employee is qualified to understand such detailed agreements. The company should allow enough time for candidates to have such agreements reviewed by their legal counsel, and this time should be factored into the offer letter acceptance timeline. It is common practice for organizations to have an expiration date for their offer for employment.

DURING EMPLOYMENT

This control objective is focused on making sure that all parties, internal and external, are aware of information security threats and vulnerabilities as they relate to their environment and their responsibility for information security matters. It also ensures that management has provided the necessary conditions to allow this to happen.

8.2.1 — MANAGEMENT RESPONSIBILITIES

Scope: Management has a responsibility to the organization to document and publish information security policies, procedures, and guidelines to protect the organization and employees. The policy should clearly describe the requirement for all parties, internal or external, to follow and adhere to the published policies, procedures, and guidelines.
Key Risk Indicator: No
Control Class: (M) Management
Key Questions:

- How does management ensure to a reasonable degree of acceptance that employees, consultants, contractors, and third-party users are following the information security policy?
- How does management communicate to all users of information facilities their requirement to follow information security policies, procedures, and guidelines?
- How does management assess the ability of users to follow prescribed information security policies?

Additional Information: If users of the information processing facilities are not clearly made aware of their information security responsibilities, how can management expect them to adhere to policy? This should not be considered a one-time event. This concept and many others can be part of the 8.2.2 (Information security awareness, education, and training) control.

8.2.2 — INFORMATION SECURITY AWARENESS, EDUCATION, AND TRAINING

Scope: All users of the organization's information processing facilities, including employees, consultants, contractors, third-party users, vendors, and partners, should receive information security awareness, education, or training that is specifically targeted for their role and function within the organization.
Key Risk Indicator: Yes
Control Class: (M) Management, (O) Operations
Key Questions:

- Does your organization have a documented and formal information security awareness, education, or training program?
- How many resources are dedicated to this program on a full-time or part-time basis?
- How does management determine which users of their information processing facilities receive what awareness, education, or training?

- How frequently are general information security awareness training sessions held for the general population?
- What events determine when new or ongoing awareness, training, or education is required for a specific group or all users in general?
- Is information security awareness included in the initial hiring process for all new employees or other external parties as appropriate? If so, when is the next time a user will receive additional training or education?

Additional Information: The context of information security education and training is not very well defined within the standard. There is no distinction between education and training and no direct mention of awareness other than within the body of the control. For the sake of clarity, it is understood that education infers learning and skills are being built by the learner. Training is typically meant to introduce new concepts to learners, and the expectation of their skill level is less than it would be for education. Awareness is designed to introduce concepts to individuals and target learners so that they are "aware" of these concepts and can associate appropriate actions with the topic. Be sure your organization is very clear about the expectations for awareness versus education versus training of information security policies, topics, and concepts.

A clear plan should be developed to target each group of users and for the type of education, training, or awareness as appropriate. Information security policies are global in nature and should be a high priority to communicate to all users on a regular basis and when any modifications or additions occur.

New legislation such as Sarbanes–Oxley, Gramm–Leach–Bliley, and HIPAA requires users to receive information security awareness training, and if your organization is a publicly traded company, ensure that these requirements are being met to the capacity outlined within the legislation.

8.2.3 — DISCIPLINARY PROCESS

Scope: Management should clearly define and publish disciplinary actions and the associated process for employees who have committed a breach of the information security policy.
Key Risk Indicator: No
Control Class: (M) Management
Key Questions:

- How does management address a breach of information security policy by an employee?
- Is the requirement to follow all information security policies clearly stated in the information security policy?
- Where in organizational documents is the disciplinary process communicated to all employees?

Additional Information: The disciplinary process is a good candidate to be a part of the general information security awareness campaign because it should help serve as a deterrent to those who may have the ability or be prone to breach security policy.

TERMINATION OR CHANGE OF EMPLOYMENT

This control objective was constructed to ensure that internal and external parties (employees, consultants, contractors, third-party users, etc.) end or change employment status in a secure manner.

8.3.1 — TERMINATION RESPONSIBILITIES

Scope: When an employee or other external user of the organization's information processing facilities is terminated or changes responsibilities, a clear process should be provided by management to ensure that a secure transition occurs.

Key Risk Indicator: No

Control Class: (M) Management

Key Questions:

- Has management defined termination and change-of-employment processes for information security?
- Is the human resources department aware of information security processes when an employee is terminated or when his or her status significantly changes?
- Does the organization have a documented termination process for non-employee resources that have access to organizational assets for information security?

8.3.2 — RETURN OF ASSETS

Scope: All users, internal or external, should be required to return all organizational assets in their possession when their employment or contract terminates or ends.

Key Risk Indicator: No

Control Class: (O) Operations

Key Questions:

- Has management sufficiently documented the requirement for employees or other external parties to return all assets belonging to the organization when their employment or contract terminates or ends?
- Are soft assets such as data and information included in the return process?
- If any personal assets were used by an employee, are procedures in place to ensure the proper removal of data, information, or applications from these devices?

8.3.3 — Removal of access rights

Scope: Access rights of all organizational users including employees and all relevant external parties should be terminated and removed immediately once they are terminated or their status significantly changes.
Key Risk Indicator: Yes
Control Class: (M) Management, (O) Operations, (T) Technical
Key Questions:

- How does management ensure that logical and physical access rights are terminated immediately upon termination or some other significant change event?
- How soon after termination does human resources notify the appropriate information technology and facilities department of the status change for that individual?
- Are employees and relevant external parties required to sign agreements during the initial employment or engagement process regarding termination of logical and physical access rights in the event of termination or some other significant change event?

SUMMARY

The concept of "Human Resources Security" is a critical part of the overall information security posture for every organization. People are central to the success of virtually every organization, and they also pose many risks. Prior to employment (8.1.1), users must be made aware of their roles and responsibilities for information security. Management must take the appropriate steps and screen (8.1.2) employees and external employees before hiring or engaging them as authorized users of organizational resources and assets. To uphold the integrity of the information security policy in the event of employee or external party abuse, management should require all parties to sign a terms and conditions agreement (8.1.3).

During the employment or engagement phase of the relationship, management has the responsibility to make users aware of their information security responsibilities (8.2.1) and provide appropriate awareness, education, and training (8.2.2) specifically targeted at their role within the organization. In the event that an employee or external party refuses to follow the published information security policy, management should document, publish, and communicate a formal disciplinary process (8.2.3).

When an employee or external party either terminates or changes their responsibility (8.3.1), management must have a documented and clear process for this transition as it relates to information security matters. All users must be required to return all assets (8.3.2) in their possession, and all logical and physical rights should be terminated (8.3.3) immediately.

REFERENCES

ISO/IEC 17799:2005 Information Technology — Security Techniques — Code of Practice for Information Security Management, International Organization for Standardization, 2005.

11 Physical and Environmental Security

Physical and environmental controls are some of the most critical safeguards an organization can implement based on results. Physical controls are historically among the most breached controls. Secure areas and equipment security concepts have been around for a long time and are some of the most widely accepted methods for security. If this last statement is generally true, why are there so many physical breaches of information security controls?

So much attention is focused on high-tech controls, and the bulk of the budget dollars are typically spent in this area as well, that some of the most basic, yet effective, controls can be overlooked.

The thirteen controls and two control objectives should be reviewed very closely by every organization, and management should ensure that they are implemented and operating at a high level of effectiveness. They are some of the most straight-forward and simple controls to implement and will continue to prove to be some of the most effective for controlling common threats.

SECURE AREAS

This control objective is designed to help organizations prevent security breaches and damages to the organization's facilities and ultimately their information, data, and systems.

9.1.1 — PHYSICAL SECURITY PERIMETER

Scope: The organization's information processing facilities perimeter should be adequately protected by physical controls such as walls, fences, manned and guarded entry, barriers, access cards, closed circuit television, etc.
Key Risk Indicator: Yes
Control Class: (O) Operations
Key Questions:

- Has the organization clearly defined security perimeters?
- Describe the physical security controls and safeguards in place today to protect the information processing facility.
- Is the information processing facility monitored for fire, smoke, water, and unauthorized entry?

- Is the building that houses information processing facilities protected by a manned reception area?
- Are visitors to the information processing facilities building(s) required to sign in and be escorted by an employee at all times when visiting?

Additional Information: In smaller companies, the more elaborate controls and safeguards might not be available or appropriate. At a minimum, the information processing systems should be contained in a safe environment with controlled access; preferably this access is auditable and can be monitored.

9.1.2 — PHYSICAL ENTRY CONTROLS

Scope: Physical entry controls should be developed and implemented to properly protect secured areas.
Key Risk Indicator: No
Control Class: (O) Operations
Key Questions:

- How does management control access to secured information processing facilities?
- Is there an audit trail maintained for secured information processing facilities?
- Does management review access rights to secured information processing facilities on a regular basis?

9.1.3 — SECURING OFFICES, ROOMS, AND FACILITIES

Scope: Offices and organizational facilities should be secured with appropriate physical controls as required.
Key Risk Indicator: No
Control Class: (O) Operations
Key Questions:

- How does management identify areas within the organization requiring physical controls?
- Are vacant areas within the facilities secured with physical controls and routinely checked to ensure the integrity of the implemented controls?
- What controls are currently in place to control the use of video and audio recording equipment?

9.1.4 — PROTECTING AGAINST EXTERNAL AND ENVIRONMENTAL THREATS

Scope: Management of an organization must protect itself and employees from disasters such as fire, flooding, and explosions, including both natural and man-made events. Physical controls should be assessed, designed, implemented, and monitored to ensure adequacy and effectiveness of these controls.
Key Risk Indicator: Yes

Control Class: (M) Management, (O) Operations
Key Questions:

- How do employees and users know they are operating in a secure area within the organization?
- How does management remain current with new threats, internal and external, and how they relate to your organization?
- Describe the actions taken by your organization to protect itself from neighboring buildings or infrastructures.
- Does your organization store information or data near materials that could be considered hazardous or prone to fire or other similar events?

Additional Information: If disaster recovery equipment is housed too close to the main facility, this may be an issue for concern. Recovery equipment, systems, backup media, and other similar items should be stored as far away as reasonably possible to be protected from the event that disrupted operations at the main facility.

9.1.5 — WORKING IN SECURE AREAS

Scope: Secure areas within an organization should be designed and implemented as a result of business or organizational requirements. These areas should possess strong physical controls, and management should develop and publish requirements for working in secure areas.
Key Risk Indicator: No
Control Class: (M) Management, (O) Operations
Key Questions:

- If your organization has secure areas, currently what controls are in place to maintain the security and integrity of such areas?
- What type of access or authorization requirements does management require for secure areas?
- Is access to secure areas monitored? If so, how?
- Is access to secure areas auditable via paper or electronic logs?

Additional Information: An organization can have secure areas for reasons unrelated to information security (e.g., personnel safety reasons, storing new equipment or purchases). No matter the reason, secure areas should have strong physical controls that are routinely monitored and have the ability to be audited.

9.1.6 — PUBLIC ACCESS, DELIVERY, AND LOADING AREAS

Scope: Public areas such as reception, delivery, and loading or other similar areas should be controlled with physical controls and monitored.
Key Risk Indicator: No
Control Class: (O) Operations

Key Questions:

- How does your organization keep unauthorized people from entering the main facility from public areas such as reception, loading, and delivery?
- What types of controls are in place to enter the main facilities from public access areas?
- Are incoming shipments and materials inspected for threats before they are moved inside the main facility?

EQUIPMENT SECURITY

Network- and computer-related equipment plays a vital role in the operations and success of organizations. Controls must be developed and implemented to prevent this type of equipment from theft or compromise. The seven controls within this subsection help protect networking and computer equipment from environmental and physical threats, thereby reducing the risk of unauthorized access or compromise.

9.2.1 — EQUIPMENT SITING AND PROTECTION

Scope: This control is designed to protect networking and computer equipment from environmental and physical threats that may exist within the organization.
Key Risk Indicator: No
Control Class: (O) Operations
Key Questions:

- What methods and measures does management take to protect networking assets and computer systems from unauthorized access and environmental hazards?
- What controls exist today to prevent unauthorized removal of computer systems and networking components from secured areas or facilities?
- Is there a written policy preventing eating and drinking in the data center or computer processing facility?
- Are temperature and humidity monitored in the computer processing facility?

Additional Information: Depending on the size and operations of the organization, a computer processing facility could range from a small locked room to a full-blown data center spanning thousands of square feet. The depth of controls implemented per this objective will range depending on the complexity of the computer processing facilities.

9.2.2 — SUPPORTING UTILITIES

Scope: Management should protect information processing systems and facilities from uninterrupted power and utility failures.
Key Risk Indicator: No

Control Class: (O) Operations
Key Questions:

- What methods has management implemented to protect the utilities (electric, gas, water, heating, ventilation, etc.) supporting core information processing systems and facilities?
- Has the organization implemented an uninterruptible power supply (UPS) or backup generator appropriate for organizational needs?
- How frequently is the UPS or generator tested?
- Does the organization have a contract with a local firm to supply fuel or other resources in the event of a sustained outage?

Additional Information: It is always a good idea to have multiple power feeds to the information processing facilities to help avoid a single point of failure in the power supply to the facilities.

9.2.3 — Cabling security

Scope: Networking and telecommunications cables should be protected from harm as well as from unauthorized tampering.
Key Risk Indicator: No
Control Class: (O) Operations
Key Questions:

- Are the power and telecommunications cabling going into the information processing facilities underground?
- In public areas, is network cabling protected from unauthorized tampering with conduit or other similar means?
- Are wiring closets secured via a manual or electronic lock to keep unauthorized users away from the cabling?

9.2.4 — Equipment maintenance

Scope: Key systems and hosts in the information processing facility should be maintained according to manufacturer guidelines to ensure their availability for authorized users.
Key Risk Indicator: No
Control Class: (O) Operations
Key Questions:

- Does management maintain service contracts on the hardware components of all critical computing, networking, and telecommunication systems?
- How does your organization ensure that only authorized maintenance personnel are allowed access to equipment in the information processing facility?

- If appropriate, what controls has management implemented for systems and devices that house confidential information and data when maintenance personnel are repairing or maintaining this equipment?

9.2.5 — SECURITY OF EQUIPMENT OFF-PREMISES

Scope: If the organization has information processing equipment off site for whatever reason, its operation should be authorized by management and properly secured as a result of a risk assessment.
Key Risk Indicator: No
Control Class: (O) Operations
Key Questions:

- Does management require a documented information security risk assessment for information processing systems located outside of organizational facilities?
- How does management implement appropriate controls to protect data and information being processed or stored on these systems?
- What controls are in place today to prevent unauthorized access or tampering with these systems and equipment?

9.2.6 — SECURE DISPOSAL OR REUSE OF EQUIPMENT

Scope: Management should require and ensure that licensed software has been properly removed from all forms of computing devices and systems containing storage media and that any data has been securely disposed of prior to disposal or reuse of equipment.
Key Risk Indicator: Yes
Control Class: (O) Operations
Key Questions:

- Describe how your organization disposes of old or unwanted computing or other devices that have organizational data and information stored on them.
- What procedures are in place today for systems that are reused within your organization?

Additional Information: Many organizations use a third-party organization to dispose of outdated or unwanted systems. It is normal and customary for these organizations to provide your firm with a certificate of destruction. These certificates should be maintained for whatever term management and legal counsel have determined is appropriate for your organization.

9.2.7 — REMOVAL OF PROPERTY

Scope: Computing systems, software, or other devices containing organizational information and data should not be removed from the organization without management authorization.

Key Risk Indicator: No

Control Class: (M) Management, (O) Operations

Key Questions:

- Has management published a policy notifying all users that equipment or systems containing the organization's software or information/data should not be removed from the facility without proper management authorization?
- How does the organization ensure that users are not improperly removing equipment and systems?
- When equipment has been properly authorized for off-site use, is there a control in place that ensures the asset will be returned by a particular time?

SUMMARY

The "Physical and Environmental Security" clause has two control objectives focusing on secure areas (9.1) and equipment security (9.2). Perimeter security controls (9.1.1) are fundamental and critical to protect an organization and its assets. A layered approach is taken with physical and environmental security, just as it should be in the logical realm. After establishing strong perimeter controls, a series of entry controls (9.1.2) should be developed, implemented, and monitored as appropriate for the organization. As needed, offices, rooms, and other areas housing sensitive or critical systems (9.1.3) should be protected by physical controls as well.

In many cases, organizations reside in a shared facilities environment or operate in very close proximity to other organizations. In these cases, it is important to develop and implement controls protecting against the threats posed by external parties and other environmental elements (9.1.4). Management should develop and implement secure areas (9.1.5) within the organization as appropriate. Employees or other authorized users should operate or possess knowledge of these areas on a need-to-know basis. Any type of public access area (9.1.6), such as reception, loading, unloading, or other similar areas, should be closely monitored and have strong controls leading into the secured facilities.

Equipment must be properly identified (9.2.1) to be protected. Information processing facilities and the associated systems and components rely on several basic utilities (9.2.2) such as air-conditioning, heating, water, sewer, and others to operate. The systems and hosts within the information processing facilities rely on cabling (9.2.3) to operate as designed. This cable should be protected from damage and unauthorized tampering. Computer systems, applications, networking devices, and telecommunications equipment need to be maintained and repaired like any other equipment. When the equipment requires repair or maintenance (9.2.4), management should have implemented the appropriate balance of controls to protect these assets from theft, interruption of services, and unauthorized tampering. If the organization has any equipment or systems operating off site (9.2.5), management should ensure that the equipment is secured with the same level of controls and safeguards as the primary equipment and systems. Eventually, systems and network devices need to be replaced or updated. When this occurs, management must have implemented a policy, process, and method to ensure that any data and information is properly destroyed or removed before the equipment is taken out of commission or repurposed (9.2.6). From time to time it may be necessary to remove key systems or components from the organization or from the information processing facility. In these cases, management should have a written and documented process to allow equipment to be taken off site (9.2.7).

REFERENCES

ISO/IEC 17799:2005 Information Technology — Security Techniques — Code of Practice for Information Security Management, International Organization for Standardization, 2005.

12 Communications and Operations Management

The "Communications and Operations Management" security clause is the largest clause in the code of practice. This clause contains 32 controls in 10 different objectives. After little consideration, it is easy to understand why this area has the most controls. Information security is highly operational and involves communications on a frequent basis. The controls within this clause are very important, and nine of the 35 key risk indicator controls are contained in this clause, making up a little over 25 percent of the total KRI controls.

OPERATIONAL PROCEDURES AND RESPONSIBILITIES

To securely operate information systems and processing facilities, a host of controls must be designed, implemented, and monitored on a regular basis. Operating procedures, guidelines, and policies are critical to secure operations. Management should develop and publish operating procedures and guidelines that support the information security policy to ensure its secure operation. The controls within this objective focus on documentation, change management, segregation, and operating environments.

10.1.1 – DOCUMENTED OPERATING PROCEDURES

Scope: Information security-related operating procedures should be developed and maintained by management for users of information systems and facilities as appropriate. Users and authorized third parties must understand all relevant security policies as well as system boundaries as prescribed by procedures and guidelines. Operating procedures within this context help support the information security policy and ensure its integrity.
Key Risk Indicator: Yes
Control Class: (M) Management
Key Questions:

- Describe the process of how management develops information security operating procedures.
- Does the information security policy require operating procedures for any segment or portion of the organization's operations?
- Does the organization have documented procedures for data backup and media handling?

Additional Information: Documented operating procedures cover a wide array of topics depending on the organization. The actual procedures should be the result of a formal risk assessment and based on several factors including information security policy, legal, regulatory, and organizational requirements.

10.1.2 — CHANGE MANAGEMENT

Scope: Changes within any controlled environment are a critical component of success. The operations and communications of an organization, regardless of its size and complexity, likely have components that need control and monitoring. Information processing facilities changes are critical to information security and should be tightly controlled and monitored.
Key Risk Indicator: Yes
Control Class: (O) Operations
Key Questions:

- Does the organization have a formal change control process?
- Describe the applications, tools, or methods used to control changes within the information processing facilities.
- Who is required to approve changes to information processing systems and equipment?
- Is the system or application owner involved in the approval and notification process for change?
- Does management require fallback or recovery procedures for changes to information processing facilities?

Additional Information: All changes should be logged and auditable. The person requesting the change should never be allowed to approve the change. There are many sides and dimensions to making changes to systems, applications, and components within the information processing environment. Management should have a formal process and procedure to fully evaluate the requested change and consider the impact and potential new threats or vulnerabilities that may result from the change.

10.1.3 — SEGREGATION OF DUTIES

Scope: Information security duties should be segregated whenever possible to help reduce the risk of unauthorized, unintended, or direct misuse of organizational assets.
Key Risk Indicator: Yes
Control Class: (M) Management, (O) Operations
Key Questions:

- Does management require segregation of duties in your organization? If so, when and under what conditions?

- Is it possible for users to modify information processing assets without detection?
- Is monitoring and auditing performed on key information processing facilities?

Additional Information: Segregation of duties is not always possible in smaller organizations, but the concept should be applied, or other compensating controls and methods should be implemented to the degree possible.

10.1.4 — SEPARATION OF DEVELOPMENT, TEST, AND OPERATIONAL FACILITIES

Scope: The development, test, and production systems and environments should be separated from each other with appropriate controls and safeguards to reduce the risk of unauthorized modifications to the systems or associated data.
Key Risk Indicator: No
Control Class: (M) Management, (O) Operations, (T) Technical
Key Questions:

- Does management require development, test, and production systems to be logically or physically separated? If so, describe how this is accomplished.
- Is application source code able to be accessed via production systems?
- Are source code editors, compilers, and other system tools available in the operational/production environment?
- Does management allow production data on test systems? If so, under what conditions and why?

Additional Information: The mixing of development, test, and production systems and environment can lead to negative and serious consequences. Special care should be taken by management to design and apply the appropriate controls to help separate and contain each of these systems and environments, particularly when the application or environment is accessible via the Internet.

THIRD-PARTY SERVICE DELIVERY MANAGEMENT

For those organizations that engage in third-party service delivery management, management should develop, implement, and monitor the service delivery act and process to ensure that the agreement is being met and that it is within the scope of the organization's information security policy.

10.2.1 — SERVICE DELIVERY

Scope: Management should ensure that third-party providers are meeting service delivery agreements and that they are within the scope of the information security policy.
Key Risk Indicator: No
Control Class: (M) Management, (O) Operations
Key Questions:

- Does your organization use third parties to deliver services or applications?
- Is information security part of the operating agreement or other agreement between the organizations?
- How does management ensure that the third party maintains sufficient service capability?

10.2.2 — MONITORING AND REVIEW OF THIRD-PARTY SERVICES

Scope: Any service, product, or information provided by a third party should be regularly audited, reviewed, and monitored to ensure accuracy and compliance with terms and conditions set forth in any agreements.
Key Risk Indicator: No
Control Class: (M) Management, (O) Operations
Key Questions:

- Does management require the review and audit of third-party services?
- Is information security included in any review or audit procedures of third parties? If so, briefly describe the scope and frequency.
- Is the third party trained in reporting information security incidents to the appropriate contacts in your organization in the event of a realized or suspected event?

Additional Information: For large organizations, management and compliance issues surrounding third parties represent a full-time job for many people and resources. Depending on the size and complexity of operations, dedicated managers may also be needed to ensure that proper monitoring and review of third parties is carried out in accordance with policy.

10.2.3 — MANAGING CHANGES TO THIRD-PARTY SERVICES

Scope: Third-party services can be critical in some organizations. Management must account for changes in third-party services that include information security. Changes can be the result of new business requirements or added functionality. In either case, information security risks should be identified to ensure that the proper controls and safeguards have been implemented and are operating to the level expected.
Key Risk Indicator: No

Control Class: (M) Management, (O) Operations
Key Questions:

- Describe how management identifies changes in third-party services.
- Does management require a formal risk assessment or reassessment of third-party services relating to information security risks?
- How are changes to third-party services communicated to key stakeholders?

SYSTEM PLANNING AND ACCEPTANCE

This control objective was developed to help organizations reduce the risk of failures relating to information processing systems.

10.3.1 — CAPACITY MANAGEMENT

Scope: Key information processing systems should be reviewed and monitored for operating levels and capacity. Management should ensure that systems have enough capacity to meet business objectives and will be available to authorized users as they need them.
Key Risk Indicator: No
Control Class: (O) Operations
Key Questions:

- Does management have a capacity management plan for information processing systems and applications? If so, describe the plan at a high level.
- Has management implemented any type of controls to detect potential problems before unacceptable capacities are exceeded?
- How does management track system usage and trends?

10.3.2 — SYSTEM ACCEPTANCE

Scope: Management should develop formal test criteria for new systems or upgrades to systems before they are placed in production.
Key Risk Indicator: Yes
Control Class: (M) Management, (O) Operations, (T) Technical
Key Questions:

- What tests does management require of a new system or upgraded system before promoting it to production status?
- Has management defined formal procedures and processes for system acceptance?
- Is a log or history maintained of the system acceptance process?

PROTECTION AGAINST MALICIOUS AND MOBILE CODE

Malicious and mobile code has the ability to create serious and negative consequences in information processing systems and across an entire enterprise if it is not handled and controlled properly. This objective helps management design controls aimed at detection, prevention, removal, and containment.

10.4.1 — CONTROLS AGAINST MALICIOUS CODE

Scope: Procedures for the containment, recovery, prevention, and detection of malicious code should be developed and published by management for all appropriate target groups.
Key Risk Indicator: Yes
Control Class: (M) Management, (O) Operations, (T) Technical
Key Questions:

- What type of controls has management implemented to address the risks of malicious code?
- Is there an information security policy addressing malicious code?
- Is the concept of malicious code included in the organization's information security awareness program?

Additional Information: Malicious code can manifest and exist in just about any system or application within the organization. It is advisable that the organization use more than one detection method or software tools to identify potential threats.

10.4.2 — CONTROLS AGAINST MOBILE CODE

Scope: Mobile code may be a viable part of the system and application environment, so special care should be taken to ensure that this code operates directly in accordance with company policy. Controls should be developed and implemented to detect unauthorized mobile code and prevent it from executing on information processing systems and applications.
Key Risk Indicator: No
Control Class: (M) Management, (O) Operations, (T) Technical
Key Questions:

- What actions and controls does your organization employ to identify and control unauthorized mobile code?
- Does your organization use mobile code to meet specific business requirements?
- If mobile code is used, does your organization use any type of encryption or authentication method to ensure that the mobile code is authorized?

Additional Information: Some organizations may be unfamiliar with the definition of mobile code. Mobile code is simply software code that is exchanged via a network connection from one system to another and then automatically executes some type of function, with or without user input on the target side. Mobile code is used in many applications to meet specific business requirements and is not intended to create a security-related event. Unfortunately, mobile code is a perfect vehicle for dishonest and malicious individuals to create a negative information security incident.

BACKUP

Management should create and publish a written strategy and set of associated procedures for information backup.

10.5.1 — INFORMATION BACKUP

Scope: Critical data and information, including application data, software, and device configurations, should be securely backed up on a regular basis according to company policy.
Key Risk Indicator: No
Control Class: (O) Operations, (T) Technical
Key Questions:

- How frequently is critical application data and information backed up?
- Has management defined a written backup policy and associated procedures?
- Does your organization back up applications and device configurations? If so, how frequently?
- How frequently are backup media tested to ensure reliability in case of an emergency?

Additional Information: Retention of information and data can be an issue for some organizations. There may be contractual, legal, or regulatory requirements that must be followed. Documented operating procedures and guidelines should guide staff through the appropriate actions.

NETWORK SECURITY MANAGEMENT

Networking equipment and components provide a critical and necessary service for organizations. Special care should be taken to protect networking systems and equipment from threats to ensure that the infrastructure will remain operational and available to support operations.

10.6.1 — NETWORK CONTROLS

Scope: Special consideration and controls should be developed for network-related components and equipment and the information payload they transmit.
Key Risk Indicator: No
Control Class: (O) Operations, (T) Technical
Key Questions:

- Does the organization have a platform or application to manage network devices separate from systems and applications? If so, please provide a brief description.
- If network devices extend beyond organizational boundaries, how does management account for their security and operations?
- Describe how your organization captures and manages security-related events on network devices and components.

External References: ISO/IEC 18028 — Information Technology, Security Techniques, IT Network Security

10.6.2 — SECURITY OF NETWORK SERVICES

Scope: Network services must be secured and should be identified in any service-level agreements whether the services are provided internally or via a third party.
Key Risk Indicator: No
Control Class: (O) Operations, (T) Technical
Key Questions:

- How does your organization identify security services in network services?
- Does your organization contract with any third party for managed security services? If so, how was the organization's information security requirements communicated to the third party?
- In the event that your organization has engaged a third party to operate or manage network services, does your agreement with the third party include the right to audit?

MEDIA HANDLING

Media, of all types, should be protected from unauthorized disclosure or removal, tampering, or destruction. Logical and physical controls should be developed and implemented by management.

10.7.1 — MANAGEMENT OF REMOVABLE MEDIA

Scope: Removable and easily transportable media are a risk, so there must be documented procedures for administration and operations staff to properly manage this type of media.

Key Risk Indicator: Yes
Control Class: (M) Management, (O) Operations
Key Questions:

- Has the organization published written procedures and guidelines for the management of removable media?
- Are the concept and associated risks of removable media included in an information security awareness program?
- Is there an audit log maintained for all media that is removed from the organization for any purpose?
- Are there any security policies published on the use of removable media?

Additional Information: Removable media examples include hard disks, USB disks, flash drives, CD-ROMs, DVDs, tapes, and printed paper.

10.7.2 − DISPOSAL OF MEDIA

Scope: Media contains company information and data that should be properly destroyed and disposed of when it is no longer required per a written set of procedures published by management.
Key Risk Indicator: No
Control Class: (O) Operations
Key Questions:

- Has your organization published written procedures for the secure disposal of unwanted or unneeded media?
- Does your organization allow the storage of sensitive or confidential information on portable drives such as USB flash or PCMCIA drives? If so, is there a specific policy in place governing the use and application of these types of devices?
- Does your organization log the disposal or destruction of media?

Additional Information: Organizations exist for the sole purpose of secure disposal of media and information such as paper, etc. If your organization uses the services of this type of firm, be sure to properly validate their procedures and be sure to get a written certificate of destruction.

10.7.3 − INFORMATION HANDLING PROCEDURES

Scope: Written procedures for the handling of all information types should be developed and published by management to protect against unauthorized misuse or disclosure.
Key Risk Indicator: Yes
Control Class: (M) Management, (O) Operations, (T) Technical
Key Questions:

- Has management published written information handling procedures for all relevant types of users within the organization as well as any applicable external third parties?
- Do the information handling procedures, if they exist, work in conjunction with the classification guidelines developed as part of 7.2.1?
- Do the information handling procedures, if they exist, include information in documents, voice communications, and other forms of non-computing media?

Additional Information: Information can be stored and transported in many different forms including computing devices, networks, written documents, mail, facsimiles, etc.

10.7.4 — Security of system documentation

Scope: Documentation for information processing facility systems should be properly secured and protected from unauthorized access to minimize the risk of system exploits and compromise.
Key Risk Indicator: No
Control Class: (O) Operations, (T) Technical
Key Questions:

- Does management require system documentation to be stored securely to prevent or minimize the risk of unauthorized access?
- Where is system documentation stored? If it is stored on a network, have the proper controls been designed and implemented to control access?
- Is an audit log maintained on system documentation access?

Additional Information: System documentation can include information that can disclose sensitive procedures or processes that could lead to system compromise or interruption. It should be protected accordingly.

EXCHANGE OF INFORMATION

Information exchanged within the organization and with external parties must be secured and compliant with all relevant contracts, laws, and regulations.

10.8.1 — Information exchange policies and procedures

Scope: Formal policies and procedures should be developed and published by management to all relevant internal and external parties covering the exchange of information.
Key Risk Indicator: No
Control Class: (M) Management, (O) Operations
Key Questions:

- How does your organization control the exchange of information within and externally to the organization?
- Does the organization include communications and the associated risks in the information security awareness program?
- Does the scope of your information exchange policy include information exchange in the form of paper, voice, and wireless communications?

Additional Information: Awareness is a key safeguard for this control. There are many forms of communications and methods to exchange a wide range of information. Management should assess organizational requirements and implement applicable policies, procedures, and awareness messages as appropriate.

10.8.2 — EXCHANGE AGREEMENTS

Scope: Written agreements should be developed and required for the exchange of information between the organization and any relevant party.
Key Risk Indicator: No
Control Class: (M) Management, (O) Operations
Key Questions:

- Does your organization have a standard written agreement when exchanging information with external parties?
- Does the agreement include requirements for notification, packaging, and receipt?
- Does the agreement include procedures in case of a security breach or incident?
- Does any relevant information include labeling per classification guideline to ensure its proper handling?

Additional Information: The policies, procedures, and agreements should directly reflect the type and classification of data. For example, it would not be a good business investment to apply unnecessary controls for public information. Conversely, it would be highly undesirable not to apply appropriate controls for highly sensitive or confidential data and information.

10.8.3 — PHYSICAL MEDIA IN TRANSIT

Scope: Media in transit should be protected against tampering, altering, and unauthorized disclosure in accordance with the information classification policy.
Key Risk Indicator: Yes
Control Class: (O) Operations
Key Questions:

- Does your organization have written policies to protect media in transit? If so, is the policy in accordance with information classification guidelines?

- Does your organization use an external company or party to transport media to a location external to your organization? If so, what type of contract or agreement is in place to ensure the integrity of the information contained on the media?
- What controls are required to protect sensitive data in transit?

Additional Information: Unless the proper controls have been implemented, there is no way to determine if sensitive or classified information has been tampered with or disclosed to unauthorized persons while away from the organization. In many cases, media is stored off site for a long period of time before being returned to the organization, if ever. Organizations should closely manage and monitor media when it is away from the organization.

10.8.4 — Electronic messaging

Scope: Electronic messages should be protected from unauthorized access, tampering, or incorrect delivery.
Key Risk Indicator: No
Control Class: (O) Operations, (T) Technical
Key Questions:

- What types of electronic messages does your organization use in key business processes (e-mail, IDI, IM, etc.)?
- What controls has your organization implemented to protect electronic messages?

10.8.5 — Business information systems

Scope: Management should create and publish policies and procedures to protect information and data associated with the operation of business.
Key Risk Indicator: No
Control Class: (M) Management, (O) Operations, (T) Technical
Key Questions:

- Does your organization have policies on the management of information in accordance with a classification scheme?
- How does management restrict the use of information systems by type of user (e.g., employee, contractor, third party)?

ELECTRONIC COMMERCE SERVICES

Electronic commerce is a high-risk business operation. Information and electronic commerce data require special controls and safeguards including management, operational, and technical dimensions to protect the integrity and availability of such information.

10.9.1 — ELECTRONIC COMMERCE

Scope: Data and information passing over public networks for electronic commerce should be protected from fraud, unauthorized disclosure, and modification.
Key Risk Indicator: Yes
Control Class: (O) Operations, (T) Technical
Key Questions:

- Does your organization conduct commerce via electronic networks? If so, describe the controls and safeguards your organization has implemented to protect from fraud, unauthorized disclosure of customer and financial data, and modification of data.
- How does your organization ensure the availability of electronic commerce services?
- What types of cryptographic controls have been implemented in the electronic commerce systems and applications?
- What types of operational controls are in place to control the risks of electronic commerce?

Additional Information: Electronic commerce over public networks poses unique and challenging risks to organizations. Special care should be taken on the part of management to appropriately assess all aspects of electronic commerce services to ensure that the proper balance of controls has been established and that the controls are performing as expected.

10.9.2 — ONLINE TRANSACTIONS

Scope: Electronic commerce transactions are at risk of being routed to the wrong destination, altered in some form, disclosed to unauthorized people, and duplicated for unauthorized inspection at a later time. Appropriate controls should be developed by the organization to address these risks and other requirements as identified by business requirements, legislation, regulations, or legal contracts.
Key Risk Indicator: No
Control Class: (O) Operations, (T) Technical
Key Questions:

- What controls are in place today to verify the client?
- How does your organization ensure that the credentials supplied by the client are valid?
- Where within the network and systems does your organization store transaction details?
- Is encryption used for electronic commerce transactions? If so, specifically where in the network connection is encryption being used?

10.9.3 — Publicly available information

Scope: Public systems and applications are under an unusual amount of risk because of the very nature of their accessibility to anyone with an Internet connection. Special care should be taken to continually assess and develop the proper balance of controls to protect information and prevent unauthorized disclosure and modification.
Key Risk Indicator: No
Control Class: (O) Operations, (T) Technical
Key Questions:

- How often does your organization test public systems and applications for weaknesses, applicable threats, and vulnerabilities?
- Does your organization have a formal process to approve and allow information and data to be made available via public systems? If so, can you describe the process?
- Are your public systems, data, or information required to comply with any laws or regulations? How often does your organization check for these types of requirements?

MONITORING

Monitoring critical systems and applications in the information processing facilities is a highly effective information security control. Special controls should be implemented to detect unauthorized activities within the information processing facilities.

10.10.1 — Audit logging

Scope: Audit logs of key systems and controls are critical to the overall security posture of organizations. The retention of audit logs should be in compliance with any applicable legislation, regulations, and contracts as appropriate; otherwise, a period of time should be published by management for retention of audit log information.
Key Risk Indicator: No
Control Class: (M) Management, (O) Operations, (T) Technical
Key Questions:

- Is there a written policy requiring audit logging and associated procedures and guidelines?
- Is time synchronization used on systems participating in audit logging? If so, what time source is used by the systems?
- How are audit logs monitored and reviewed?

Additional Information: Audit logs can contain sensitive information such as user account information, and special care should be taken to protect the audit logs from unauthorized disclosure and tampering.

10.10.2 — MONITORING SYSTEM USE

Scope: Systems and applications in the information processing facility should be monitored for proper use and operation. Monitoring results should be reviewed regularly as appropriate for the amount of risk to the organization.
Key Risk Indicator: No
Control Class: (M) Management, (O) Operations
Key Questions:

- What type of monitoring is currently used for the information processing facilities?
- How frequently are monitoring events and data reviewed?
- Were the monitoring procedures the result of a written risk assessment provided to management? If so, how often is this risk assessment performed and by whom?

Additional Information: Security monitoring should be the result of a risk assessment. The persons reviewing the monitoring data must understand the threats to the systems and environment to identify potential dangers.

10.10.3 — PROTECTION OF LOG INFORMATION

Scope: Audit and security event log information must be protected from unauthorized tampering or access to ensure the integrity of the information and data.
Key Risk Indicator: No
Control Class: (O) Operations, (T) Technical
Key Questions:

- What controls are in place today to protect security and audit logs?
- How does your organization ensure that audit and security logs are not being altered or tampered with?
- How long does your organization require audit and security logs to be retained? Are the audit and security logging systems checked on a regular basis to ensure that there is enough capacity?

10.10.4 — ADMINISTRATOR AND OPERATOR LOGS

Scope: System administration and operator actions should be logged and monitored external to their control to ensure compliance with company policy and security of the systems.
Key Risk Indicator: No
Control Class: (O) Operations, (T) Technical
Key Questions:

- What type of logging and monitoring does your organization have for IT administration and operator actions?

- How frequently are these logs reviewed?
- Does your company monitor IT system administration and operator actions? If so, how?

Additional Information: Admin-level access is a required part of business operations, but it carries a large risk if an unauthorized or ill-willed person has access to systems and applications. For security reasons, some type of intrusion detection system should be implemented and out of the control of the administration staff.

10.10.5 − FAULT LOGGING

Scope: System and application errors should be logged and monitored.
Key Risk Indicator: No
Control Class: (O) Operations, (T) Technical
Key Questions:

- Does your organization require system or application errors to be reported and tracked in a formal system? If so, please describe.
- Who reviews the fault or error logs, and how frequently?
- Does the company require systems and applications to enable error logs by default?

Additional Information: Errors can be security related; therefore, all faults and errors should be logged and monitored for suspicious activity.

10.10.6 − CLOCK SYNCHRONIZATION

Scope: Time synchronization is an important element in information security because it ensures that all security logs report the correct time the event happened in relation to the other network devices. Time is important for security events because it can communicate the path of the unauthorized intruder.
Key Risk Indicator: No
Control Class: (M) Management, (T) Technical
Key Questions:

- What time source does your organization use for network devices and components?
- What systems and devices are included and excluded for external time synchronization?
- How frequently is the time synchronization checked on the critical devices and systems in the information processing facility?

Additional Information: An external time source should be used to synchronize the time for all critical network devices and components. The time on each device should be checked frequently to ensure that all devices are operating in synchronization.

SUMMARY

The "Communications and Operations Management" security clause is the largest clause in the Code of Practice with 32 controls and 10 control objectives. The 10 control objectives—operational procedures and responsibilities (10.1), third-party service delivery management (10.2), system planning and acceptance (10.3), protection against malicious and mobile code (10.4), backup (10.5), network security management (10.6), media handling (10.7), exchange of information (10.8), electronic commerce services (10.9), and monitoring (10.10)—are a comprehensive set of objectives covering the full spectrum of communication and operational aspects of information security including internal and third-party external operations and communications.

REFERENCES

ISO/IEC 17799:2005 Information Technology — Security Techniques — Code of Practice for Information Security Management, International Organization for Standardization, 2005.

13 Access Control

The "Access Control" clause is the second largest clause, containing 25 controls and 7 control objectives. This clause contains critical controls because authorized access to information processing facilities, logical or physical, is proven to be a key element in the security of these systems and applications. Organizations should place special emphasis on developing policy on many of these critical controls to set the expectation and requirements for all users—internal and external.

BUSINESS REQUIREMENTS FOR ACCESS CONTROL

Information is a business commodity and it should be protected and controlled. A series of access-related controls should be developed and implemented by management, ranging from policies, guidelines, and processes to actual safeguards that control access to information and data.

11.1.1 — ACCESS CONTROL POLICY

Scope: Management should develop and publish an access control policy meeting organizational requirements including legal, regulatory, contractual, and any other special case as appropriate.
Key Risk Indicator: Yes
Control Class: (M) Management, (O) Operations
Key Questions:

- Has management developed and published a written access control policy? If so, when, and what is the scope of the policy?
- Do access control procedures and policies exist to support the access control policy?
- How frequently are access controls reviewed and by whom?
- What is the process for developing access controls?
- Is there a formal procedure for removing access rights for a terminated employee, consultant, contractor, or authorized third party? If so, please describe.

Additional Information: Access control is a key concept in information security, and organizations should take a very close look at their operations and compare their current environment against the controls in this objective to find areas for further improvement.

USER ACCESS MANAGEMENT

Users of the organization's information processing facilities should be authenticated and authorized in accordance with a formal policy and method. The method should take the information classification guideline into consideration and take the least-privilege approach when granting rights and permissions.

11.2.1 — USER REGISTRATION

Scope: Management should develop a clear set of procedures driven by policy to create and delete users from their information processing systems and applications.
Key Risk Indicator: Yes
Control Class: (M) Management, (O) Operations, (T) Technical
Key Questions:

- Is there any case where unique user accounts are not required within your information processing systems or applications?
- Does the organization have written procedures for the creation (registration) and deletion (deregistration) of user accounts?
- How is the level of access for each user account determined?
- Are users required to sign access agreements?
- Is the HR department involved in the registration and deregistration process? If so, how?
- Does management provide users with a written statement of their access rights on the organization's information processing systems?

Additional Information: Organizations should consider developing and implementing a role-based account system based on job function to help maximize time and resources required to properly implement this series of controls.

11.2.2 — PRIVILEGE MANAGEMENT

Scope: Once a valid user account is created to access the information processing systems, privileges should be restricted and controlled in accordance with published policy and guidelines.
Key Risk Indicator: No
Control Class: (O) Operations, (T) Technical
Key Questions:

- How does your organization control privilege management for information systems and applications?
- What types of records or logs are maintained for privilege allocation?
- How are privileges granted within your organization?

Additional Information: The concept of privilege is important to information security because it is based on trust.

11.2.3 — User password management

Scope: Password management is an important component in controlling and managing access to information processing facilities. A formal policy and set of procedures should be developed and implemented for user password management.
Key Risk Indicator: No
Control Class: (M) Management, (O) Operations, (T) Technical
Key Questions:

- What type of management process does your organization have for passwords?
- Are users required to sign an agreement to keep their passwords confidential and private from all others?
- When a new account is created, is the user required to change his or her password to a new password conforming to company policy? If so, what is the company policy on password assignment?
- Are default password for systems, devices, or applications allowed anywhere in your information processing facilities? If so, under what circumstances?
- If the IT administration staff has to reset a user's password, what type of validation checks are performed before resetting the password?

11.2.4 — Review of user access rights

Scope: Access rights should be reviewed on a regular basis by qualified staff not responsible for account creation to ensure that the rights are in alignment with roles and responsibilities.
Key Risk Indicator: No
Control Class: (M) Management, (O) Operations
Key Questions:

- How frequently are user access rights reviewed?
- Is a formal process or method used to review user access rights? If so, please describe.
- Do you review accounts with additional privilege more frequently?
- When modifications are made to privileged accounts, how is this process carried out and is the modification maintained in a log?

USER RESPONSIBILITIES

People can be one of the best lines of defense in information security. Authorized users should be aware and trained in their responsibilities to help prevent unauthorized user access leading to an undesirable event.

11.3.1 – Password use

Scope: The organization's password structure should be the result of company policy based on good password practices. Users should not be allowed to override the policy.
Key Risk Indicator: No
Control Class: (M) Management, (O) Operations, (T) Technical
Key Questions:

- Does the organization require users to keep their passwords confidential? If so, how is this accomplished?
- Describe the organization's password policy (length, special characters, reuse, etc.).
- How frequently are users forced to change their passwords?

11.3.2 – Unattended user equipment

Scope: When systems and application are left unattended, management should develop controls to ensure that the unattended equipment is appropriately secured and protected.
Key Risk Indicator: No
Control Class: (O) Operations, (T) Technical
Key Questions:

- How does the organization make users aware of the security risks that arise when they leave their systems or devices unattended when logged in?
- Does the organization have any type of system override to automatically lock the system after a period of inactivity? If so, please describe.

11.3.3 – Clear desk and clear screen policy

Scope: When people are away from their work area for an extended amount of time (overnight, out for meetings, etc.), their work area should be secured and no sensitive information should be accessible in any form (paper, electronic, etc.).
Key Risk Indicator: No
Control Class: (M) Management, (O) Operations
Key Questions:

- Has the organization published a clear desk and clear screen information security policy? If so, what is the scope?
- Does management audit or monitor the operating facilities for compliance with the clear desk and clear screen policy?

NETWORK ACCESS CONTROL

Network services provide critical and trusted services for the organization. Special care should be taken to prevent unauthorized access to networked services.

11.4.1 — POLICY ON USE OF NETWORK SERVICES

Scope: Management should develop and create a written policy informing users that they should use only the network services they have been specifically granted.
Key Risk Indicator: No
Control Class: (O) Operations, (T) Technical
Key Questions:

- Has management developed and published a written policy on the use of network services? If so, what is the scope of the policy?
- What type of authorization is required to access the network or network services?
- If a new network connection is established at the organization's facilities, what process is required to activate the network connection?

Additional Information: Network connections and particularly Internet and wireless connections have the ability to introduce significant and unidentified risks in the environment. Management should develop a clear policy on the use and creation of networks and routinely monitor the environment to ensure that no new networks have been implemented without management approval.

11.4.2 — USER AUTHENTICATION FOR EXTERNAL CONNECTIONS

Scope: A secure form of authentication should be used to control external network connections to the information processing facility.
Key Risk Indicator: No
Control Class: (O) Operations, (T) Technical
Key Questions:

- How does your organization control access and authentication of remote network connections to the information processing facilities?
- Does your organization allow VPN, dial-up, or broadband access to the information processing environment?

11.4.3 — EQUIPMENT IDENTIFICATION IN NETWORKS

Scope: As appropriate, equipment can be a secure means to authenticate network communications from a specific controlled environment and piece of equipment.
Key Risk Indicator: No
Control Class: (T) Technical
Key Questions:

- Does your organization authenticate any remote network devices based on location or equipment? If so, how is this accomplished and were all other methods determined to be inappropriate?
- If remote authentication is allowed based on location, is the remote location properly secured physically and logically?

11.4.4 − Remote diagnostic and configuration port protection

Scope: Diagnostic and remote ports to networking and telecommunications equipment should be closely controlled and protected from unauthorized access.
Key Risk Indicator: No
Control Class: (O) Operations, (T) Technical
Key Questions:

- Does your organization allow the use of remote diagnostic ports? If so, are external vendors or third parties allowed to access the system via the remote ports?
- Does your organization use modems for remote port connection? If so, please describe the process for modem use.
- For equipment with diagnostic or remote port management installed by default, how does your organization manage this risk?

11.4.5 − Segregation in networks

Scope: Services on the network should be segregated in logical networks when possible to increase the depth of controls.
Key Risk Indicator: Yes
Control Class: (O) Operations, (T) Technical
Key Questions:

- How does your organization segregate Internet services from the internal network?
- Does your organization allow wireless networking? If so, is wireless network traffic segregated in any way? If so, describe how.
- Does your organization require segregation in network services? If so, under what circumstances?
- Has management published a written policy on segregation of network services and associated procedures or guidelines?

Additional Information: Network services are simply network-based services such as Internet services, internal networking, wireless networking, IP telephony, video broadcasting, etc.

11.4.6 − Network connection control

Scope: When networks extend beyond organizational boundaries, special care should be taken to implement safeguards and controls to limit user connectivity and access to the network.
Key Risk Indicator: No
Control Class: (O) Operations, (T) Technical
Key Questions:

- Does your organization's network extend beyond your facilities and direct control? If so, is this section of the network required to comply with other network controls such as the access control policy, etc.?
- Specifically, what type of technical and operational controls does your organization implement for networks extending beyond the direct control of the organization?
- Has management published written guidelines or procedures for connection or interconnecting with networks beyond the direct control of the organization?

Additional Information: Controlling network connections to third-party vendors or external business partners can be challenging from an information security perspective and is often overlooked because they may be considered trusted network connections.

11.4.7 — NETWORK ROUTING CONTROL

Scope: Logical control of network routes can be critical to control the flow of data and information. Network routing control should be developed in conjunction with the access control policy of specific applications and services.
Key Risk Indicator: No
Control Class: (T) Technical
Key Questions:

- Does your organization's network extend to external parties or vendors? If so, how does management control the flow of traffic to and from the external source?
- If network routing controls have been implemented, what type of logging is used and how often are the routing controls reviewed to ensure that they are operating as designed?

Additional Information: Network routing control is a highly technical subject and, typically, only a very select few individuals in the IT department possess the knowledge to design and implement this type of control. This control is a prime candidate for validation by an external subject matter expert.

OPERATING SYSTEM ACCESS CONTROL

Operating systems are the core systems in which business applications function and perform the services required to operate the business. Special care should be taken to develop the appropriate layer of controls to protect the operating systems from unauthorized access, modification, or interruption.

11.5.1 — Secure log-on procedures

Scope: Operating systems should be controlled and protected by secure log-on and authentication procedures.
Key Risk Indicator: No
Control Class: (O) Operations, (T) Technical
Key Questions:

- How does your organization control access to information processing facility operating systems?
- Does your organization publish a general notice message during log-on stating that the computer should only be accessed by authorized users? If so, has this notice been reviewed and approved by your legal advisers?
- What type of alert and logging is performed for access to operating systems?
- How frequently is each critical systems access log reviewed?

11.5.2 — User identification and authentication

Scope: Each user of the organization's information processing system should have his or her own unique user account, and a secure method should be used to validate the user's identity before allowing access to the system.
Key Risk Indicator: No
Control Class: (T) Technical
Key Questions:

- Does your organization require unique user accounts for each individual? If not, under what circumstances?
- For circumstances where the identity of the user requires more than a name and password, how does your organization handle this?
- What types of authentication methods are used by your organization besides passwords?

Additional Information: There are a limited number of circumstances where a group user ID is appropriate, but they should be used only after a full risk assessment has been performed.

11.5.3 — Password management system

Scope: An automated system should be used to manage passwords and ensure that the password policy is enforced.
Key Risk Indicator: No
Control Class: (T) Technical
Key Questions:

- How does your organization manage user account passwords?

- Does your organization have a policy for password architecture? If so, does your password management system have the ability to enforce the requirements?
- How often does your password management system require the user to enter a new password?
- Does your password management system retain a record of previous passwords to prevent the user from using the same password again? If so, what is the management's system retention policy?

Additional Information: Password management systems are generally associated with the network, but they also apply to applications and databases.

11.5.4 — USE OF SYSTEM UTILITIES

Scope: Any utilities or tools that have the ability to override the control of the system should be closely controlled and monitored.
Key Risk Indicator: No
Control Class: (O) Operations, (T) Technical
Key Questions:

- Does your organization allow the installation of utilities or tools that can override system settings? If so, under what conditions?
- If system utilities are allowed, who has access and will existing monitoring and logging capture the use of these utilities and tools?
- Does the organization publish written procedures or guidelines for the use of system utilities?

11.5.5 — SESSION TIME-OUT

Scope: After a predetermined amount of time, operating systems and terminals should lock to prevent unauthorized access.
Key Risk Indicator: No
Control Class: (T) Technical
Key Questions:

- Does your organization require that unattended systems be locked after a predetermined amount of time? If so, what amount of time?
- If the operating system or terminal locks after a predetermined time, how is this accomplished?
- Is it possible for the user to override the automatic locking procedure?

11.5.6 — LIMITATION OF CONNECTION TIME

Scope: High-risk applications should have restrictions on connection time before locking or disconnecting.
Key Risk Indicator: No

Control Class: (T) Technical
Key Questions:

- Does your organization require any type of special controls for time-out or disconnection for high-risk applications? If so, are procedures or guidelines provided by management?
- What policies exist for controlling high-risk applications? Do any of these policies include the concept of limitation of connection time?

APPLICATION AND INFORMATION ACCESS CONTROL

Applications have the ability to store and process sensitive and critical data and information. Controls should be developed and implemented by management to prevent unauthorized access or tampering with such data and information.

11.6.1 — INFORMATION ACCESS RESTRICTION

Scope: Information contained in business systems and applications should be protected in accordance with the organization's access control policy and any applicable business application requirements.
Key Risk Indicator: No
Control Class: (M) Management, (O) Operations, (T) Technical
Key Questions:

- Does the organization document the class and type of information by application and system? If so, when is this process performed and how frequently is it reviewed for modification?
- How is sensitive and confidential data protected from unauthorized access and tampering at the application level?
- How is application and system output controlled?

11.6.2 — SENSITIVE SYSTEM ISOLATION

Scope: Highly sensitive systems should be isolated, tightly controlled, and monitored. Application or system owners should provide the requirement for isolation.
Key Risk Indicator: No
Control Class: (O) Operations
Key Questions:

- Does your organization provide a method or process for application owners to request or define the need for isolated systems? If so, please describe.
- If your organization provides the means for isolated systems, what special provisions are provided by management to allow the fulfillment of isolated systems?

MOBILE COMPUTING AND TELEWORKING

Mobile computing users present unique risks to the organization because they operate outside of the highly controlled network. Special controls and considerations should be given to these types of users.

11.7.1 — MOBILE COMPUTING AND COMMUNICATIONS

Scope: Special policies and safeguards should be developed as the result of a risk assessment to protect the organization against the risks posed by mobile and remote network communications.
Key Risk Indicator: No
Control Class: (M) Management, (O) Operations, (T) Technical
Key Questions:

- Does the organization allow the use of mobile devices such as handheld computers, laptops, and mobile phones to transmit organizational data and information?
- Has the organization published written policies, procedures, and guidelines for mobile and remote computing users? If so, what is the scope of the policies?
- Does the organization allow the use of wireless networking for mobile computing users? If so, specifically what technology and operational controls have been implemented to address the known threats with this technology?

11.7.2 — TELEWORKING

Scope: Remote workers require access to organizational resources including internal applications and information. Specific controls and safeguards must be developed and implemented to address the vulnerabilities associated with accessing resources external to the organization.
Key Risk Indicator: Yes
Control Class: (M) Management, (O) Operations
Key Questions:

- Has management published a policy for telecommute workers or third parties? If so, what is the scope of the policy?
- Is the network session between the remote connection and your organization's network secured and encrypted? If so, provide the technical details on how the network connection is secured.
- What special training do remote or telecommute workers or third parties receive?
- Are the concept and associated risks of remote access and telecommuting included in the organization's information security awareness program?

SUMMARY

"Access Control" is the second largest security clause with 25 controls and 7 control objectives. This security clause is comprehensive, covering business requirements for access control (11.1), management of user access (11.2), responsibilities of users regarding access control (11.3), special considerations for network-based access control (11.4), operational controls addressing access control risks (11.5), application-level access control of information and data (11.6), and mobile and remote telecommuting access control concepts (11.7).

REFERENCES

ISO/IEC 17799:2005 Information Technology — Security Techniques — Code of Practice for Information Security Management, International Organization for Standardization, 2005.

14 Information Systems Acquisition, Development, and Maintenance

The "Information Systems Acquisition, Development, and Maintenance" security clause has a total of 16 controls in 6 control objectives. The controls in this clause cover the validity of information and data, cryptography, protection of systems test and operational data as well as source code, safeguards that should be considered in software development, and the identification and control of technical vulnerabilities.

SECURITY REQUIREMENTS OF INFORMATION SYSTEMS

This clause was developed to help make managers aware of the importance of including information security in the business process and that security should be included in the design and acquisition stages of a project and not as an afterthought. This clause suggests that information security should be a normal part of the business justification process.

12.1.1 — SECURITY REQUIREMENTS ANALYSIS AND SPECIFICATION

Scope: Information security requirements and controls should be identified and specified prior to the implementation of a new system or as part of an upgrade process as appropriate.
Key Risk Indicator: Yes
Control Class: (M) Management
Key Questions:

- How does your organization identify information security controls for new or upgraded systems?
- Does management require the identification and application of information security controls and safeguards as part of the business process for new or upgraded systems and applications? If so, please describe the process.
- Does your organization have a published policy and set of procedures for including information security requirements and controls?

Additional Information: Information security controls are most effective when they are part of the design process and not an afterthought.

CORRECT PROCESSING IN APPLICATIONS

Information and data are the heart and soul of business applications. Information should be properly protected from unauthorized access, misuse, and modification in accordance with the data classification class.

12.2.1 — INPUT DATA VALIDATION

Scope: When data is inputted into a system or application, controls should be developed and implemented to validate the input for correctness and appropriateness.
Key Risk Indicator: No
Control Class: (O) Operations, (T) Technical
Key Questions:

- Does your organization require the inspection of input data for key applications? If so, please describe the process.
- As part of the input data validation procedures, does your organization check for missing data or data that is considered out of range or invalid?
- Are any checks performed on the source data to ensure that no modifications have taken place to alter the input to the system?

Additional Information: Data validation is very common in the software development process, but it is less common when information and data are acquired via some type of automated capture process.

12.2.2 — CONTROL OF INTERNAL PROCESSING

Scope: Applications should be developed to check for errors during processing and be able to perform validation checks designed for the type of input the system will accept.
Key Risk Indicator: No
Control Class: (O) Operations, (T) Technical
Key Questions:

- Does your organization require that errors be identified during processing as part of the software development process?
- Does your organization publish guidelines or procedures for software developers to help them include control of internal processing? If so, please describe.
- Does your organization perform any type of checks on the source data before inputting into the system?

12.2.3 — Message integrity

Scope: Many applications use internal messages to operate and process. These application messages should be protected and safeguarded to ensure that unauthorized modification or tampering of data does not take place.
Key Risk Indicator: No
Control Class: (M) Management, (O) Operations, (T) Technical
Key Questions:

- Describe how your organization protects application message integrity.
- Is message integrity included in any of your organization's preassessment activities or processes? If so, when? Please describe.

Additional Information: Application message integrity can be internal to an application or between applications. For example, if an n-tier Web application is properly designed and deployed, the Web server is separated from the database server by design. The messages between the Web server and the database server should be protected and properly secured.

12.2.4 — Output data validation

Scope: Output from key applications should be validated to ensure that it is accurate and appropriate for the processing system.
Key Risk Indicator: No
Control Class: (O) Operations, (T) Technical
Key Questions:

- What type of plausibility checks does your organization perform on data from key systems and applications?
- Has management published a requirement and associated procedures for output data validation?
- In the event that an error or anomaly is detected during an output data validation check, has management defined and published operating procedures to properly handle this type of circumstance?

CRYPTOGRAPHIC CONTROLS

Cryptographic controls are some of the best-known safeguards for protecting information and data from unauthorized access or tampering. As appropriate, management should develop and publish cryptographic-based information security policies, procedures, and guidelines for staff.

12.3.1 — Policy on the use of cryptographic controls

Scope: Management should develop and implement written policies on the application and use of cryptographic safeguards and controls based on the information classification guideline.

Key Risk Indicator: Yes
Control Class: (M) Management, (O) Operations
Key Questions:

- What formal policies has management published on cryptography?
- Has management published operating procedure and guidelines for staff to use during business operations?
- Does your organization have a policy and procedure for managing cryptographic keys?

Additional Information: Cryptographic controls can be very effective for protecting the integrity and confidentiality of information and data, but should be used as the result of a risk assessment.

12.3.2 — KEY MANAGEMENT

Scope: Cryptographic keys should be protected from theft, misuse, and modification by a formal management system.
Key Risk Indicator: No
Control Class: (O) Operations, (T) Technical
Key Questions:

- How does your organization manage cryptographic keys?
- How does your organization protect cryptographic keys?
- What type of special controls does your organization employ for system storing cryptographic keys?

SECURITY OF SYSTEM FILES

System files and source code require special protection from modification and deletion to ensure the integrity of the system and associated applications and data.

12.4.1 — CONTROL OF OPERATIONAL SOFTWARE

Scope: Management should develop tight controls and safeguards to ensure that only authorized applications can be installed on operational information processing systems.
Key Risk Indicator: Yes
Control Class: (M) Management, (O) Operations, (T) Technical
Key Questions:

- What type of controls and safeguards does your organization have to ensure that only authorized software and application are installed on systems?

- Does your organization perform any type of application audits? If so, how often and what is the scope?
- Does your organization inspect program source code libraries for accuracy?

12.4.2 — PROTECTION OF SYSTEM TEST DATA

Scope: Test data has a history of leading to negative security events and must be carefully selected, controlled, and inspected on a frequent basis to ensure that test data conforms to policy and guidelines developed by management.
Key Risk Indicator: Yes
Control Class: (O) Operations, (T) Technical
Key Questions:

- Does your organization have a written policy on the application and use of system test data? If so, please describe.
- How does your organization ensure that sensitive or classified production data is not used for test data in an environment less secure than the production environment?
- What type of procedures or guidelines exists for the use of system test data?

12.4.3 — ACCESS CONTROL TO PROGRAM SOURCE CODE

Scope: Application and program source code should be protected from unauthorized access, modification, or alteration.
Key Risk Indicator: No
Control Class: (O) Operations, (T) Technical
Key Questions:

- Does your organization have a written policy and associated procedures or guidelines to protect application and program source code?
- Where does your organization store program source code libraries?
- What special controls exist to safeguard source code?

Additional Information: For organizations that develop custom applications, the control of the source code should be of major concern. An unauthorized knowledge-able programmer could install a wide range of unauthorized modifications to the source code, leading to very serious and negative security-related events.

SECURITY IN DEVELOPMENT AND SUPPORT PROCESSES

Managers responsible for systems and applications in their area should ensure that the security of systems and applications and their environments are controlled and monitored.

12.5.1 — CHANGE CONTROL PROCEDURES

Scope: Changes to systems, applications, data, and networking devices should be closely controlled via a formal change control process.
Key Risk Indicator: No
Control Class: (M) Management, (O) Operations, (T) Technical
Key Questions:

- What type of change control system and process does your organization employ?
- What is the scope of your change control system?
- Who is allowed to approve a requested change?
- How frequently is the change control journal audited and reviewed?
- How does the organization ensure that change modifications were submitted by authorized users?

12.5.2 — TECHNICAL REVIEW OF APPLICATIONS AFTER OPERATING SYSTEM CHANGES

Scope: After changes are made to core operating systems, a formal review of the key applications should be conducted to ensure that no adverse conditions or information security issues exist.
Key Risk Indicator: No
Control Class: (O) Operations, (T) Technical
Key Questions:

- Does your organization have a written set of procedures or guidelines for updating the operating systems of key hosts? If so, please describe.
- Is there any type of written policy requiring specific actions for operating system modifications or upgrades?
- How does your IT staff install new operating system patches and upgrades?

12.5.3 — RESTRICTIONS ON CHANGES TO SOFTWARE PACKAGES

Scope: Purchased software applications from vendors and manufacturers should operate with as few modifications as possible to help control unidentified or unpredictable security-related vulnerabilities.
Key Risk Indicator: No
Control Class: (M) Management, (O) Operations, (T) Technical

Key Questions:

- Is there any type of policy, procedure, or guideline for modification of purchased applications? If so, please describe.
- If modifications are authorized and implemented, how does your organization control and assess security-related risks?
- If changes and medications are necessary and approved, what process does your organization follow to deploy the proposed changes?

12.5.4 — INFORMATION LEAKAGE

Scope: Information leakage from media, applications, systems, and other sources can lead to serious and negative consequences for the organization. Special care should be taken to design and implement controls to prevent and control information leakage.

Key Risk Indicator: No

Control Class: (O) Operations, (T) Technical

Key Questions:

- Does your organization have a written policy addressing information leakage?
- What types of controls are in place to control or prevent information leakage?

Additional Information: Information can be leaked in many different forms including logically over a network connection or a small piece of media such as a flash drive or physically on paper or other forms of physical media.

12.5.5 — OUTSOURCED SOFTWARE DEVELOPMENT

Scope: The development of applications and software external to the organization requires special attention and controls. Management should develop policy and procedures guiding staff on the proper practices and use of external software development.

Key Risk Indicator: No

Control Class: (M) Management, (O) Operations, (T) Technical

Key Questions:

- Does your organization develop software or applications external to your organization? If so, what policies, procedures, and guidelines exist today for this practice?
- How are licensing, code ownership, and intellectual property rights handled?
- How is the source code inspected for information security–related vulnerabilities?

TECHNICAL VULNERABILITY MANAGEMENT

Applications and systems produced by manufacturers have well-known vulnerabilities associated with each version of the system or application. Management should ensure that these published vulnerabilities are properly handled to reduce risks to the operations environment.

12.6.1 — CONTROL OF TECHNICAL VULNERABILITIES

Scope: Organizations should subscribe to vendor vulnerability notification systems and promptly inspect their systems to quantify the organization's exposure.
Key Risk Indicator: Yes
Control Class: (M) Management, (O) Operations, (T) Technical
Key Questions:

- How does your organization identify new vulnerabilities to systems within the operating environment?
- Is there a written policy or associated procedures on system or application vulnerabilities?
- Does your organization maintain a current inventory of all systems and applications in the information processing environment including the version of the operating system and applications installed?
- How are your key information processing systems and applications patched for security vulnerabilities?

SUMMARY

Information security requirements (12.1.1) should be part of normal business operations to ensure the integrity and availability of key systems. Applications are at the heart of operations, and input (12.2.1) and output (12.2.4) information and data should be closely controlled and monitored to ensure accuracy and protection. The processing system and environment should be closely controlled (12.2.2) and monitored, and any message at the system or application layer (12.2.3) should be protected and controlled to reduce the risk of information corruption, tampering, or unauthorized use.

Cryptographic controls (12.3.1) are well-known safeguards to protect the integrity and authenticity of information and data. Management should develop written policies and procedures guiding staff of the selection and use of cryptography (12.3.2).

Information systems and applications in the information processing facility (12.4.1) should be closely controlled and monitored for security-related threats and vulnerabilities. System test data (12.4.2) and access to source code (12.4.3) should be controlled and protected from unauthorized access, tampering, and modification.

Organizations should develop formal change control procedures and systems (12.5.1) to control unauthorized modifications to key systems in the operations environment. Qualified IT staff should inspect (12.5.2) any changes to core operating systems as well as key applications (12.5.3). Special policies and controls should be developed by management on information leakage (12.5.4) and outsourced software development (12.5.5).

Management should have a formal process and policy on the identification of new threats and vulnerabilities (12.6.1) to the information processing systems and applications.

REFERENCES

ISO/IEC 17799:2005 Information Technology — Security Techniques — Code of Practice for Information Security Management, International Organization for Standardization, 2005.

15 Information Security Incident Management

The "Information Security Incident Management" clause is new in the second edition, but it is mostly composed of existing controls. The five controls and two control objectives focus on notification, containment, and management of information security incidents. Management should closely review this clause to ensure that their environment and operations fully address the controls in this clause.

REPORTING INFORMATION SECURITY EVENTS AND WEAKNESSES

Information security incidents can quickly elevate to organizationwide catastrophes and, therefore, management should develop and implement a formal mechanism to report and manage all information security weaknesses and incidents.

13.1.1 — REPORTING INFORMATION SECURITY EVENTS

Scope: Identified or suspected information security events should be reported to well-known management channels as quickly as possible. All users should be keenly aware of the security incident reporting process and aware of the scenarios and events that define an incident.
Key Risk Indicator: Yes
Control Class: (M) Management, (O) Operations
Key Questions:

- Does the organization have a formal information security incident reporting process and mechanism? If so, please describe the program and process.
- How are all organizational users and relevant third parties trained and made aware of their responsibilities for quickly reporting information security incidents?
- How frequently is the information security incident process tested?

Additional Information: Information security incident reporting is not a stand-alone process. This should be a part of a larger business process. Most organizations reference this type of process as an incident response system, emergency response plan, etc. The number one objective is for all users (employees, consultants, contractors, vendors, etc.) to be aware of, and trained on, the process of reporting security incidents through appropriate channels. As I previously stated in the awareness control, it is not enough for users to be aware of how to perform this mission-critical task. They should be trained on the process, and regular and random testing should occur to ensure that the users are trained and understand the process.

This is a difficult control because it cannot be implemented on its own, as it needs to be a part of the larger incident response system as I briefly outlined in the preceding paragraph. Designing, implementing, and training the users on a formal incident response system is a large undertaking, even for smaller organizations. For larger organizations, the cost can be aggressive and the information security management team will be expected to design and provide the scope for this type of project.

13.1.2 — REPORTING SECURITY WEAKNESSES

Scope: All suspected or identified security weaknesses should be reported to management through a formal process. Every user or relevant third party associated with the organization should bear this responsibility and be aware of the process.
Key Risk Indicator: No
Control Class: (M) Management, (O) Operations
Key Questions:

- Does your organization require all users to report suspected and identified security weaknesses?
- What type of training does your organization provide to the entire user body on the concept of security weaknesses?
- Do all users understand what to do, and not to do, if a suspected security weakness is identified?

Additional Information: There are two dimensions to this control. The first is to create an environment and associated process to enable users of the organization's information systems and facilities to report any observed or suspected weaknesses or threats to the proper authority. The second dimension is awareness and education. Users must be continually reminded of the type of threats and weakness that they might be exposed to. Many of the high-priority topics could be covered in the organization's information security awareness and education campaign. The point of departure for this control is to identify the weakness or threat quickly and to match the discovery with the proper authority. A trained and aware staff is one of the best information security investments any organization can ever make. People are the missing link for information security. A balance of technical and operational controls is necessary, and an aware user base is equally important to the information security protection strategy.

MANAGEMENT OF INFORMATION SECURITY INCIDENTS AND IMPROVEMENTS

Managing information security incidents is challenging and stressful. Clear documentation outlining responsibilities and actions should be provided by management for the handling of information security incidents.

13.2.1 — RESPONSIBILITIES AND PROCEDURES

Scope: Information security-related incidents can create panic and stress for all parties. Management responsibilities and associated procedures should be developed when there are no incidents under way to allow for clear thinking and the development of effective procedures.

Key Risk Indicator: No
Control Class: (M) Management, (O) Operations
Key Questions:

- Does your organization have written procedures for handling information security incidents? If so, are all users, including management, fully aware and trained on their responsibilities?
- How does your organization monitor for potential information security incidents?
- When is the last time management tested procedures for incident management?

13.2.2 — LEARNING FROM INFORMATION SECURITY INCIDENTS

Scope: Management should develop a method and system to ensure that information is properly collected during an incident to ensure that it can be analyzed after the incident for learning and evaluation for improvement.

Key Risk Indicator: No
Control Class: (M) Management
Key Questions:

- What type of methods or processes has management developed and published to collect all key information during an incident?
- Is there a process in place for management to review an incident after it is fully eradicated?

Additional Information: In many cases this type of analysis may be a part of the incident response and management system. If not, a separate process should be developed to quantify the direct and indirect costs to the organization so that management can be properly informed. A formal report should be produced as a result of this process and exercise. The resulting information can help the management team identify any patterns that require immediate attention. In addition, the information security management team can utilize the information to review the associated control to ensure that they are appropriate in scope and applied. Furthermore, any associated information security policies should be reviewed and updated if necessary.

13.2.3 — COLLECTION OF EVIDENCE

Scope: Many times, information security incidents can have legal implications. Special care should be taken by management to develop and publish procedures and guidelines for the collection of evidence.
Key Risk Indicator: No
Control Class: (M) Management, (O) Operations, (T) Technical
Key Questions:

- How does your organization handle the collection of evidence during an information security incident?
- How does your organization make users aware that evidence is a part of the information security incident process?

SUMMARY

"Information Security Incident Management" is a new security clause for the second edition, but the concept and some controls were carried over from the first edition. Management should develop and publish a clear set of procedures and guides for the reporting of security incidents (13.1.1) and weaknesses (13.1.2). Management must be clear on its responsibilities (13.2.1), and there should be a mechanism for learning (13.2.2) from incidents as well as an awareness and procedures for collecting evidence (13.2.3).

REFERENCES

ISO/IEC 17799:2005 Information Technology — Security Techniques — Code of Practice for Information Security Management, International Organization for Standardization, 2005.

16 Business Continuity Management

The "Business Continuity Management" security clause has a total of five controls and one control objective. There are many information security–related elements of business continuity management that an organization should consider. The controls in this clause will help managers identify and quantify areas within their respective programs that need improvement or modification.

INFORMATION SECURITY ASPECTS OF BUSINESS CONTINUITY MANAGEMENT

When business operations are interrupted, the protection and integrity of the recovered environment should operate with the same controls and safeguards as the production environment and systems.

14.1.1 — INCLUDING INFORMATION SECURITY IN THE BUSINESS CONTINUITY MANAGEMENT PROCESS

Scope: Management should ensure that information security is included in the business continuity process and recovery plan.
Key Risk Indicator: Yes
Control Class: (M) Management, (O) Operations
Key Questions:

- Does management formally include information security in the business continuity management plan and strategy? If so, please describe.
- How are information security risks identified in the recovered business continuity operation's environment?

14.1.2 — BUSINESS CONTINUITY AND RISK ASSESSMENT

Scope: The concept of business continuity should be included in an organization's risk assessment processes that also link information security-related risks to business continuity.
Key Risk Indicator: No
Control Class: (O) Operations, (T) Technical

Key Questions:

- How does your organization include information security in the business continuity strategy and plan?
- How often is the business continuity plan evaluated and reviewed for effectiveness and applicability?

14.1.3 − DEVELOPING AND IMPLEMENTING CONTINUITY PLANS INCLUDING INFORMATION SECURITY

Scope: When the business continuity plan is carried out, information security controls should have been assessed and implemented to ensure the secure operation of the recovered systems, applications, and environment.
Key Risk Indicator: No
Control Class: (M) Management, (O) Operations
Key Questions:

- Was the assessment of information security controls and safeguards for the recovered environment part of the business continuity planning process?
- How will the organization ensure that information security controls are functioning as designed in the recovered systems, applications, and environment?

14.1.4 − BUSINESS CONTINUITY PLANNING FRAMEWORK

Scope: Management should maintain a single planning architecture and framework for business continuity to ensure that information security is part of the process as appropriate.
Key Risk Indicator: No
Control Class: (M) Management, (O) Operations
Key Questions:

- If more than one business continuity plan exists because of organizational requirements, how is consistency maintained to the master plan?
- When individual business continuity plans are required or appropriate, how are information security risks evaluated for the recovered environment and systems?

14.1.5 − TESTING, MAINTAINING, AND REASSESSING BUSINESS CONTINUITY PLANS

Scope: Because of the risks to the organization, business continuity plans should be frequently reviewed and tested to ensure that the plans are current and effective.
Key Risk Indicator: No
Control Class: (O) Operations, (T) Technical

Key Questions:

- Does the organization have a formal testing methodology and schedule for business continuity? If so, please describe.
- How frequently is the business continuity plan tested, and to what extent is the plan tested?
- Are information security controls assessed during test plans to ensure their effectiveness as designed?

SUMMARY

Business continuity management has many ties to information security. There are many opportunities for controls and safeguards to break down during this time of crisis, leaving the organization vulnerable and at risk. Information security should be a fundamental part (14.1.1, 14.1.3) of the business continuity plan and framework (14.1.4). Information security (14.1.2) and business continuity should be part of a formal risk assessment process when developing recovery plans and strategies. The business continuity plan and information security controls within the recovered environment should be tested (14.1.5) and evaluated to ensure effectiveness.

REFERENCES

ISO/IEC 17799:2005 Information Technology — Security Techniques — Code of Practice for Information Security Management, International Organization for Standardization, 2005.

17 Compliance

The "Compliance" security clause has far-reaching implications for public or regulated organizations because of the changes in the legal and regulatory requirements over the last five years. Many of the laws and regulations that are applicable today did not exist when the first edition of the standard was developed. There are a total of ten controls and three control objectives for this clause. Executive management should take ample time reviewing the controls and concepts presented in this clause to identify any missing elements in their organization and operations.

COMPLIANCE WITH LEGAL REQUIREMENTS

Executive management must take special care and continually evaluate its organization and operating environment for the applicability of laws and regulations to avoid breaches of legal requirements.

15.1.1 — IDENTIFICATION OF APPLICABLE LEGISLATION

Scope: It is the responsibility of executive management to identify all relevant regulatory, statutory, and contractual requirements and develop and publish a strategy dealing with these requirements.
Key Risk Indicator: Yes
Control Class: (M) Management
Key Questions:

- How does executive management identify applicable and relevant regulatory, contractual, and statutory requirements?
- How often is management's plan and strategy reviewed?

15.1.2 — INTELLECTUAL PROPERTY RIGHTS (IPR)

Scope: Management should develop policy and procedures to ensure compliance with all applicable intellectual property rights.
Key Risk Indicator: No
Control Class: (M) Management, (O) Operations
Key Questions:

- Has management published written policies and procedures for intellectual property rights?
- How is the use and acquisition of software handled in your organization?

- Is the concept of intellectual property rights included in your organization's information security awareness program?
- How frequently does your organization audit for unauthorized application software?

15.1.3 — PROTECTION OF ORGANIZATIONAL RECORDS

Scope: Management should develop and implement appropriate controls within the organization to protect organizational records from unauthorized access, modification, destruction, and tampering.
Key Risk Indicator: No
Control Class: (M) Management, (O) Operations, (T) Technical
Key Questions:

- How does your organization protect sensitive and critical organizational records?
- What does your organization include in the scope of protection for this control?
- Has management evaluated protection requirements against statutory and regulatory requirements?

15.1.4 — DATA PROTECTION AND PRIVACY OF PERSONAL INFORMATION

Scope: Personal information of employees and clients must be protected in accordance with all relevant legislation and regulations.
Key Risk Indicator: Yes
Control Class: (M) Management, (O) Operations, (T) Technical
Key Questions:

- Does your organization have a published data protection privacy policy? If so, please describe the scope of the policy.
- How often does management evaluate laws and regulations against the internal environment and operations?
- Who is responsible for the privacy and protection of personal information?

15.1.5 — PREVENTION OF MISUSE OF INFORMATION PROCESSING FACILITIES

Scope: Controls and safeguards should be implemented by the organization to prevent and deter the misuse of information processing facilities.
Key Risk Indicator: No
Control Class: (O) Operations, (T) Technical
Key Questions:

- Does your organization publish a written policy on the proper use of information processing systems and facilities? If so, please describe the scope of the policy.

- Is the concept of proper and improper use of information processing systems and facilities included in the organization's information security awareness program?
- Does the organization include any type of warning message when logging on to a system or application? Was the message reviewed and approved by legal counsel?

15.1.6 — REGULATION OF CRYPTOGRAPHIC CONTROLS

Scope: Cryptographic controls can be governed by federal or international laws. Management should ensure that all cryptographic controls and policies are used in compliance with all relevant legislation and regulations.
Key Risk Indicator: No
Control Class: (M) Management
Key Questions:

- How does management ensure that cryptographic controls and policies operate within all relevant legislation and regulation requirements?
- Does your organization import or export computer hardware or software? If so, do you check for cryptographic requirements?
- Does your organization have any type of encrypted network connection to any other locations outside of the United States? If so, was legal counsel contacted to ensure that the proper use of cryptography was being used?

COMPLIANCE WITH SECURITY POLICIES AND STANDARDS, AND TECHNICAL COMPLIANCE

The organization's information processing systems and applications should be checked to ensure compliance with all relevant security policies and standards published by management.

15.2.1 — COMPLIANCE WITH SECURITY POLICIES AND STANDARDS

Scope: Managers should review their area of responsibility to ensure compliance with organizational security policy.
Key Risk Indicator: No
Control Class: (M) Management, (O) Operations
Key Questions:

- What types of checks are carried out for checking compliance with organizational security policies and standards in the information processing environment?
- Are departmental managers held responsible for compliance with the organization's information security policies in their area?
- Is there a written process for managers to follow when a noncompliance item is detected or discovered?

15.2.2 — Technical compliance checking

Scope: The organization's information processing systems and applications should be checked to ensure compliance with all relevant security policies and standards published by management.
Key Risk Indicator: Yes
Control Class: (O) Operations, (T) Technical
Key Questions:

- What types of technical checks are carried out for checking compliance with organizational security policies and standards in the information processing environment?
- If technical checks are performed, who executes the tests?
- What type of report or output is required of the testers?
- How often does the organization engage external unbiased subject matter experts to validate compliance with security policy?

INFORMATION SYSTEMS AUDIT CONSIDERATIONS

Management should develop an audit process that does not interfere with business operations while still meeting all of the audit requirements and objectives.

15.3.1 — Information systems audit controls

Scope: When production systems are audited, special care should be taken not to disrupt business operations.
Key Risk Indicator: No
Control Class: (M) Management
Key Questions:

- How are audit requirements determined for each system or application?
- Does your organization have an internal audit department? If so, does the internal audit manager work with system owners on coordinating audit activities?
- When was the last time your information processing systems and facilities were audited by an external firm? How did they coordinate the audit?

15.3.2 — Protection of information systems audit tools

Scope: Audit tools have the ability to reveal protected and private information. Special care should be taken to prevent unauthorized use or abuse of audit tools. *
Key Risk Indicator: No
Control Class: (O) Operations, (T) Technical
Key Questions:

- Are there any audit tools installed on any of the organization's hosts or systems? If so, please describe.

- How does management monitor for or control the risk of abusing audit tools?
- Who in your organization has access to audit tools?
- If unauthorized staff or persons installed audit tools and software on the organization's systems, is there a process and method in place to detect this unauthorized software?

SUMMARY

The "Compliance" security clause is a critical clause because it deals with the identification (15.1.1) of relevant and applicable legislation and regulations. Intellectual property rights (15.1.2) are reviewed and the protection of the organization's private records (15.1.3) is addressed along with the protection and privacy of personal information (15.1.4). Organizations should have controls in place addressing the misuse of information processing facilities (15.1.5) and use of cryptographic controls (15.1.6).

Managers should be responsible for adherence to all security policies (15.2.1) within their area of responsibility, and the organization should perform technical checks (15.2.2) to ensure that the information processing systems and environment are in compliance with information security policies and standards.

Audit tools have the ability to interrupt production systems, and special care should be taken by management to ensure that this does not happen (15.3.1). Appropriate measures and controls should be implemented to identify the misuse and detection of unauthorized audit software and tools (15.3.2).

REFERENCES

ISO/IEC 17799:2005 Information Technology — Security Techniques — Code of Practice for Information Security Management, International Organization for Standardization, 2005.

Appendix A

ISO STANDARDS CITED IN ISO/IEC 17799:2005

- ISO/IEC Guide 2:1996 "Standardization and related activities — General vocabulary"
- ISO/IEC Guide 73:2002 "Risk management — Vocabulary — Guidelines for use in standards"
- ISO/IEC 9796-2:2002 "Information technology — Security techniques — Digital signature schemes giving message recovery — Part 2: Integer factorization based mechanisms"
- ISO/IEC 9796-3:2000 "Information technology — Security techniques — Digital signature schemes giving message recovery — Part 3: Discrete logarithm based mechanisms"
- ISO 10007:2003 "Quality management systems — Guidelines for configuration management"
- ISO/IEC 11770-1:1996 "Information technology — Security techniques — Key management — Part 1: Framework"
- ISO/IEC 12207:1995 "Information technology — Software life cycle processes"
- ISO/IEC 13888-1:1997 "Information technology — Security techniques — Non-repudiation — Part 1: General"
- ISO/IEC 14516:2002 "Information technology — Security techniques — Guidelines for the use and management of Trusted Third Party services"
- ISO/IEC 14888-1:1998 "Information technology — Security techniques — Digital signatures with appendix — Part 1: General"
- ISO/IEC 15408-1:1999 "Information technology — Security techniques — Evaluation criteria for IT security — Part 1: Introduction and general model"
- ISO 15489-1:2001 "Information and documentation — Records management — Part 1: General"
- ISO/IEC 18028-4 "Information technology — Security techniques — IT network security — Part 4: Securing remote access"
- ISO/IEC TR 18044 "Information technology — Security techniques — Information security incident management"
- ISO 19011:2002 "Guidelines for quality and/or environmental management systems auditing"

Appendix B

GENERAL REFERENCES

Anderson, A.M., Comparing risk analysis methodologies, Proceedings of the IFIP TC11 Seventh International Conference on Information Security, North Holland, New York, NY, Amsterdam, 1991, pp. 301–311.

Anderson, A.M., The risk data repository: A novel approach to security risk modelling, Proceedings of the IFIP TCII Seventh International Conference on Information Security, North Holland, New York, NY, Amsterdam, 1993, pp. 185–194.

Baskerville, R., Information systems security design methods: Implications for information systems development, *ACM Computing Surveys,* 25, 373–414, 1993.

Baskerville, R., Risk analysis as a source of professional knowledge, *Computers & Security,* 10, 1991.

Bennett, S.P. and Kailay, M.P., An application of qualitative risk analysis to computer security for the commercial sector, Proceedings of the Eighth Annual Computer Security Applications Conference, IEEE Computer Society Press, Los Alamitos, CA, 1992, pp. 64–73.

Birch, D.G.W., An information driven approach to network security, Second International Conference on Private Switching Systems and Networks, Institution of Electrical Engineers, London, 1992.

Birch, D.G.W. and McEvoy, N.A., Risk analysis for information systems, *Journal of Information Technology,* 7, 1992.

Bodeau, D.J., A conceptual model for computer security risk analysis, Proceedings of Eighth Annual Computer Security Applications Conference, IEEE Computer Society Press, Los Alamitos, CA, 1992, pp. 56–63.

Caelli, W., Longley, D., and Shain, M., *Information Security Handbook,* Macmillan, Basingstoke, 1991.

Clark, R., Risk management—A new approach, Proceedings of the Fourth IFIP TCII International Conference on Computer Security, North Holland, New York, NY, Amsterdam, 1989.

Eloff, J.H.P., Labuschagne, L., and Badenhorst, K.P., A comparative framework for risk analysis methods, *Computers & Security,* 12, 1993.

FIPS 79, *Guideline for Automatic Data Processing Risk Analysis,* FIPS PUB 65, National Bureau of Standards, U.S. Department of Commerce, 1979.

Garrabrants, W.M., Ellis, A.W. III, Hoffman, L.J., and Kamel, M., CERTS: A comparative evaluation method for risk management methodologies and tools, Sixth Annual Computer Security Conference, IEEE Computer Society Press, Los Alamitos, CA, 1990.

Katzke, S.W., A government perspective on risk management of automated information systems, Proceedings of the 1988 Computer Security Risk Management Model Builders Workshop, 1987, pp. 3–20.

Mayerfeld, H.T., Framework for risk management: A synthesis of the working group reports, First Computer Security Risk Management Model Builders Workshop, NIST, Gaithersburg, MD, 1989.

Moses, R., A European standard for risk analysis, Proceedings of COMPSEC International, Elsevier, Oxford, 1993.

Saltmarsh, T.J. and Browne, P.S., Data processing—risk assessment, *Advances in Computer Security Management,* 2, 1983.

Wong, K. and Watt, W., *Managing Information Security: A Non-technical Management Guide,* Elsevier Advanced Technology, Amsterdam, 1990.

Index

A

Access control, 101–105, 173
  application and information access control, 105, 182
  business requirements for, 101, 173
  equipment identification in networks, 103
  information access restriction, 105
  limitation of connection time, 104
  mobile computing and teleworking, 183
  network access control, 103, 176–179
  network connection control, 103
  network routing control, 103–104
  and network services use, 103
  objectives in ISO/IEC 17799 standard, 74
  operating system access control, 104, 179–182
  password management system, 104
  password use, 102
  policy, 101, 173
  privilege management, 102
  remote diagnostic port and configuration protection, 103
  secure log-on procedures, 104
  segregation in networks, 103
  sensitive system isolation, 105
  session time-out, 104
  system utilities use, 104
  unattended user equipment, 102
  user access management, 101–102, 174–175
  user authentication for external connections, 103
  user identification and authentication, 104
  user password management, 102
  user registration, 102
  user responsibilities, 102, 175–176
Access control lists, 40
Access control policy, 66
Access rights, removal of, 62, 91–92, 145
Accidental threats, 26
ACL configuration criteria, 41–42
Adaptability, as security criterion, 20–21
Administrator and operator logs, 101, 169–170
Analysis and findings, in ISE process, 53
Anti-virus solutions, 40

Application access control, 105, 182
  information access restriction, 182
  sensitive system isolation, 182
Application firewalls, 40
Application information security assessment, 11
Asset identification, xxiii, 59
Asset management, 73, 88–89, 133
  classification guidelines, 89
  information classification, 89, 135–137
  responsibility for assets, 88, 133–135
Assets
  acceptable use of, 88, 134–135
  return of, in human resources security, 144
Assets inventory, 60, 88, 133–134
Assets ownership, 88, 134
Audit considerations, 113
Audit controls, 113, 206
Audit logging, 100, 168
Audit standards, xxi–xxii
Audit tools, 113
  protection of, 206–207
Authorities, contact with, 86, 129
Authorization process, for information processing facilities, 86, 128
Automation, management desire for, 20–21

B

Background investigations, 61
Backup, 97, 161
Bank of America, security breaches by, xxxi
Banking industry, 24
Best practice guidelines, 29, xxxii
  encryption, 67
Big 4 public accounting firms, xxviii
BITS Kalculator, 23
Business continuity management, 110–111, 199–201
  continuity plan development, 200
  criteria, 42
  objectives in ISO/IEC 17799 standard, 75
  plan maintenance and testing, 200–201
  planning framework, 200
  and risk assessment, 199–200

H

I